ENGLAND
The state of the regions

Edited by John Tomaney and John Mawson

First published in Great Britain in July 2002 by

The Policy Press
34 Tyndall's Park Road
Bristol BS8 1PY
UK

Tel +44 (0)117 954 6800
Fax +44 (0)117 973 7308
e-mail tpp@bristol.ac.uk
www.policypress.org.uk

British Library Cataloguing in Publication Data
A catalogue record for this book is available from the British Library

ISBN 1 86134 375 2 paperback
A hardcover version of this book is also available

John Tomaney is Professor of Regional Governance at the Centre for Urban and Regional Development Studies at the University of Newcastle upon Tyne and **John Mawson** is Director of the Local Government Centre, Warwick Business School, University of Warwick.

Cover design by Qube Design Associates, Bristol.
Front cover: Map of Oxford supplied by kind permission of the Science Photo Library

Printed and bound in Great Britain by Hobbs the Printers Ltd, Southampton

Contents

List of tables and figures

Tables

Figures

Acknowledgements

The chapters in this volume are based on papers presented at a seminar held at the University of Newcastle-upon-Tyne in the autumn of 2001. The seminar was sponsored jointly by the university's Jean Monnet Centre and the Centre for Urban and Regional Development Studies, University of Newcastle upon Tyne. We are grateful to Ella Ritchie, Director of the Jean Monnet Centre, for agreeing to support the seminar, and to Janet Sharpe for her excellent organisational skills. The event brought together academics, civil servants and journalists from around England and beyond. We are grateful to those who made the journey to Newcastle and to the staff and postgraduates of the University of Newcastle-upon-Tyne for their contributions during the seminar. Several of the papers in this volume draw on two major research programmes sponsored by the Leverhulme Trust ('Nations and regions: Understanding the dynamics of constitutional change') and by the Economic and Social Research Council ('Devolution and constitutional change'), led respectively by Robert Hazell of the Constitution Unit at University College London, and Charlie Jeffrey at the University of Birmingham. We are indebted to both for their support. Finally we are grateful to Rowena Mayhew, Dawn Rushen, Ailsa Grant Ferguson and the staff of The Policy Press in Bristol for their professionalism, patience and support in seeing this volume through to publication.

List of contributors

John Adams, Senior Research Fellow, Institute for Public Policy Research, London.

Sarah Ayres, Aston Business School, Aston University, Birmingham.

Paul Benneworth, Centre for Urban and Regional Development Studies, University of Newcastle upon Tyne.

Tom Bridges, Arup Economics and Planning, Ove Arup and Partners, London.

Paul Foley, Graduate Business School, De Montfort University, Leicester.

Benito Giordano, Department of Geography, University of Manchester.

Peter John, School of Politics and Sociology, Birkbeck College, University of London.

Peter Jones, *The Economist*, London.

Simon Lee, Department of Politics and International Studies, University of Hull.

Paul McQuail, Constitution Unit, University College London.

John Mawson, Local Government Centre, Warwick Business School, University of Warwick.

Steve Musson, School of Geographical Sciences, University of Bath.

Graham Pearce, Aston Business School, Aston University, Birmingham.

Wendy Russell Barter, Local and Regional Government Research Unit, Office of the Deputy Prime Minister, London.

Mark Sandford, Constitution Unit, University College London.

Adam Tickell, School of Geographical Sciences, University of Bristol.

John Tomaney, Centre for Urban and Regional Development Studies, University of Newcastle upon Tyne.

Neil Ward, School of Geography, University of Leeds.

ONE

Introduction

John Tomaney

This book examines aspects of the governance of England in a devolved (or *devolving*) United Kingdom. On the face of it, devolution is a process, which has yet to impact on England directly. In contrast to Scotland, Wales and Northern Ireland, the English have tended to remain indifferent to the appeal of devolved institutions. England, because of its size, has dominated the UK, while generally acknowledging the national traditions and aspirations of its other components, especially Scotland. Unlike Scotland or Wales, there has been little demand for the (re)creation of an English Parliament in the past century. The lack of interest of the English in a parliament of their own helped to scupper initiatives such as 'Home Rule All Round' prior to the First World War. From time to time over the past century or so, commentators have suggested a federal system in which England would form one element alongside Scotland and Wales. However, this solution has generally been rejected as unsustainable. An English Parliament representing a population of 45 million, compared to Scotland's population of five million and Wales' population of three million, would overshadow any federal parliament.

At the same time, it is frequently argued that England lacks traditions of regionalism or, as Harvie (1991) puts it, English regionalism is "the dog that never barked". It is certainly true that the English political class has shown itself uninterested in the kind of issues that arouse great passions in Scotland. It is sometimes argued that this is because England can boast a 'one thousand-year history' of integrated governance stretching back to the Norman Conquest. In 1885 the celebrated constitutional theorist A.V. Dicey could argue:

> Two features have at all times since the Norman Conquest characterized the political institutions of England.... The first of these features is the omnipotence or undisputed supremacy throughout the whole country of the central government.... The second, which is closely connected with the first, is the rule or supremacy of law. (Quoted in Weir and Beetham, 1999, p 6)

Such a constitutional theory would appear to leave little space for regionalism within English political culture and administration. Attempts were made to introduce regional planning structures into England in the 1960s and 1970s by Labour governments. However, these were weak bodies and remained very much the creatures of central control, and did not survive the election of Margaret Thatcher's Conservative government in 1979 (although in 1994 the

Major government did create Government Offices [GOs] in order to integrate the activities of central government in the regions). It is only recently in the modern period that English regionalism has begun to be a significant political force.

Proposals for the reform of English regional governance began to circulate within the Labour Party in the 1980s. In opposition, the Labour Party accumulated a range of ill-specified commitments as far as the English regions were concerned. Their 1992 Manifesto committed the party to elected regional government in England, alongside proposed reforms in Scotland, Wales, Northern Ireland and London. However, little detailed policy work was undertaken on the subject, although the statement was enough to stir signs of interest in regions such as the North East. Under the leadership of Tony Blair, Labour drew back from its previous commitments and made a more tentative promise of action where there was demonstrable demand. Meanwhile, John Prescott, the party's deputy leader, won the party over to the idea of creating Regional Development Agencies (RDAs), ostensibly to tackle regional inequalities, but also implicitly as a *quid pro quo* for English MPs' acquiescence in the devolution debate.

New Labour and the English Question

Thus, the 'English Question' – that is, how will England be governed in a devolved, let alone federal UK? – was left largely unanswered by New Labour in its first term of office. As Bogdanor notes, "England is hardly mentioned in the devolution legislation, and yet England is, in many respects, the key to the success of devolution" (1999, p 265). In New Labour's initial devolution programme the absence of England was a gaping one (see Tomaney, 1999a, for extended discussion). Much concern was expressed about the possibility of an 'English backlash' to Scottish and Welsh devolution but, to date, the attitude of mass opinion in England appears to express benign indifference. There is no guarantee that the English will continue to adopt this attitude as the wider implications of devolution for the UK become more apparent. For this reason, the 'English Question' continues to be raised and solutions proffered. One solution to the 'English Question' lies in proposals for an English Parliament. This option is now favoured, in one form or another, by the Conservatives. The other option, to which the Labour Party is ambivalently committed, sees the solution to the 'English Question' in the form of regional governments *within* England. This option is supported in the more peripheral regions, especially those abutting Scotland and Wales which tend to see an English Parliament as just another form of London government.

Although the New Labour government paid comparatively little direct attention to the needs of England and, more especially, its regions in its first term, it did initiate some changes. Within England the government, largely as a result of the initiative of John Prescott established eight RDAs. Each RDA has a board of directors selected from within its respective region. Ministers in London, however, appoint these boards on the advice of civil servants. The government has also encouraged the formation of Regional Chambers, primarily from local authority associations, but incorporating interest groups such as business, unions and voluntary organisations. However, these organisations were given only a consultative role and have no statutory basis or direct powers, and therefore looked very weak compared to the institutions created in Scotland and Wales. The New Labour government announced its intention to legislate for English regional government, but only where demand for it existed, although it did notably little itself to stimulate such demand in its first term.

One area where the government did legislate is in relation to London, where it created an elected mayor and accompanying assembly of 25 members. While the Greater London Authority (GLA) model represents a constitutional innovation, insofar as it introduces the concept of the directly elected mayor, it represented a relatively weak form of devolution. Unlike the Scottish Parliament or Welsh Assembly, the GLA takes over few central government activities, does not have a single block grant to fund its activities, and is subject to the veto of the Secretary of State over most of its actions. The mayor has *responsibilities* in areas such as transport, policing and planning that are of great import to the London public. It is less clear that the mayor has the *powers* necessary to make progress on these issues. The mayor, however, is able to claim a large mandate, and this has proved to be a recipe for tension, especially over transport, between the incumbent mayor, Ken Livingstone and the central government. New Labour's worries here echo those it had in Wales. There, in late 1999, the Labour Party became embroiled in an unseemly squabble to ensure that its candidate for the post was, above all, suitably loyal to the New Labour project.

Historians will judge devolution as one of the lasting legacies of the first Blair government, but as Tony Wright MP observed the English were, initially at least, "spectators at the devolutionary feast" (2000, p 11). New Labour left the 'English Question' largely unanswered in its first term. The high tide of its engagement with the 'regional question' in its first term came with the creation of RDAs and the promotion of voluntary local authority-led Regional Chambers in 1997. Labour made no moves on the commitment – made in its 1997 Manifesto – to legislate for elected regional assemblies ("where there is demand"). But in the run-up to the General Election, New Labour began to deepen its engagement with the English regions, not least because of the widening range of political pressures compelling it to do so. However, as its first term ended, there were signs that the 'regional question' was beginning to move up the government's agenda. The governance of England was finally becoming an explicit political issue. During the General Election campaign of 2001, the Labour Party promised to publish a White Paper on English regional government, which would put forward proposals on English Regional Assemblies.

The structure of this book

Despite a growing focus on regionalism, there have been few attempts to describe its evolution across England. This book seeks to fill that gap.

In the following chapter, Wendy Russell Barter presents an overview of the issues surrounding regional government (Chapter Two). She reviews the literature on regional government in England and sets this in an international context. The chapter identifies four arguments for regional government: democracy, economic development pressures, European imperatives, and technocratic requirements. However, the debate on regional government has tended to be based on assertion rather than evidence-based proposals. The research evidence on the form and function of regional government in England – in terms of both existing and potential developments – is sparse. The remainder of this book introduces evidence to the debate.

In Chapter Three John Tomaney describes in detail the evolution of regional policy and governance under New Labour. The chapter notes that existing structures – notably GOs, RDAs and voluntary Regional Chambers (or Assemblies) – were gradually strengthened during the period 1997-2001. The chapter also notes that these bodies lie at the heart of a more complex system of regional governance, comprising the regional arms of central government, quangos and other bodies. Since 1997, a slow and low profile growth of regionalisation has occurred within England. At the same time, central government – both in the form of important New Labour figures and key elements of the civil service – remained ambivalent at best about regionalism. Nevertheless, the commitment to produce a White Paper on elected Regional Assemblies during the 2001 General Election campaign represented a significant step forward for the regionalist argument within government.

Chapters Four to Eleven outline the conditions in each English region. Each chapter seeks to address the same broad questions:

- What are the main social and economic challenges facing the region?
- How well matched are the evolving regional strategies to meeting these challenges?
- How have the new regional institutions settled in each region?
- How are key stakeholders responding to the new institutional terrain?
- What have been the main controversies to date?
- Have distinctive regional policy issues begun to emerge?
- How are social and political interests in the regions responding to the prospect of elected regional government?
- What evidence is there of genuine civic interest in the new regionalism?
- How is the media covering the regional issue?

The individual regional experiences are diverse and the general questions have a different purchase in each case. This diversity reflects different social and economic structures, uneven regional identities and diverse emerging political trajectories. Regional economic performance varies considerably in the UK (see Figure 1.1).

Broadly speaking, regional prosperity diminishes the further one travels from London. Of course, disparities *within* regions can be as significant as those *between* them. Underlying economic circumstances help to frame the conditions

Figure 1.1: Regional gross domestic product per capita (1999)

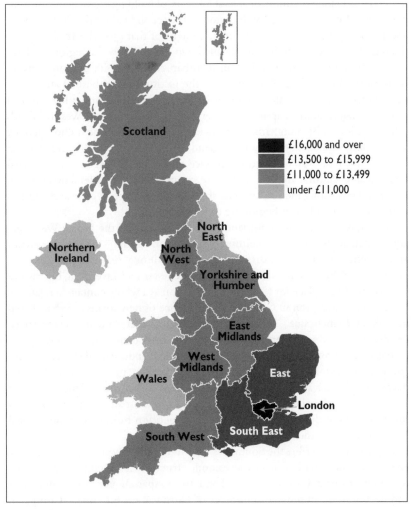

£16,000 and over
£13,500 to £15,999
£11,000 to £13,499
under £11,000

Source: ONS

in which regional institutions operate and broader regionalism can develop. For instance, in Chapter Four, Simon Lee notes that Yorkshire is a disadvantaged region, containing some of the most deprived communities in the UK. Lee measures the regional strategies developed in Yorkshire against the scale of these problems. He suggests that the capacity of the new regional institutions to improve social and economic conditions will remain vulnerable to external economic shocks. Lee charts the emergence of regional institutions, noting that the region has a record of regional institution building and close relationships between the main actors. However, he notes that in the period after 1997, regionalism had a relatively low civic and popular profile, with the regional press hostile to claims for devolution.

In Chapter Five, John Tomaney and John Mawson note that the West Midlands has a relatively long tradition, of at least 50 years, of building regional institutions. The West Midlands was a growth region in the second half of the 20th century and planning was focused on the management of that growth. In the 1980s, the region's traditional industries declined rapidly, and now the region contains some very deprived communities in its urban core. Despite the longevity of regional working in the West Midlands, the institutions established after 1997 got off to a shaky start, reflecting tensions between the RDA and other regional actors. A major factor shaping the pattern of regionalism in the West Midlands is the position of Birmingham. A multi-ethnic city of over one million people, and the largest local authority in England, Birmingham, which is reinventing its economic base as an international service centre, has its own complex internal political and cultural dynamics that are regarded with puzzlement by those living and governing the surrounding shire counties. Explicit civic and political regionalism are only just beginning to be visible.

In Chapter Six, Benito Giordano looks at the case of the North West. He argues that, despite having a tradition of institution building, the region remains ambivalent about regionalism. This ambivalence reflects real internal geographical division, notably between Manchester and Liverpool, but also in terms of finding a place for Cumbria. The region as a whole contains a relatively fast growing subregion in Cheshire and evidence of new forms of urban-based growth in Manchester. However, it is a region that contains severe social disadvantages and social tensions, as the riots of 2001 demonstrated. Liverpool, in particular, presents an example of exceptional industrial decline. In this context, the region began to develop regional working prior to 1997. This has developed further since, notably in the form of a concordat signed between Liverpool and Manchester in 2001. Regionalism, as broader civic and political force, appears in the North West to face competition from strong subregional – especially city – identities.

Tom Bridges describes the South West case in Chapter Seven. A geographically extensive region, with a diverse economic structure, it stretches from the hi-tech industry of Bristol on the one hand, to the sparsely populated rural areas and declining tin mining communities of Cornwall on the other. Compared to the northern regions, Bridges stresses the poor institutional inheritance of the South West and the virtual absence of regional working prior to 1997. The diversity of the region means much emphasis is put on subregional partnerships as the mode of working in the South West. All of these have posed specific challenges for regional working here. The South West does display an interest in civic and political regionalism, but the picture is complicated. A special feature is Cornwall's claim to nationhood, in which an active nationalist party has a number of representatives in local government.

In Chapter Eight, Neil Ward and John Tomaney examine the East of England. They note that this region is a relatively artificial construction, a point made by most key actors in the region. The region combines the East Anglian counties of Norfolk, Suffolk and Cambridgeshire, with the south eastern counties of Bedfordshire, Hertfordshire and Essex. The former group shares a common rural identity, while the most populous parts of the latter group are linked socially, economically and culturally to London. For instance, Watford has many of the characteristics of a London borough. The region is one of the most prosperous in England, with Cambridge as a centre of hi-tech industry. The new regional institutions have struggled to cope with the lack of regional identity, while important actors in the region (such as the press) have been actively hostile to regionalism. Nevertheless, the RDA has sought to forge a vision of the region as a hi-tech powerhouse and to promote this image internally and externally. County councils (and county identities) remain strong. In part it was these interests which led to the East of England being the first region where public conflict occurred between the new RDA and its corresponding voluntary chamber. A type of technocratic regionalism is emerging in the East of England, but there are few signs, as yet, of a broader political and civic regionalism developing.

If the East Midlands and East of England are said to provide unpropitious conditions for regionalism, then it is typically assumed that the South East region is even less fertile ground. The South East is generally regarded as amounting to little more than lines on official maps. In Chapter Nine, Peter John, Steve Musson and Adam Tickell suggest that there is more mobilisation and institution building than the stereotype implies. They suggest that the South East is characterised by a higher degree of economic coherence than is often assumed, and that there is a degree of shared economic problems – notably the need to upgrade the region's infrastructure if it is to maintain its international competitiveness. The new regional institutions, notably the RDA, emphasise how the South East needs to improve its international position, which may reflect a defensive position in relation to the other English regions, as much as real fears about its declining status. Although regionalism in the South East has a low public profile, it is interesting because it is being driven by Conservative local government leaders.

In Chapter Ten, John Tomaney and Paul Benneworth look at the case of the North East, which is often seen as being at the opposite end of the regionalist spectrum to the South East. The North East, by most measures, is the most disadvantaged English region, but one with a relatively long history of institution building and the strongest regional identity. The region has tended to be at the leading edge of demands for stronger regional institutions. The severity of the region's economic problems has been the backdrop to regionalism, but also places constraints on what the region itself can achieve. A theme of the debate in the North East has been the territorial distribution of public expenditure, which is seen as underpinning some of the region's problems, helping to fuel the debate on regionalism. The North East is the only region where the prospects for regional government are regularly debated in the press.

The East Midlands is another region not noted for the strength of its regional identity. It is a region with a diverse social and economic structure and polycentric urban form. It has no longstanding tradition of regional working, although some modest efforts in this direction were initiated prior to 1997. However, as Paul Foley notes in Chapter Eleven, the new regional structures bedded down quickly in the East Midlands. Indeed in some respects the East Midlands has proved itself an innovator, especially in terms of attempting to integrate the various regional strategies. The reasons for this may be that a regional agenda is new to the East Midlands, with little accompanying baggage, which has allowed rapid progress.

The final three chapters sketch out future issues surrounding English regionalism. As existing regional institutions take root, the question of elected Regional Assemblies gains greater salience. In Chapter Twelve, John Tomaney looks in more detail at how the existing structures of regional governance operate in practice in England. Looking at North East England, he asks what, if anything, constitutes the governance problem in the regions. The chapter focuses on the problem of institutional fragmentation and the impact that this might have on public policy outcomes.

The desire for more integrated public policy at the regional level, along with greater democratic accountability, are driving forces in the debate about elected regional government in England. In Chapter Thirteen, Paul McQuail and Mark Sandford examine what elected Regional Assemblies in England could look like. They sketch out three models of elected regional government. These models build on the institutional arrangements that already exist in the English regions. Each of the models has a different range of powers, from a model with purely strategic activities, through to an assembly with powers broadly equivalent to the National Assembly for Wales. Between these is a model that has both strategic and executive functions. McQuail and Sandford's analysis suggests that the 'strategic/executive' model could be a plausible ambition for those who favour further reform of regional governance in the direction of elected assemblies.

In Chapter Fourteen, Peter Jones shows how debates about the territorial distribution of public expenditure are moving up the political agenda. His focus is the Barnett Formula. As he notes, this is a widely misunderstood mechanism for determining *changes* in the distribution of public expenditure between the nations of the UK. The operation of the system over time has resulted in Scotland receiving a relatively generous settlement in terms of expenditure per capita. This advantage looks particularly unfair to those English regions that have higher levels of need than Scotland. In this context, the chapter outlines some measures that could be taken in the English regions to raise their level of resources.

Chapter Fifteen, takes a forward look, focusing particularly on the outlook for strategies and regional governance in England.

The debate about English regional governance is still in its infancy. Policy makers legislate and commentators opine, often without a good understanding of the diversity of political and economic conditions in England. This volume aims to help fill the knowledge gap. Its focus is unashamedly empirical. It paints a more detailed and comprehensive picture of the condition of English regionalism than is generally available: one of varied regions and growing political assertiveness beyond the metropolis. The task of research and analysis is just beginning.

References

Bogdanor, V. (1999) *Devolution*, Oxford: OPUS.

Harvie, C. (1991) 'English regionalism: the dog that never barked', in B. Crick (ed) *National identities*, Oxford: Blackwell.

Tomaney, J. (1999) 'New labour and the English Question', *The Political Quarterly*, vol 70, no 1, pp 74-82.

Wright, T. (2000) 'England, whose England?', in S. Chen and T. Wright (eds) *The English Question*, London: Fabian Society, pp 7-17.

TWO

Regional government in England: reviewing the evidence base

Wendy Russell Barter[1]

Introduction

The government was elected in 1997 with a commitment to a fundamental devolution of power, responsibilities and resources to the UK's constituent nations and regions. Alongside the most obvious manifestations of the 'UK devolution project' (Roberts, 2000), the establishment of the Scottish Parliament and the creation of directly elected Assemblies in Wales and Northern Ireland, England has frequently been portrayed as the "silent and uninvited guests at the devolutionary feast" (Wright, 2000, p 11). With the publication, in May 2002, of the White Paper *Your region, your choice*, the government's plans for taking forward its manifesto commitment to establish elected regional assemblies in England have now been set down (Cabinet Office/DTLR, 2002).

The focus of this chapter is the evidence base available for developing policy on elected regional assemblies within England. In recent years there has been a relative outpouring of research and (more often) commentary on different aspects of the 'regional agenda', with much debate focused on the 'English question': the implications of devolution for England and the desire (or otherwise) for an English tier of regional government. This chapter provides a brief review of the contribution of this research to some aspects of the debate surrounding the introduction of regional government. It is in no way intended to provide an exhaustive overview. Rather, it seeks to set down something of the wider research context within which policy decisions regarding elected regional assemblies have been made.

While the explicit focus of this chapter is about the research context within which decisions regarding English regional government policy were made, there is an important subtext relating to the operationalising of the government's commitment to evidence-based policy. Previous work has reviewed the availability of evidence regarding the rationale for, and purpose of, regional assemblies (Russell Barter, 2000), the findings of which stressed the range of approaches and experiences between countries and quite often within them. Overseas experience provides some evidence on which to draw, although analysis of international systems reveals that the form of regional government is not fixed and that there is no consensus on what regional tiers should look like nor how they should operate. Of necessity, therefore, key decisions surrounding the introduction of regional government within England – as with other countries that have regionalised – have been taken in the knowledge that research does not provide clear lessons for action. Evidence-based policy demands that those making policy decisions are receptive to research and willing to reflect on its implications for the decisions to be taken. By turn, it is also important that a body of research continues to emerge – both in terms of analyses of overseas experience and appraisals of options and their implications – in order to inform the process of rolling out regional assemblies within England.

This chapter briefly reviews the rise of the new regionalism body of research, before considering the evidence concerning the rationale for introducing regional government. Subsequent sections consider the findings of available research in terms of boundaries and what regions might look, the functions of regional government and, finally, the process of implementation.

Regions and the 'New Regionalism'

After at least two decades in the shadows, the relatively recent proliferation of research and commentary concerned with the role and impact of the region has been termed the 'New Regionalism'. This term has been coined to refer to the body of literature which claims that regions are the territorial sphere most suited to the interaction of economic, political and social processes within the context of globalisation (Tomaney and Ward, 2000). In this respect, the notion includes both the observation that the region is becoming an increasingly important element in economic development, as well as the normative view that the region *should* be the prime focus of such policy activity (cf Lovering, 1999).

A number of distinct themes can be identified within this literature. Conceptual work has focused on the extent to which the region provides the appropriate crucible for promoting and coordinating economic growth. From an economic perspective, a number of authors have argued that the economic success of a region is dependent on a series of social, cultural and institutional structures, as well as economic factors. Thus, it has been argued, regional government is a key driver of economic development, since it provides the necessary 'devolved institutional capacity' (Amin and Thrift, 1995). This has been accompanied by the emergence of a network paradigm (Cooke and Morgan, 1998), in which the region is seen as providing the necessary level of spatial clustering and interaction, between private and public sector activities, to facilitate this economic growth. These economic arguments have been accompanied by a body of literature that argues that the political importance of regions has grown in the context of globalisation and the restructuring of the nation state. Thus, it has been argued, economic pressures have forced nations to devolve powers both to supra-national structures and sub-national bodies in order that they are more responsive to global change, with a resultant 'hollowing out of the state' (Jessop, 1994).

Alongside this conceptual work, a body of research and literature has focused on the importance, for economic, political or functional reasons, of effective regional structures (although a characteristic of much of this literature is a lack of clarity about the definition of such regional structures). This work places an emphasis on the need for greater regional management arising from, in part: the fragmentation of the public sector, persistence of regional economic disparities, the traditionally limited regional presence of central government departments, and the (perceived) imperative driven by a Europe of the Regions. As a backdrop to this, political concerns have been expressed about the accountability and openness of many existing *governance* structures at the regional level (see, for example, Labour Party, 1995, 1996).

The rationale for regional government

Previous work has stressed the plethora of literature concerning the rationale for regional government (Russell Barter, 2000). Much of the literature comprises advocacy papers and thinkpieces from particular organisational or ideological perspectives (for example, Fabian Society, 1990; Constitution Unit, 1996; LGIU, 1997), and the debate to date has yet to produce a clear consensus. Instead it remains polarised between those who favour, and those who oppose, a regional tier of government.

To briefly summarise this literature, there are four main foci concerning the rationale for regional government: democratic arguments, economic development pressures, European imperatives, and administrative requirements, each of which reflect different perspectives of the debate and often implicitly reflect different notions of the form of regional government. In many respects, these arguments can be viewed as mutually reinforcing. The lack of any formal consensus within the literature reflects not only the inadequacy of any one set of arguments to provide a definite basis on which to build, argue Stoker et al (1996), but also the very ambiguity of the term 'regional government'. Like is not necessarily being compared with like. The sections below review the main thrusts of the various arguments deployed in the literature.

Democratic arguments

Democratic arguments are premised on, first, the potential role of regional government in adding accountability through devolving powers from central government and unelected bodies and, second, through permitting a more direct forum for the expression of diverse regional identities and needs. Advocates of regional government often focus on the centralised nature of government within England and argue that regional government would deliver accountability, democracy and greater efficiency to an ad hoc, uncoordinated and unelected regional tier (Coulson, 1990; Davis and Stewart, 1993; Straw, 1995), and provide a basis on which to reverse the democratic deficit (Morgan and Roberts, 1993).

Critics of this argument focus primarily on the relevance and practicality of regional government within existing structures, given that the current confusion of boundaries and agencies do not easily lend themselves to an autonomous regional tier of government (Hogwood, 1996). Critics also question whether regional government will necessarily increase accountability given the potential for the upward transfer of functions from local government to the regional level (CLD, 1995; Tindale, 1995). From this perspective, regional government is perceived as "centralism ... genuine decentralisation should be to local government, not to regional government" (Jones, 1988, p 5).

A second strand of the democratic argument relates to the notion of regional identity and the extent to which these differences demand a means of expression. Counterarguments question whether regional identity can be said to exist in England and, in any case, whether there should necessarily be political consequences of regional identity. Survey evidence remains inconclusive. This does not preclude, of course, the possibility that regional government itself may be an important facilitator of regional identity and that support may emerge once a regional tier of government is in place, although this is not necessarily borne out by international experience.

Economic imperative arguments

Economic arguments rest on notions of regional government as a key driver of economic performance through development of economic strategies and coordination of development needs. A large body of literature has emerged in recent years exploring the enhanced economic importance of regional units (for example, Porter, 1990; Krugman, 1991; Keating, 1998). The best mechanism for achieving a successful regional economic policy, it is argued, is the development of indigenous strengths through activities undertaken within individual regions (HM Treasury/DTI, 2001). A number of commentators argue, therefore, that regional government enables a wider 'brokerage' role to be undertaken, and provides scope to produce coherent strategies for economic growth, coordination of development needs, and provide a voice for regional economic concerns (Coulson, 1990; cf Martin and Pearce, 1993; Hutton, 1995; Wiehler and Stumm, 1995). Evidence supports the importance of institutional capacity in regional development (Morgan, 1986; Minns and Tomaney, 1995), although critics argue that the case for regional government (as distinct from regional intervention) is unclear. They further argue that the effect of political devolution may exacerbate *unhelpful* interregional competition, since it is generally accepted that regions with devolved institutions are more able to adopt competitive policies (and perhaps perceive greater legitimacy for so doing) (Keating, 1998). Indeed, the experience in Spain illustrates that those regions which have been granted more extensive powers have implemented more advanced and aggressive development strategies, notably through the use of *vacaciones fiscales* (Rodríguez-Pose, 1996). This begs the question of whether enhanced levels of interregional competition, and any associated growth in regional imbalances, are an acceptable outcome of political devolution.

The European imperative

European arguments rest on notions of the increased importance of the regions within the EU and their enhanced capacity to access funding and decision making (Martin and Pearce, 1993; Taylor, 1995). Critics argue that the role of the regions has been overstressed: the nation state remains pre-eminent and those countries without a regional tier of government do not appear to be disadvantaged. There is some evidence to support this argument: analysis of the role of the French regions in attracting EU Structural Funds indicated that they were not included in the process and that the regional *Préfet* (central government administrators in the regions) undertake the task (Le Galès and John, 1997). In any case, critics suggest, the pressures are not sufficient to justify reconfiguration of domestic systems of governance, particularly given that European funding levels are small relative to monies spent by the British government.

The administrative arguments

A persistent theme within research on regional governance has been the density of regional decision making across the public and quasi-public sectors within England, the sum total of which is a wide variety of different structures in form and scale, in administrative boundaries and in range of functions. Administrative arguments are drawn from the perception of regional government representing 'good' government in terms of efficiency and effectiveness, and that certain functions demand a more strategic coordinated approach. The current multiplicity of regional administrative arrangements, alongside the emergence of cross-cutting issues – with which local authorities may currently not possess all required competencies to deal – has led to arguments for the development of regional government in order to respond appropriately to these pressures (Norton, 1994; Council of Europe, 1998). Counterarguments stress the lack of any clear role for regional government within current local government arrangements given that relative to other European countries, England has a large-scale local government system. European evidence does not indicate a clear relationship between the size of a regional authority and its capacity for effective and efficient management; there is not a simple way of identifying the right size or tier to exercise government competencies.

What might regions look like?

The introduction of a regional government tier requires either the creation of new boundaries or the inheritance of existing ones. Traditionally, there has been a density of regional decision making within England, with a wide variety of regional structures: in form and scale, in administrative boundaries and in range of functions (Hogwood, 1996), although more recently there has been an increasing number of agencies adopting Government Office boundaries as the basis on which to operate. The White Paper sets down proposals for implementing assemblies on the basis of existing Government Office/Regional Development Agency (RDA) boundaries, in part because they are the established unit of administration for an increasing number of public and private functions, because they command a reasonably high level of public recognition and they represent a credible size to support a regional assembly.

There is a debate within the literature about the most appropriate form of boundaries, although it is clear that this will be affected by the nature of functions ascribed to a regional tier (Stewart, 1995; Stoker et al, 1996; Sandford and McQuail, 2001). Regional identity is a key factor in the political significance ascribed to regional government, yet it is clear that England does not have, even in the case of the North East, the sort of historical identity and sustained devolutionary pressures that existed in Scotland. Indeed, there are some parts of England which, by any criterion, do not clearly belong to any region (Sandford and McQuail, 2001).

International evidence, however, appears to indicate that it is not necessary to have an historic identity in order to create a modern political one (Keating, 1996; Stoker et al, 1996). It is possible to find examples of highly artificial regions maintaining a coherent identity (for example, the French region Rhône-Alpes and many of the German *Länder*), as well as traditional regions (for example in the south of Italy) being hardly able to establish an identity and develop their own strategies. On this basis, Stoker et al (1996) argue that other cultural dimensions are more important than a pre-existing sense of regional identity, including: social stability, established processes of democratic participation, and the existence of social and economic relationships.

Aside from the issue of regional identity, others argue that regional boundaries should be based on areas which not only facilitate the democratic process, but also enable services to be provided economically and efficiently, and as close as possible to the individual (Norton, 1994; Council of Europe, 1998). There does not appear a need for administrative consistency among regions. There is no precedence internationally that authorities with similar powers need to be of a similar geographical or demographic size, and there are numerous European examples of significant diversity in the size of regions.

What would regional government do?

Inevitably, much of the debate around the rationale for the introduction of regional government gravitates towards the issue of what regional government will do and what value-added it will bring. Indeed, without a clear understanding of the potential functions envisaged for regional government, the debate concerning the merits (or otherwise) of its introduction can, at times, become sterile. The White Paper has outlined a largely strategic role for elected regional assemblies. They are to provide a strategic vision for improving the quality of life in their regions, in particular improving economic performance. But they will have important powers to ensure delivery of their strategies, notably through the sponsorship of their RDA.

In terms of the evidence base on which to draw, there has been limited attention paid in the research to the specific policy areas in which regional government might best operate, the administrative mechanisms by which it might best exercise that responsibility, and the appropriate degree to which it might operate with discretion over those functions. In short, there is no clear delineation as to what functions are best carried out at the regional level. We know, for example, that the functions undertaken by regional government vary significantly, from narrow administrative capacities (for example, France), to broad remits entrenched in written constitutions (for example, Spain and Germany). Similarly, international experience demonstrates the range of distinct administrative capacities of regional assemblies, from direct service provision, strategic powers and other powers in relation to existing institutions, such as scrutiny powers. In the English context, the White Paper sets down proposals that regional assemblies should have a range of *executive* functions, for example responsibility for the RDAs, and financial responsibility for functions such as housing and tourism. In addition, they are to have a much wider *influencing* role, including: scrutiny (of RDAs), appointment responsibilities for the Learning and Skills Councils, advisory role in respect of local transport funding, and strategic responsibilities in terms of planning and public health.

Implementing regional government

Reviews of international systems of regional government suggest that the form is not fixed: it is a process rather than an event, whose 'end-state' is not necessarily known at the beginning and which may take decades to reach. Furthermore it is clear that approaches and practice across countries, and regions within them, to regional government, differs considerably. In terms of the domestic literature on the implementation of regional government, it is only recently that this has begun to progress beyond the rhetoric of regional devolution (notably Sandford and McQuail, 2001).

The phasing and speed of introduction

The model of English devolution presented within the White Paper very clearly states that regional assemblies will only be introduced where people in a region vote to have one. By definition, therefore, the process (if not the outcome) will be asymmetric: there may be a period of time during which some regions will have elected regional assemblies and others will not. Such an approach is certainly not atypical. Indeed, the UK is already an example of differential levels of devolution being granted to different areas at different times.

Other European examples of regionalisation demonstrate that not all regions are required to move at the same pace or need to be involved in every stage of change (Newlands, 1998). In Italy, the five *special status* regions have more functional competencies, greater financial powers and a higher degree of autonomy than other regions. The development of *Autonomous Communities* in Spain, with its broad distinction between nations and regions, is regarded as a prototype of an asymmetric regionalisation process in which the 'historic nations' were accorded wide economic and political status while the remaining regions have a more modest devolution of powers and functions. Conversely, in France, a consistent structure of regional government is uniform across the whole country.

Supporters argue that this asymmetry allows reflection both of different regions' capacity to carry out functions and the political support for doing so. Critics argue that there are costs associated with such asymmetric or incremental approaches, in that they may impede regional cooperation and therefore reduce efficiency in the conduct of intergovernmental relations. International evidence suggests that in most cases, special arrangements designed to meet the demands of a small number of regions have been quickly followed by a similar structure for the whole country, a phenomenon termed *fiebre autonómica* (autonomy fever) in Spain.

The resource implications of introducing regional government

The issue of finance cannot be considered independently of the purpose which regional government is intended to serve. The nature of its functions will determine both the scale of resource required and the extent to which regions are able to exercise self-determination. The White Paper sets down the proposal that regional assemblies will be funded primarily by central government grant which they will have the freedom to spend as they deem best, subject to helping to achieve certain agreed targets. In addition, regional assemblies will be able to raise additional resources via a precept on the Council Tax, an arrangement that currently exists for the Greater London Authority.

Advocates argue that for regional government to operate requires access to regional tax revenues rather than complete reliance on transfers, although international evidence points to the variety of financial arrangements, and degree of autonomy, in place. In Germany, the *Länder* have tax raising powers, although this represents a small proportion of their income, while in Italy, the resources of *regioni* are distributed largely via central government in the form of block and tied grants.

Discussion of the extent of regional financial autonomy, however, cannot be divorced from consideration of interregional economic imbalances. The ability of regions to raise revenue is largely reflective of their different socioeconomic and demographic characteristics. As a result, any increase in regional financial autonomy may serve to exacerbate regional inequalities, unless explicit national policies of redistribution are implemented to counter them. Drawing on the case of Poland, for example, where regions have autonomy to levy and spend one third of their regional budget, the revenue-raising capacity of those regions near the country's eastern frontier is much lower than more prosperous regions further west (Dawson, 1999; Regulski, 1999).

Conceptually, it is possible that the introduction of financial autonomy could be progressed in stages, and Tindale (1995) proposes a three-stage process in which regional government was initially funded by grants, then, in the medium term, to allocate regions a share of taxes collected locally and then, in the longer term, there may be a case for giving regions power to vary those tax rates. It is, nevertheless, supposed that local authorities are unlikely to welcome regional authorities being given a share of their taxable resources (Tindale, 1995; LGIU, 1997).

Relationships between regional assemblies and other tiers of government

It is clear that the introduction of elected regional assemblies into England will have implications for existing government structures and organisations. The White Paper stresses the need for regional assemblies to work with local authorities and others in order to establish effective working arrangements. There has been little analysis to date of the implications of introducing regional government within England on existing governance arrangements.

A relatively large body of advocacy work exists examining the implications for local government of an additional tier of sub-national government (notably Jones, 1988; Stewart, 1995; LGIU, 1997). The thrust of this work essentially argues that the relationship with local government may initially be tense if there are perceived or actual loss of functions to regions. International experience appears to add some credence to these fears, although in the longer term, European evidence reveals significant levels of interaction and joint working. The Council of Europe (1998) suggest it may be prudent for local authorities to have a judicial remedy to protect themselves from interference, allied with a need for flexibility about the most appropriate tier to perform different functions across regions. It remains, however, that local–central relations may become more complex.

The development of regional government challenges both the powers and existence of sub-regional intermediate organisations. There is little domestic literature examining the impact, although there is an implicit assumption that regional government constitutes an improvement on the current disaggregation of (unaccountable) activities. Critics question this point, highlighting the (political) need for central monitoring of regional government and arguing that it merely replaces one set of structures with another. Whether the value-added of regional government takes the form of partnership synergy *writ large*, or whether there are more fundamental issues, has not yet been explored within the research.

Conclusions

Decisions regarding the introduction of regional government within England have, of necessity, largely been taken in the absence of any comprehensive empirical or comparative analysis of the options for it. While the domestic literature concerning the justifications for regional government is relatively extensive, there remain a number of significant gaps in connection with detailed form and function issues, although it is acknowledged that many of the issues are not amenable to any clear research statement. In contrast, literature about international forms of regional government is more developed and contains much detail about existing systems. This provides evidence that an evolutionary and incremental approach to the introduction of regional government can be adopted. It also indicates the breadth of international experience in terms of size of regions, and constitution and powers of elected bodies, such that there is no obvious overseas model which might be applied to England.

The government is of the view that regional government within England has a strong role to play in overcoming fragmentation of existing policy and institutions, and will bring strength, clarity and accountability to the existing web of governance structures operating within regions. Timely and accessible research will be important in this rolling out, in terms of analysis of the ways in which assemblies might operate, and the implications of pursuing different courses of action. Research, like the implementation of elected regional assemblies, is a process not an event.

Note

[1] The views in this chapter are those of the author and do not necessarily reflect those of the government.

References

Amin, A. and Thrift, N. (1995) 'Globalisation, "institutional thickness" and the local economy', in P. Healey et al (eds) *Managing cities: The new urban context*, Chichester: John Wiley & Sons, pp 91-108.

Cabinet Office/DTLR (Department for Transport, Local Government and the Regions) (2002) *Your region, your choice: Revitalising the English regions*, Cm 5511, London: DTLR.

CLD (Commission for Local Democracy) (1995) *Taking charge: The rebirth of local democracy*, London: CLD.

Constitution Unit (1996) *Regional government in England*, London: Constitution Unit.

Cooke, P. and Morgan, K. (1998) *The associational economy*, Oxford: Oxford University Press.

Coulson, A. (1990) *Devolving power: The case for regional government*, London: Fabian Society.

Council of Europe (1998) *Regionalisation and its effects on local self-government*, Local and regional authorities in Europe series No 64, Strasbourg: Council of Europe.

Davis, H. and Stewart, J. (1993) *The growth of government by appointment: Implications for local democracy*, Luton: Local Government Management Board.

Dawson, A. (1999) 'The transformation of Polish local government', *Public Administration*, vol 77, no 4, pp 897-902.

Fabian Society (1990) *Devolving power: The case for regional government*, London: Fabian Society.

HM Treasury/DTI (Department for Trade and Industry) (2001) *Productivity in the UK: The regional dimension*, London: HM Treasury/DTI.

Hogwood, B. (1996) *Mapping the regions: Boundaries, coordination and government*, Bristol/York: The Policy Press/Joseph Rowntree Foundation.

Hutton, W. (1995) *The state we're in*, London: Jonathan Cape.

Jessop, B. (1994) 'Post-Fordism and the state', in A. Amin (ed) *Post-Fordism: A reader*, Oxford: Blackwell, pp 251-79.

Jones, G. (1988) 'Against regional government', *Local Government Studies*, vol 14, no 5, pp 1-11.

Keating, M. (1996) 'Regional devolution: the West European experience', *Public Money & Management*, vol 16, no 4, pp 35-42.

Keating, M. (1998) 'What's wrong with asymmetrical government?', *Regional and Federal Studies*, vol 8, pp 195-218.

Krugman, P. (1991) *Geography and trade*, Cambridge, MA: MIT Press.

Labour Party (1995) *A choice for England*, London: Labour Party.

Labour Party (1996) *A new voice for England's regions: Labour's proposals for English regional government*, London: Labour Party.

Le Galès, P. and John, P. (1997) 'Is the grass greener on the other side? What went wrong with French regions, and the implications for England', *Policy & Politics*, vol 25, no 1, pp 51-60.

LGIU (Local Government Information Unit) (1997) *Mapping the future: A local perspective on English regional government*, London: LGIU.

Lovering, J. (1999) 'Theory led by policy: the inadequacies of the "new regionalism"', *International Journal of Urban and Regional Research*, vol 23, pp 379-95.

Martin, S. and Pearce, G. (1993) 'European regional development strategies: strengthening meso-government in the UK?', *Regional Studies*, vol 27, no 7, pp 681-5.

Minns, R. and Tomaney, J. (1995) 'Regional government and local economic development: the realities of economic power in the UK', *Regional Studies*, vol 29, no 2, pp 202-7.

Morgan, K. (ed) (1986) *Regionalism in European politics*, London: Policy Studies Institute.

Morgan, K. and Roberts, E. (1993) *The democratic deficit: A guide to quangoland*, Papers in Planning Research 144, Cardiff: Department of City and Regional Planning, University of Wales.

Newlands, D. (1998) 'Limits to the economic powers of regional government', Paper presented to the Regional Science Association Annual Conference, York, September.

Norton, A. (1994) *International handbook of local and regional government: A comparative analysis of advanced democracies*, Cheltenham: Edward Elgar.

Porter, M. (1990) *The competitive advantage of nations*, London: Macmillan.

Regulski, J. (1999) *Building democracy in Poland: The state reform of 1998*, Local Government and Public Service Reform Initiative Discussion Paper No 9, Budapest: Open Society Institute.

Roberts, P. (2000) *The new territorial governance: Planning, developing and managing the United Kingdom in an era of devolution*, London: TCPA.

Rodríguez-Pose, A. (1996) 'Growth and institutional change: the influence of the Spanish regionalisation process on economic performance', *Environment and Planning C: Government and Policy*, vol 14, no 1, pp 71-87.

Russell Barter, W. (2000) *Regional government in England: A preliminary review of literature and research findings*, London: DETR.

Sandford, M. and McQuail, P. (2001) *Unexplored territory: Elected regional assemblies in England*, London: Constitution Unit, UCL.

Stewart, J. (1995) 'Reflections on regional government', *Political Quarterly*, vol 66, no 4, pp 269-77.

Stoker, G., Hogwood, B. and Bullman, U. with Osei, P. and Cairney, P. (1996) *Regionalism*, Luton: Local Government Management Board.

Straw, J. (1995) 'Labour and the regions of England', Regional Studies Association Guest Lecture, Labour Party Press Release, London: Labour Party, 28 September.

Taylor, K. (1995) 'European Union: the challenge for local and regional government', *Political Quarterly*, vol 66, no 1, pp 74-83.

Tindale, S. (1995) *Devolution on demand – Options for the English regions and London*, London: IPPR.

Tomaney, J. and Ward, N. (2000) 'England and the "New Regionalism"', *Regional Studies*, vol 34, no 5, pp 471-8.

Wiehler, F. and Stumm, T. (1995) 'The powers of regional and local authorities and their role in the European Union', *European Planning Studies*, vol 3, no 2, pp 227-50.

Wright, T. (2000) 'England, whose England?', in S, Chen and T. Wright, *The English question*, London: Fabian Society.

THREE

New Labour and the evolution of regionalism in England

John Tomaney

Introduction

In New Labour's first term its action in the regional field was restricted to the establishment of Regional Development Agencies (RDAs) in 1999 and the promotion of voluntary Regional Chambers. However, New Labour did not deliver on the promise, contained in its 1997 Manifesto, to introduce directly elected Regional Assemblies, where there was demonstrable demand (Tomaney, 2000). The period before the General Election of 2001 saw the government act to strengthen the main regional institutions within England. These included additional resources, and the promise of increased financial flexibility, for RDAs and new central government resources for Regional Chambers. New Labour's deepening engagement with the issue culminated in the commitment on the part of the government to publish a White Paper on English regional government. However, the first Queen's Speech after the election failed to mention the English regions. Moreover, in the aftermath of the election, significant changes in Whitehall departmental responsibilities occurred which had implications for the governance of the English regions. New Labour's engagement with the English regions continued to reveal an ambivalence about devolution in general and English regionalism in particular.

This chapter outlines the evolution of the new thinking emerging within the government as far as the English regions are concerned, and reports on the development of RDAs, Regional Chambers and the various civic campaigns for devolution that have sprung up in parts of England. The chapter also examines the ways in which the concerns of the English regions have been addressed in Westminster and Whitehall. Although the political space for regionalism may have expanded within England, its shape and progress remain uneven and hotly contested. The chapter concludes by assessing the issues that confronted the government as far as the English regions are concerned.

The regional debate

The evolution of the regional debate was punctuated by a series of interventions by senior Labour figures in the period after July 2000. These interventions followed a call by the party's National Policy Forum for the government to bring forward a White Paper on regional government (Tomaney, 2000). A series of ministerial statements also prepared the way for new resources and responsibilities for RDAs and Regional Chambers. Ministers' statements also helped to stake out the territory upon which the government's White Paper on regional government will be produced.

The leading government figure in the promotion of regional policy and regional government during this period was – and remains – the Deputy Prime Minister, John Prescott. A significant development in the run-up to the General Election of 2001, however, was the sound of new voices in the debate. Chief among these was that of the Chancellor of the Exchequer, Gordon Brown, who, in a number of speeches, began to make the case for greater action at the regional level to alleviate socio-economic disparities. Gordon Brown's interventions were prefigured by those of his Chief Economic Advisor, Ed Balls, who began to sketch out arguments in favour of greater regional autonomy in the field of economic development policy. Balls contributed to a pamphlet in which he made the case for a 'new approach' to regional policy:

> Our new regional policy is based on two principles – it aims to strengthen the essential building blocks of growth – innovation, skills and the development of enterprise – by exploiting the indigenous strengths in each region and city. And it is bottom-up not top-down, with national government enabling powerful regional and local initiatives to work by providing the necessary flexibility and resources. (Balls, 2000, pp 12-13)

This new approach of promoting regional initiative raises questions of accountability:

> [T]he new resources and flexibilities for RDAs will require greater regional and local accountability and public scrutiny – to ensure the regional strategies are responding to the needs and helping to ensure that decisions of RDA boards are consistent with regional and local strategies. (Balls, 2000, p 15)

The Chancellor echoed these themes in a speech made in Manchester at the end of January 2001. In the speech he called for a regional policy based on local initiative and focused on the promotion of 'indigenous measures' aimed at the promotion of enterprise, skills, technological change and job creation (Brown, 2001; see also Tomaney and Hetherington, 2001b, for further discussion). This would provide the basis for 'a Britain of nations and regions'. The Chancellor argued that stronger regional initiative requires greater local accountability based both on strengthened Regional Chambers and changes to the House of Commons.

> By extending the scope for region by region initiatives and by complimenting these with greater accountability at a regional level and through the select

committee system in the Commons, we are proving our ability to ensure that
regionally set objectives are met. (Brown, 2001)

The Chancellor connected his approach to a wider set of constitutional concerns:

We are moving away from the old Britain of subjects where people had to
look upwards to a Whitehall bureaucracy for their solutions – to a Britain of
citizens where region to region, locality to locality we are ourselves in charge
and where it is up to us. (Brown, 2001)

Although Chancellor Brown stopped short of raising the issue of directly elected
assemblies, the press coverage of the speech suggested it was the first step to his
endorsement of an idea hitherto associated with John Prescott. A report in the
London *Evening Standard* (29 January 2001) noted that the content of the
Chancellor's remarks had little or no connection with his Treasury
responsibilities:

Instead, it outlined plans to increase the accountability of regional development
agencies as *a first step toward elected assemblies* for the English regions. The
policy has its keenest supporter in Deputy Prime Minister John Prescott, into
whose turf it falls. There is little suggestion, however, of Mr Brown's choice of
subject sparking protests from Prescott. Instead there were claims that the
two men are forging new links with polling day rapidly approaching. (emphasis
added)

The *Financial Times* (29 February 2001) also claimed that talk of increased
accountability of RDAs was "an interim measure before elected assemblies are
created in English regions". The more immediate effects of the Chancellor's
new-found interest, however, were increased funds and flexibility for RDAs
and central government resources for Regional Chambers.

Other developments during early 2001 also suggested that a space for
regionalism was opening up. For instance, Department for Environment,
Transport and the Regions (DETR) ministers implied that they had dropped
New Labour's previous stipulation that unitary local government was a prerequisite of moves to regional government. In the House of Commons in
January, John Prescott made it clear that moves to regional government were
not dependent on a preceding reform of local government (*Hansard*, 16 January
2001, col 184). Beverley Hughes, the junior minister in the DETR, reiterated
this approach in a debate in Westminster Hall in January 2001 (*Hansard*, 17
January 2001). It was a commitment, which ministers repeated publicly on
subsequent occasions. Such statements contributed to a perception that the
government was preparing to act on Regional Assemblies in its second term.
Thus, the *Financial Times* reported the minister's statement "was certain to have
been cleared by John Prescott" and represented "the clearest signal yet" that the
government would move on elected assemblies ('Labour signals rapid regional
referendums', *Financial Times*, 11 May 2001).

Irrespective of whether or not the Chancellor's speech signalled his conversion to regional assemblies, the background to the new concern with regional policy appears to be twofold. On the one hand it reflects the persistence of regional disparities within England. In November 2000, the then Trade and Industry Secretary, Stephen Byers – another new voice in the debate – argued:

> The economic differences between UK regions are clear and indicate that a winners' circle is emerging, with some regions keeping up and staying in touch while others slip further behind. These are the underlying causes we need to tackle through a strong, radically reformed regional policy, simply tinkering at the edges will not be enough. (DTI Press Release, P/2000/761, 15 November 2000)

Underpinning this concern about persistent regional disparities is an essentially 'Keynesian' analysis of their economic consequences – that is the view that unused social and economic resources in lagging regions represent a constraint on the output growth of the national economy. In a later speech, Byers sought to link the goals of "social justice and economic efficiency" in the field of regional policy in a more or less explicitly Keynesian way:

> We do so out of a sense of social justice but also because our future economic success as a country depends on all parts and all people of the United Kingdom achieving their full potential. (Byers, 2001)

This concern with a 'winners' circle', however, probably also reflected a more practical political concern with the condition and mood of New Labour's electoral heartlands in the run-up to the General Election. Senior New Labour figures were motivated by the need to mitigate a perception in some regions that New Labour was mainly responding to the concerns of Middle England, and had little specific to offer its traditional bastions. A number of episodes contributed to this perception over the preceding period. The impact of the Bank of England's interest policy – aimed at restricting the growth of consumer demand in the South but impacting severely on those regions disproportionately dependent on manufacturing industry – had become an issue for some RDA chairs and for the media in some regions. In addition, the Prime Minister's intervention in late 1999, which appeared to cast doubt on the existence of the North/South divide, provoked a strong backlash in the northern regions – and a swift retraction.

The perception that New Labour was open to arguments in favour of regionalism was reinforced when a further influential voice was added to the debate. In a speech in his Hartlepool constituency at the end of March 2001, the former Northern Ireland Secretary Peter Mandelson made a powerful call for North East regional government. Describing himself as a convert to the cause, he argued that "we cannot achieve economic revitalisation in the North East without modernising the means of delivering our economic policies, and this means renewing the region's political institutions". He continued:

"The first step is to introduce a democratically elected element into the existing regional chamber by establishing a regional authority for the North East that is tight in numbers and focus. The elected element would need to be based on proportional representation drawing together all the political parties and areas of the region." (Quoted in Tomaney and Hetherington, 2000b, p 26)

The speech appeared to give a powerful New Labour endorsement to regionalism, albeit in a partially elected form. Given the proximity of Peter Mandelson to the heart of the New Labour project, his intervention was seen by some as a strong signal of likely future trends.

Institutions of regional governance

The evolving debate on regional governance provided the backdrop for a number of developments in the institutions of regional governance in the period before, and just after, the General Election of 2001. Most attention focused on the activities of RDAs, Regional Chambers/Assemblies and Government Offices (GOs). However, events during the period also drew attention to the activities of other public bodies in the regions and the ways in which these have a bearing on the governance of the English regions.

Regional Development Agencies (RDAs)

RDAs represented the centrepiece of New Labour's policies for the English regions in its first term. In the final year of the last government New Labour acted to strengthen their capacity to address regional economic problems. These moves reflected, in part, a response to criticisms – not least from business leaders – that RDAs lacked the resources and flexibility to make an impact on regional problems. At the centre of the criticism was the accusation that RDAs had too many Whitehall paymasters enforcing their priorities over regional strategies (see, PIU, 2000; Tomaney, 2000).

At the same time, however, and as I mentioned earlier, moves to bolster the activities of RDAs reflected a genuine belief on the part of the Chancellor that they could play a key role in achieving his ambition of full employment. The first indication of the expanded role of RDAs came in the Spending Review 2000, which announced increased resources for RDAs (see Table 3.1).

In addition to increased resources, the Spending Review also contained proposals to extend the financial flexibility afforded to RDAs. This was to be achieved by creating "a single cross departmental funding framework" in order to overcome the problems of 'Departmentalitis' that were identified by the Performance and Innovation Unit (PIU, 2000). In return, it was announced, that RDAs would be given "challenging outcome targets" (HM Treasury, 2000a). The Chancellor expanded on the new approach in his Pre-Budget Report in November 2000. This claimed that RDAs "provide a key element in the delivery of the Government's strategy for improving UK productivity" (HM Treasury, 2000b). The report also provided details of how the single programme (also

Table 3.1: Spending allocations for RDAs in the 2000 Spending Review (SR2000) (£ million)

	2000/01	2001/02	2002/03	2003/04
Total programme before SR2000	1,182	1,271	-	-
Total programme after SR2000	1,242	1,445	1,550	1,700
New single budget of which:				
DETR existing	1,114	1,183		
DETR additional	60	150		
DfEE existing	49	49		
DfEE additional	0	8.5		
DTI existing	19	39		
DTI additional	0	15		

Source: DETR News Release 489, 21 July 2000

known as 'the single pot') would work. He announced that RDAs would be able to transfer up to 20% out of any programme to another programme, so long as it was consistent with delivery objectives. He also announced the inception of a new Strategic Programme, which would allow RDAs to promote innovative schemes that meet their economic, and other strategic aims, as a test-bed for the Single Budget and new project appraisal processes to be introduced in 2002 (HM Treasury, 2000b).

The Department of Trade and Industry's (DTI) White Paper on enterprise, skills and innovation published in March 2001, further endorsed the evolving role of RDAs (DTI, 2001). It ascribed a prominent role to regional policy in meeting the government's wider industrial policy. The White Paper claimed to adopt a new approach to regional policy concerned with "building the capability of regions and communities":

> Government must equip all regions and communities with the means to build on their own distinctive cultures, know-how and competitive advantages. This must be a bottom–up approach: the role of central Government must be to ensure that all regions and communities have the resources and capability to be winners. Strong regional policies have shown their worth in other European economies and in the USA. (DTI, 2001, para 3.3)

The White Paper proposed the notion of industry 'clusters' as the basis of its new approach to promoting economic development. Cluster development has been taken up as a major theme of the work of RDAs subsequently. (The debate around the White Paper also signalled the future shift of responsibility for RDAs from the DETR to the DTI; this is discussed later in this chapter.)

RDA chairmen, however, remained sceptical about the degree of the government's commitment to letting RDAs off the leash (Tomaney and Hetherington, 2000). Graham Hall, the chairman of Yorkshire Forward, writing at the end of 2000, offered a series of challenges to the government:

Firstly, the concept of the 'single pot' must be made a reality. This concept is so counter-cultural to the way Parliament votes money, the accountability mechanisms and the 'command and control' nature of large parts of Whitehall that it is not as simple as it first seems. This must consist of a clear corporate planning process, whereby the Government 'buys' a single set of outcomes – one Public Service Agreement – from RDAs, and sensible monitoring of review arrangements. It must not consist of separate corporate plans, prescriptive guidance, an excessive degree of details in planning and reporting, mid year initiatives involving RDA bidding and outputs so specific as to make any flexibility mythical. This is our biggest current challenge for Ministers.

The financial accountability arrangements should be changed to reflect the devolution of responsibility to RDAs. RDA Chief Executives should take sole responsibility as Accounting Officers and Departmental Permanent Secretaries should lose their dual responsibility. This will help to relax the present 'control' culture of the Civil Service. A more fundamental review of the Civil Service may be also needed in the medium term. (Hall, 2000, p 27)

The tensions reached a high point in January 2001 when RDA chairs met senior officials at the DETR to discuss the shape of the 'single pot'. RDA chairs accused Whitehall officials of dragging their feet. One said:

The concept of the 'single pot' is so counter-cultural (to the civil service) and the accountability mechanisms, the command and control nature of Whitehall, that it makes it a quite difficult thing to get through.... [T]hey find it incredibly difficult to deal with things across more than one department. Part of the argument for why you have to have RDAs is because you cannot control things from a distance and have to be on the ground where things really happen. There is a real issue here about the modernisation of Whitehall and I have to say the jury is out at present. (Quoted in Tomaney and Hetherington, 2001a, p 9)

Notwithstanding these tensions, at a meeting with RDA chairs in Middlesbrough in March 2001, John Prescott and Gordon Brown jointly announced further details of the new scheme. (Simultaneously they announced proposals to enhance the scrutiny functions of Regional Chambers, discussed later in this chapter.) The Single Budget arrangements were to be in place by April 2002. In the immediate aftermath of the General Election, with RDAs now a responsibility of the DTI, the new Trade Secretary Patricia Hewitt, announced the system of general outcome targets that would apply from April 2002. These covered the areas of regional business performance, employment creation, skill formation and the recycling of brown-field land. Although the details of the agreements between the government and the individual RDAs had yet to be finalised, RDA chairs, by July 2001, were more confident that Whitehall officials would avoid too much day-to-day interference in their work, although whether this reflected the wider views of business was unclear (Tomaney et al, 2001).

Regional Chambers/Assemblies

Regional Chambers (or 'Assemblies' as most style themselves) are the other new actors in the English regions that are the product of New Labour's policies since 1997 (see Tomaney, 2000). The central task of Regional Chambers remains that of providing a level of scrutiny of RDAs. The role of chambers, however, expanded in many regions during the period July 2000 to July 2001, and announcements by ministers presaged an even greater role in the future.

The first indication of the government's ambitions for Regional Chambers was contained in the government's Planning Policy Guidance Note on Regional Planning, published in October 2000. In this note, the government proposed that Regional Chambers should assume responsibility for the preparation for Regional Planning Guidance (RPG) from regional planning conferences of local authorities. It argued:

> Given the representation of a range of regional stakeholders on each Regional Chamber, and the latter's role in relation to the RDA under the RDAs Act, it makes sense for the Chamber to take on the regional planning function. Indeed a Chamber supported by a full time regional planning, monitoring and review team would be in an ideal position to provide the necessary leadership to produce and implement an integrated spatial strategy for the region. However, the arrangements to be adopted in any particular region must be for the region to decide. (DETR, 2000, para 2.4)

In most regions, chambers moved to assume the role of Regional Planning Conferences. In other regions, such as the West Midlands, powerful local authorities initially kept control of the regional planning process, although subsequent developments are loosening their grasp (discussed later in this chapter).

A further major development occurred at the meeting between John Prescott, Gordon Brown and the RDA chairs in Middlesbrough in March 2001 (as I mentioned earlier). At the meeting John Prescott proposed offering central government resources to assist Regional Chambers in their job of scrutinising RDAs and ensuring that their strategies and activities mesh with the wider framework of strategies for the region. A DETR discussion paper, published at the same time, offered suggestions of how the resources might be used:

> [B]y way of illustration, the way forward could involve the chambers establishing a stronger analytical or research capacity to monitor and evaluate the RDAs' plans in relation to the region's performance and to the wider strategic context within the region. In doing so they will, for example, need to lock into the work of the Regional Observatories [which monitor local social and economic conditions] and consider the links with the work on monitoring implementation of Regional Planning Guidance. It could also involve the chambers holding hearings at which the RDAs could formally explain and answer questions on their performance against their strategies

and targets. In turn, the chambers will need to feed back their conclusions to the RDAs and to communicate developments to the wider regional community. (Quoted in Tomaney and Hetherington, 2001b, pp 15-16)

Following a consultation, the government announced a £15 million fund for Regional Chambers in July 2001, amounting to £5 million per annum for the next three years, with each chamber receiving £500,000 per annum and £1 million available for joint initiatives. The consequence of the changes was to raise the profile of Regional Chambers as regional actors. One immediate effect, for instance, was to reopen the debate – in those regions that had not already done so – about chambers taking over the responsibilities of Regional Planning Conferences, as the government's own Planning Policy Guidance had suggested.

Independent of government announcements, chambers were already beginning to assert themselves as political actors in their respective regions, carrying out three distinctive roles:

• holding RDAs to account;
• representing regions in conflicts with central government;
• policy integration.

Regional Chambers are developing a diversity of structures in pursuit of these aims, as represented in Table 3.2.

The most public effort by a chamber to call its RDA to account occurred in the East of England. According to the *Local Government Chronicle*, "The East of England is not noted for its political turbulence" ('Opinion', 12 April 2001). The paper suggested, therefore, that, "It comes as something of a surprise that the first insurrection against the government's fudged regional policy should emanate from the east". The 'insurrection' came about when, on 5 April 2001, New Labour and Conservative members on the East of England Regional Assembly (EERA) refused to endorse a revision of the East of England Development Agency's (EEDA) Regional Economic Strategy (RES). EEDA is the only RDA to undertake a major revision of its RES, but chose to do so in the light of new research and the evolving institutional architecture in the region. Members of the assembly were reportedly concerned about the environmental impact of its 3.2% growth target, its alleged failure to take account of subregional differences, the arrangements for partnership working, and a concern that questions of social inclusion had not been properly dealt with. EEDA had adopted its first version in October 1999, but agreed to revise it after EERA had voiced what its chair, John Kent, described as "severe reservations". Concerns raised by subregional partnerships prompted the assembly to reject the strategy. Mr Kent accused EEDA of "ducking the difficult decisions" needed to stimulate development (quoted in Tomaney and Hetherington, 2001b, p 16). Rejection of the revised RES came about because EERA had previously given only its qualified endorsement to the first version of the strategy.

Table 3.2: Regional Chambers in England: basic data

	East of England	East Midlands	Yorkshire and Humberside	North West	North East	West Midlands	South West	South East
Name:	Regional Assembly	Regional Assembly	Regional Chamber	Regional Assembly	Regional Assembly	Regional Chamber	Regional Assembly	Regional Assembly
Composition:								
Size	42	105	35	80	63	100	117	111
Local authority (%)	66	63	63	70	66	68	75	70
Stakeholder representation	14	35	13	24	19	32	38	34
Budget 2000-01	The Assembly sets no levy and has no budget	Combined LGA and Assembly – £800,000. Assembly – £140,000	£1.2m including full RPG budget (£240,000) dedicated to Regional Chambers	£1.1m which includes the RPG Budget and secondees for waste and sustainability	£861,000 combined	c.£100,000 in cash or in kind	Combined £300,000	£1.2 m.

Source: Authors' research

EEDA reacted angrily. Its chief executive, Bill Samuel, accused EERA of being "reluctant to commit to firm and positive action to move the region's economy forward" (p 16). Although EERA eventually endorsed a revision of the RES, the events in the East of England represented the first public flexing of (admittedly) limited muscle by a Regional Chamber. Of course, as the *Local Government Chronicle* noted, the assembly had no right of veto over the RES: it is answerable to the Secretary of State. However, many of the issues that surround the government's approach to the accountable governance of the English regions are highlighted in the 'eastern insurrection', and it may very well be, as the *Local Government Chronicle* put it, "a very small-scale dress rehearsal for future battles".

An example of a Regional Chamber being drawn into conflict with central government comes from the South East. The South East Regional Assembly (SERA), along with the South East England Development Agency (SEEDA), clashed with the government over the latter's decision to block plans for two proposed bypasses at Hastings on the Sussex/Kent border in July 2001. The rejection was announced in a letter to Councillor David Shakespeare, leader of the Regional Assembly, in which the Secretary of State, Stephen Byers, maintained that the economic benefits of the proposed scheme did not outweigh the environmental costs. The bypasses would have damaged two sites of Special Scientific Interest and an Area of Outstanding Natural Beauty in the South Downs.

The bypasses had been a recommendation of a government sponsored multi-modal transport study, aimed at assisting the regeneration of Hastings, a run-down seaside town. The bypass proposal had been incorporated into broader planning priorities for the area and adopted by the assembly (which is responsible for RPG), the RDA and local authorities. Environmental campaigners welcomed the announcement. However, the Regional Assembly "expressed fears for the successful regeneration of Hastings and the South Coast" and questioned "the Government's commitment to the delivery of urban renaissance in the region's coastal towns" (quoted in Tomaney et al, 2001, pp 14-15). A paradoxical effect of the decision may have been to stimulate regionalism among the business sector in the South East, with local business leaders arguing that the scheme would have gone ahead if the decision had been delegated to an elected Regional Assembly (*Financial Times*, 16 July 2001).

Finally, some Regional Chambers sought to establish a role for themselves as a body that can integrate public policy within the region. A good example of this is the East Midlands Regional Assembly (EMRA). EMRA launched its Integrated Regional Strategy (IRS) in June 2001. This is intended to provide a framework for the proliferation of regional strategies – in the fields of the economy, culture, environment, energy, spatial development, social inclusion, transport and housing – while placing a concern with sustainability at their heart. The principle underlying the IRS means that when the assembly or RDA considers an issue they do not do it in isolation to other areas of concern (see Chapter Eleven).

Government Offices (GOs)

GOs remain important, if low profile, actors in the region. The period July 2000 to July 2001 saw their roles significantly strengthened. Following the recommendations of the PIU, the government sought to increase the range of Whitehall departments represented in GOs. The first moves came in July 2000, when the then Agriculture Secretary, Nick Brown, announced that senior staff from the Ministry of Agriculture, Fisheries and Food (MAFF) would be moved into GOs in order to improve MAFF's regional policy making capacity. At the same time the Department of Culture, Media and Sport (DCMS) and the Home Office made additional appointments in the form of Regional Cultural Directors and Crime Reduction Teams, headed by Regional Crime Reduction Directors. The administrative integration of GOs will be facilitated by the introduction of a 'single pot' to meet its running costs, with some local discretion on how this is spent. The combined running costs of GOs are in the order of £100 million per annum, in support of programmes that are worth £5-6 billion. However, GOs will not have the kind of flexibility to move money between programmes that has been accorded to RDAs.

In September 2001, GOs incorporated a presence from the following departments:

- Transport, Local Government and the Regions;
- Trade and Industry;
- Education and Skills;
- Environment, Food and Rural Affairs;
- Culture, Media and Sport;
- Home Office.

The restructuring of GOs, was badly affected by the Foot and Mouth Disease (FMD) crisis. GO officials played a central role in the fight against FMD in those regions that were most badly affected – notably the North East, North West (Cumbria) and the South West (Devon). Although MAFF regional directors moved into GOs, with the aim of ensuring the work of GOs incorporated a rural perspective, the scale and endurance of the rural problems resulting from FMD inevitably slowed down this development. However, GOs are likely to acquire further powers in the future. The evolving role of GOs will include providing a regional base for National Connections (the government's new 'joined-up' youth policy), Sure Start, the Children's Fund and the Neighbourhood Renewal Unit. GOs may also have a role in monitoring Local Strategic Partnerships and local Public Service Agreements (Tomaney and Hetherington, 2001b).

A further significant development occurred in April 2001, with the launch of the Regional Co-ordination Unit (RCU) within Whitehall. The creation of the RCU was an outcome of a report of the PIU of the Cabinet Office (PIU, 2000). The aim of the RCU is to oversee the work of GOs and influence central government departments' dealings with the regions. The RCU is relatively small, comprising currently about 50 staff drawn from a range of departments across Whitehall. It incorporates the previous elements of the Whitehall machinery concerned with the financing and personnel aspects of GOs. The number of policy specialists is relatively modest, comprising about half of the RCU's total complement. In the new regime all departments are formally required to consult the RCU when introducing any new Area-Based Initiative (ABI). Although the Director General of the RCU is the 'line manager' of GO directors, the RCU preferred to see itself standing at the heart of what he terms "the Government Office Network", with RCU relying heavily on Regional Directors for power and influence within the Whitehall machine (interview, May 2001).

Regionalisation

Taken together, the changes to the RDAs, Regional Chambers and GOs represent a significant strengthening of the apparatus of governance in the English regions. However, these bodies are only the most prominent in what is currently a fractured governance. A study for the North East Regional Assembly (Tomaney and Humphrey, 2001) showed that over 20 organisations were involved in the preparation of at least 12 regional strategies, which affected many aspects of the region's life. Although the RDA, Regional Assembly and, especially, the GO were heavily involved in the preparation of regional strategies, many other government departments, non-departmental government bodies and other agencies were also involved. The dominant trend among these bodies is toward the creation, or strengthening, of regional structures in order to better assist them to contribute to regional strategy making. This quiet regionalisation of government structures, and simultaneous proliferation of regional strategy making is a relatively unnoticed feature of the governance of the English regions. The senior decision makers within these organisations assume the trend will grow rather than diminish. In particular, the move to regional strategy making was seen positively, but frustrations exist about the failure to 'join-up' individual strategies and the lack of capacity to properly implement them. In addition there was a broad acceptance of the need for greater accountability of the existing structure of regional governance. In short, the study revealed both the potential and current limits of existing regionalism.

Civic regionalism

With the exception of the North East of England, the English regions, until recently, have not been characterised by the presence of broadly based and vigorous regional campaigns. In 2000-01, however, that picture began to change with the emergence of regional campaigns and conventions across England (see Table 3.3). The rate of development differs substantially between regions. The North East stands out as the region with the most active debate, but developments can be seen across the other northern regions, and also in the West Midlands and South West. In each case the forces promoting (and resisting) regionalism are different. The divide between 'official' regionalism (as represented by chambers, for example) and 'civic' regionalism (as represented by campaigns and conventions) is being blurred in some regions. The joint working of the North East Constitutional Convention (NECC) and the North East Regional Assembly (NERA) in the production of an agreed plan for regional government exemplifies this convergence. The NECC had been formed originally, in part at least, to broaden the debate about regional government beyond the usual political channels into wider civic arenas. In the West Midlands, on the other hand, the convention chair Councillor Phil Davis (leader of Telford and Wrekin council) was elected chair of the West Midlands Regional Chamber in mid-2001. The broad pattern of development is summarised in Table 3.3.

Table 3.3: Civic regionalism 2001

Region	State of civic regionalism
North East	Campaign for a North East Assembly formed in 1992. NECC formed in 1999. NECC working with Regional Assembly producing case for regional government. Polls typically indicate increasing support. Little active opposition. Major issue for regional media.
North West	North West Constitutional Convention established by local authorities in 2000 and endorsed by some stakeholders. No civic campaign, but moves are underway to establish one. Low media profile.
Yorkshire	Active regional campaign (Campaign for Yorkshire and the Humber, see www.cfy.org.uk) established in 1999. Convention begun in 2000, to undertake detailed work on regional government. Low public awareness, but increasing media attention.
South West	Campaign for Regional Assembly just started. Convention launched in May 2001. Chaired by Bishop of Exeter and supported by key stakeholders, notably Liberal Democrats. Low public awareness and media interest. Boundary problems (specifically the Cornish question, where active movement exists). Strongly opposed by active UK Independence Party (UKIP).
West Midlands	Campaign for a West Midlands Assembly established in 1999. Constitutional Convention launched in July 2001, funded by Cadbury Barrow Trust. Key stakeholders becoming involved. Launch of convention in July 2001. Emerging media interest. Active public opposition from Conservative MPs and UKIP. The weight of Birmingham means that the debate about elected mayors overshadows the regional issue.
East Midlands	Stakeholders showing interest in regionalism. Moves afoot mainly by Liberal Democrats to establish a campaign for regional government. Minimal media interest.
Eastern	Some stakeholders showing interest. Minimal public interest. Media coverage ranges from the disinterested to the actively hostile.
South East	Some stakeholders showing interest. No civic interest. Negligible media interest.

Whitehall

Throughout New Labour's first term the main locus of regional policy was the Department of Environment, Transport and the Regions (DETR), presided over by the Deputy Prime Minister John Prescott. DETR sponsored RDAs, Regional Chambers, planning policy and sponsored most of the other non-departmental public bodies that had a strong regional presence. The regional brief, however, formed only one component of this vast department. The thinking behind the creation of DETR in 1997 was that it brought together policy areas that embodied considerable spillovers. A persistent criticism of DETR, throughout its existence, was that it proved too big, with Prescott himself having a brief that was too wide to be effective. In the period before the General Election of 2001, the future of DETR was subject to much speculation, with predictions that, in line with their evolving role in relation to the government's industry policy, RDAs would become a responsibility of the DTI. Further speculation suggested that John Prescott would move to a new role in the Cabinet Office, keeping the regional portfolio and a range of other responsibilities.

Shortly after the General Election, the Prime Minister announced major changes to the machinery of government, which had implications for the governance of the English regions (see Tomaney et al, 2001, for further discussion). The relevant changes were outlined in a press statement (10 Downing Street, Press Release, 8 June 2001):

- An **Office of the Deputy Prime Minister** was established in the Cabinet Office. The Deputy Prime Minister (DPM), John Prescott, will chair a number of key Cabinet Committees. These include a new Committee of the Nations and Regions, which, among other things, will develop policy on the English regions. The DPM will oversee the delivery of the Manifesto pledges, as well as dealing with important cross-departmental issues, including social exclusion. The RCU, the GOs in the regions, along with the Social Exclusion Unit, now report to the DPM in the Cabinet Office. The DPM will also retain final responsibility for the production of the White Paper on regional government.

- A new **Department for the Environment, Food and Rural Affairs (DEFRA)** was created to promote green issues and the countryside. In addition to taking over responsibility for agriculture, the food industry and fisheries from MAFF, it took on the environment, rural development, countryside, wildlife and sustainable development responsibilities of the former DETR. It sponsors the Environment Agency, the Countryside Agency and English Nature. It will also take on responsibility for animal welfare and hunting, previously a responsibility of the Home Office.

- A new **Department for Transport, Local Government and the Regions (DTLR)** is, according to the Prime Minister,"designed to give sharper focus" to the old DETR's responsibilities for transport, as well as local government, housing, planning, regeneration, urban and regional policy. It assumed responsibility for the fire service and electoral law from the Home Office.

- The **Department of Trade and Industry (DTI)** assumed responsibility for the RDAs, where they will sit alongside the department's regional economic responsibilities. The DTI also assumed sponsorship of the construction industry, which had hitherto rested with the DETR.

One important outcome of these changes concerned the production of the government's White Paper, with responsibility being divided between the new Office of the Deputy Prime Minister and the new DTLR, headed by a new Secretary of State, Stephen Byers, and his Regions Minister, Nick Raynsford. Although both ministers were quick to promise action on regional government, they also acknowledged that they would need to balance this priority against others, such as local government reform and transport improvements.

Outlook

The General Election of 2001 saw New Labour's Manifesto reaffirm its commitment to legislating for Regional Assemblies "where there is demand" (Labour Party, 2001). The Manifesto was pored over by commentators and campaigners alike in the search for runes to read. In the event it sent yet more mixed signals. The Manifesto revived the stipulation that "predominantly local government" was a condition for legislative action. This appeared to be at odds with statements of DETR ministers over the previous period. This was taken by some as a signal the cooling of New Labour's ardour. On the other hand, hardly any attention was given to the fact that the stipulation that Regional Assemblies should involve no additional public expenditure was dropped.

An additional innovation in the election campaign was the launch of a document entitled *Ambitions for our regions* (Prescott, 2001), which set out New Labour's past and future policies. While containing no surprises, it represented a radical shift in approach compared to 1997 when the English regions did not figure as a concept in New Labour's election campaigning. The document was launched at a meeting in Wakefield on 30 May 2001, which was jointly addressed by John Prescott and Gordon Brown. The meeting appeared to put the seal on a growing accord between the two about the importance of the regional issue, albeit one narrowly focused on economic development. John Prescott used the occasion to restate his commitment to English Regional Assemblies, which would be concerned with 'strategic' issues, such as economic development, planning and transport (Prescott, 2001). The launch was followed by the launch of 'regional manifestos' in some of the English regions. The most detailed of these was published in the North East (*Ambitions for the North East*), although it was largely a reheated version of other party documents. Taken together, these developments appeared to provide further evidence of New Labour's new, but tentative, engagement with the regional issue.

The 'English Question' in the period after the General Election of 2001 looked set to be dominated by the politics of producing the White Paper on regional government. On the one hand, the government's commitment to producing the White Paper signalled a new engagement with the English regions. On the other hand, some actors saw the absence of a mention for the English regions in the Queen's Speech as evidence of an enduring ambivalence on the part of the government, notwithstanding the statements of Gordon Brown and others. The Queen's Speech debate in the House of Commons was notable for the interventions of former ministers – typically liberated by the post-election reshuffle – calling for swift government action on the issue. Ministers were at pains to stress their commitment to progressing English regional government. In an interview with *The Journal* of Newcastle upon Tyne, Stephen Byers suggested legislation could be brought forward in the 2002 Queen's Speech:

> What I want to do is have a White Paper, then for colleagues to agree there should be a slot in the Queen's Speech next year. I will be pushing for that. I do think it's right that if local people want to have a regional assembly we have got to be prepared to act on that. We are working on the White Paper, we will make good progress, and certainly the plan is to do it within the next six months. (*The Journal*, 13 July 2001)

Ministers are likely to act when they feel pressured to do so. A key question is where the political pressure points lie? These might be found in the interventions in the Queen's Speech debate by ex-ministers. Freed of the ordinance of silence, and not easily dismissed as members of the 'awkward squad', these interventions by ex-ministers suggested a rockier backbench ride on the issue for the government in its second term. The architect of New Labour, Peter Mandelson, could not have been plainer in a speech given to the Centre for Urban and Regional Development Studies at the University of Newcastle-upon-Tyne on the day after the Queen's Speech:

> I believe that if a second term Labour Government fails to act on regional devolution it will leave the constitutional settlement enacted by New Labour dangerously unbalanced. Indeed, it might lead some to question the legitimacy of those constitutional changes. More importantly, it will fail to address how we improve the capacity of the state to act. (Mandelson, 2001)

A further factor, already in play by the summer of 2001, was rising manufacturing job losses in New Labour's northern heartlands, some in the constituencies of prominent ministers. While hardly news in regions like the North East, they promised a return to the politics of the North/South divide in the public's attention and provide grist to the mill of devolution campaigners.

References

Balls, E. (2000) 'Britain's new regional policy', in E. Balls and J. Healey (eds) *Towards a new regional policy: Delivering growth and full employment*, London: The Smith Institute, pp 6-23.

Balls, E. and Healey, J. (eds) (2000) *Towards a new regional policy: Delivering growth and full employment*, London: The Smith Institute.

Brown, G. (2001) 'Enterprise and the regions', Speech by Gordon Brown MP, Chancellor of the Exchequer at UMIST on 29 January, HM Treasury News Release 02/01, 29 January (www.hm-treasury.gov.uk/press/2001/p02_01.html).

Byers, S. (2001) 'Turning change into opportunity: the next steps for industrial policy', Speech to the Social Market Foundation, 4 May (www.dti.gov.uk/ministers/speeches/byers040501.html).

Department of the Environment, Transport and the Regions (DETR) (2000) *Planning Policy Guidance Note 11: Regional Planning*, (www.planning.detr.gov.uk/ppg11/index.htm).

Department for Trade and Industry (DTI) (2001) *Opportunity for all in a world of change: A White Paper on enterprise, skills and innovation*, London: DTI/Department for Education and Employment, (www.dti.gov.uk/opportunityforall).

Hall, G. (2000) 'Rising to the challenge', in E. Balls and J. Healey (eds) *Towards a new regional policy: Delivering growth and full employment*, London: The Smith Institute, pp 24-30.

HM Treasury (2000a) *Spending Review 2000: Prudent for a purpose. Building opportunity and security for all*, London: HM Treasury (www.hm-treasury.gov.uk/sr2000/report/index.html).

HM Treasury (2000b) *Building long-term prosperity for all. Pre-Budget report*, Cm 4917, London: HM Treasury (www.hm-treasury.gov.uk/pbr2000/report/Contents.htm.).

Labour Party (2001) *New ambitions for our country*, Election Manifesto, London: Labour Party.

Mandelson, P. (2001) 'Keynote address', *The State of the English Regions Seminar*, University of Newcastle-upon-Tyne, 21 June 2001.

PIU (Performance and Innovation Unit) (2000) *Reaching out: The role of central government at the regional and local level*, London: Cabinet Office.

Prescott, J. (2001) *Ambitions for our Regions*, London: Labour Party.

Tomaney, J. (2000) 'Regional governance in England', in R. Hazell (ed) *States and Nations Review: The first year of devolution in the United Kingdom*, Exeter: Imprint Academic, pp 107-31.

Tomaney, J. (2001) 'Identity and politics – the regional government debate in the North East', *Northern Economic Review*, vol 31, pp 56-69.

Tomaney, J. and Hetherington, P. (2000) *Monitoring the English Regions. Report No 1* (November), Centre for Urban and Regional Development Studies (CURDS), University of Newcastle upon Tyne, (www.ucl.ac.uk/constitution-unit/leverh/index.htm).

Tomaney, J. and Hetherington, P. (2001a) *Monitoring the English Regions: Report No 2* (February), CURDS, University of Newcastle upon Tyne, (www.ucl.ac.uk/constitution-unit/leverh/index.htm).

Tomaney, J. and Hetherington, P (2001b) *Monitoring the English Regions: Report No 3* (May), CURDS, University of Newcastle upon Tyne, (www.ucl.ac.uk/constitution-unit/leverh/index.htm).

Tomaney, J. and Humphrey, L. (2001) *Powers and functions of a Regional Assembly. A study for the North East Regional Assembly*, CURDS, University of Newcastle upon Tyne, (www.northeastassembly.org.uk/publications/subpage/reggov.pdf).

Tomaney, J., Hetherington, P. and Humphrey, L. (2001) *Monitoring the English Regions: Report No 4* (August), CURDS, University of Newcastle upon Tyne, (www.ucl.ac.uk/constitution-unit/leverh/index.htm).

FOUR

Yorkshire (and the Humber)

Simon Lee

The main social and economic challenges facing Yorkshire: the competitive disadvantage of the region

Yorkshire is England's largest county. With the administrative areas of North Lincolnshire and North East Lincolnshire, the hybrid region of Yorkshire and the Humber embraces a population of five million, a workforce of 2.3 million, or just under 9% of the UK total, with more than 1,500 foreign firms employing 130,000 workers in the region. In 1998, the region accounted for 7.5% of the UK's GDP but an average GDP per capita of only 88% of the UK average, South Yorkshire recorded a deteriorating GDP per capita of only 74% of the European Union (EU) average (GOYH, 2000, p 2). The main social and economic challenges confronting Yorkshire and the Humber have remained those that arose from the deindustrialisation of the 1980s and early 1990s. Yorkshire's remaining deep mines, including those of the Selby coalfield, have come under renewed threat during the Blair government's first term, while the steel industry and the region's defence manufacturers have faced major restructuring. To these have been added new challenges arising from the impact of flooding and Foot and Mouth on the region's agricultural and tourist industries.

As the most recent statistics for regional GDP (1999) have shown, Yorkshire and the Humber recorded a GDP of £57.5 billion, yielding a per capita income of £11,404 – only 88% of the UK figure, 86% of the English, and 91% of the Scottish (ONS, 2001, table 2). This meant that the region was the third poorest in England. When a 1999 Cabinet Office report sought to highlight the variations in economic and social conditions within the English regions, it drew attention to the fact that, while South Yorkshire (where 1.3 million of the region's 5 million population live) had qualified for £740 million of Objective 1 EU funding – because its GDP had fallen below the 75% of the EU average threshold – the other parts of the region had all performed "slightly better" than the rest of the UK in improving their percentage of the national average of GDP per capita between 1981 and 1996 (Cabinet Office, 1999, p 19). However, this lost sight of the fact that the region as a whole had seen only a very marginal improvement in its GDP per capita from 90.8% of the UK average in 1991, to 91.2% in 1997. In many indicators of economic and social conditions, only the North East prevents Yorkshire and the Humber from being the most deprived English region. As the Cabinet Office report noted, 31.6% of Yorkshire and the Humber was located in areas ranked among England's 50 most deprived districts, and 52.6% of the region within the 100 most deprived districts (Cabinet Office, 1999, p 40). There is also considerable variation in economic and social conditions within Yorkshire and the Humber: in 1995, GDP per capita (UK average = 100) in the region varied between 127 in York, and 65 in Barnsley, Doncaster and Rotherham (Cabinet Office, 1999, p 12).

Robert Huggins' Index of Regional Competitiveness in the UK (Huggins, 2000) ranked Yorkshire and the Humber tenth (out of 12) among the constituent nations and regions of the UK, with a score of 93.4% of the UK average. Only Wales (90.7%) and the North East (88.8%) were ranked lower (Huggins, 2000, p 14). In his Index of Regional Knowledge-Based Business in the UK, Huggins ranked Yorkshire and the Humber eighth (out of 11), achieving 76% of the UK average. Once more, only the North East ranked below it (72.6%) (Huggins, 2000, p 15). Using the International Institute for Management Development's 1999 World Competitiveness Scoreboard as a benchmark to rank the UK's nations and regions, Huggins also found that Yorkshire and the Humber, with a score equivalent to 69.27% of that of the USA, would be ranked between Spain (69.4%) and Israel (67.8%) in 23rd and 24th places respectively. Again, only the North East (65.87%) ranked lower among the English regions (Huggins, 2000, p 17).

The government has recently identified the main source of inequalities in regional GDP per capita as regional variations in labour productivity levels, with differences in demographics, unemployment and participation rates also playing a role. To achieve its objective of "regionally balanced growth, led by the regions themselves" (HMT/DTI, 2001, p 6), the government has based its regional policy for its second term on two principles. The first is that "exploiting indigenous strengths in each area is likely to be the most effective way of strengthening the essential building blocks of growth-innovation, skills and the development of enterprise" (HMT/DTI, 2001, p 6). The problem for Yorkshire and the Humber is that, whichever of these benchmarks is chosen, the region is struggling to remain competitive. For example, in terms of innovation, at £256 million or 0.4% of regional GDP, Yorkshire and the Humber had the lowest percentage of regional GDP devoted to research and development among the English regions in 1998 (Cabinet Office, 1999, p 47). In terms of skills, for a region aspiring to be competitive in a knowledge-based economy, the biggest challenge is its very poor standards of educational attainment. In 1997/98, only 37.9% of the region's pupils attained five GCSEs or SCEs grade A-C, with only 21.4% of Kingston-upon-Hull's pupils attaining this standard – the worst performance in England, and less than half the English national average. In 1998/99, no fewer than 7.0% of the region's pupils recorded "no graded results" (Cabinet Office, 1999, pp 20, 53, 54) (albeit a significant improvement on the 9.9% of 1996/97) – the joint worst performance in England (with the North East). Paradoxically, the region achieved the highest score for average A/S level point scores with 18.2 points, compared to an English average of 17.3 (Cabinet Office, 1999, pp 20, 53, 54). The region also found itself at the top of the national league tables for average class sizes in both its primary and secondary schools. In spring 1998, 20.3% of the region's population of working age possessed no qualifications, compared to an English average of 17.6% (Cabinet Office, 1999, p 56).

In terms of the development of enterprise, Huggins' rankings have been confirmed by the government's VAT registrations, which have shown that 19 out of 21 local authority districts in Yorkshire fall below the UK average for business start-up rates (HMT, 2000, pp 3-10). In 1999, business start-up registrations outnumbered deregistrations in every region of England except Yorkshire and the Humber, where a net loss of 700 businesses was recorded (ONS, 2001, table 21). In January 2001, 67% of the region's manufacturing firms were working below capacity, the highest figure among the UK's nations and regions, and well above the UK average of 57% (ONS, 2001, table 18). To redress this competitive disadvantage, the Regional Development Agency (RDA) has recently identified clusters of businesses in the food and drink (including agriculture), digital industries, advanced engineering and metals, chemicals and bioscience sectors as "the key industries in the region which are best-placed to drive forward Yorkshire and Humber's economy" (YF, 2001a). Yorkshire Forward (YF) has been awarded £1.66 million from the government's Innovative Cluster Fund to fund seven cluster developments across Yorkshire and the Humber, which it is hoped will generate 70 new businesses and 850 jobs (YF, 2000a). It has also confirmed the establishment of a £25 million venture capital fund which will provide more than 20 small businesses with access to funding of up to £250,000 and "if needed, follow-on funding up to a maximum of £500,000 per company" (YF, 2001b). Despite its best intentions, and having already put in place most of the elements of an effective supply-side policy, YF at present lacks the resources to lever the step change in productivity and competitiveness to which it aspires.

The second principle of the government's regional policy is that "the best mechanisms for achieving this are likely to be based in the regions themselves, and so national Government must enable regional and local initiatives to work by providing the necessary resources within a national framework". Although the RDAs have been identified as "the key agents in drawing forward this new industrial policy", it is hard to see how Yorkshire Forward can fulfil this role when it possesses a budget controlling less than 1% of total public spending in the region – equivalent to about 0.4% of regional GDP (HMT/DTI, 2001, p 6). The region remains overly dependent upon a range of national and supranational funding streams for regeneration and competitiveness. For example, in 1999/2000, the region received £15 million in Regional Selective Assistance to help fund capital investment of £207 million which would create or safeguard 6,200 jobs. In a similar vein, EU funding of more than £148 million was approved in the hope of creating 19,500 new jobs in the region. In overall terms, the Government Office (GO) dispensed £531.5 million to the region in 1999/2000, including £182.3 million for regeneration, £164.1 million for business, enterprise and skills, and £70.3 million for planning, transport and environment (GOYH, 2000, p 1). In March 2001, the region received £300 million of Objective 2 funding, which is expected to attract an additional £550 million of public and private funding, and thereby create 36,000 new jobs and support 9,500 firms (YF, 2001c). However, the Campaign for the English Regions has recently noted that per capita identifiable public spending in Yorkshire and the Humber at £4,224 in 1999/2000 was £1,047 or less than in Scotland and that, on its calculations, Yorkshire and the Humber would require an additional £5.235 billion to raise spending to Scottish levels (www.cfer.org.uk/content/lib_barnett2.html). While Yorkshire and the Humber continues to experience such a large fiscal disadvantage, it is difficult to see how it can hope to fulfil the government's objectives of regionally balanced growth. How well matched are the evolving regional strategies to meeting these challenges?

Meeting the challenges

A recent report from the Select Committee on Trade and Industry has suggested that "RDA strategies tend to be broadly aspirational" (TISC, 2001, para 9). This is not an unfair description of *Advancing Together Towards a World Class Region*, the Regional Economic Strategy (RES) for Yorkshire and the Humber (YF, 1999a), in the preparation of which YF claimed to have consulted with more than 6,000 organisations and individuals. Yorkshire Forward's Head of Strategy and Policy has described the RES as taking "a classic change management approach" to the task of achieving "a radical improvement in the Yorkshire and Humber economy" (YF, 2000, p 16). Laudable as this may be, the ambition and commitment is not matched by an equivalent commitment of resources or control over policy – both of which have remained tightly prescribed by Whitehall. To a certain extent, Yorkshire and the Humber had a headstart over most other English regions in that most of the priorities defined in the RES had already been identified by the extensive process of consultation of regional stakeholders which had preceded the publication of the Regional Assembly's *Yorkshire and Humberside: Advancing Together into the Millennium* (RAYH, 1998). The fact that the region had been developing its own sector-based Regional Innovation Strategy (RIS) since November 1996 had also helped, because the RIS has subsequently been incorporated into the work of YF. As a consequence, over the ten year period covered by the RES, YF has identified its aims as:

- the creation of 150,000 new jobs;
- a doubling of the rate of business start-ups;
- a trebling of manufacturing investment by foreign firms;
- the training of three million people with IT skills;
- a halving in the number of deprived wards in the region;
- the cutting of pollution (greenhouse gases) by over one fifth (YF, 2000b, p 16).

There has been little evidence of dissent from these aims by regional stakeholders. A more salient issue is whether the aims are deliverable given the resources available to YF. The scale of the task of regenerating those parts of Yorkshire which have suffered massive deindustrialisation has been recognised at the supranational level by the award of Objective 2 and, more recently, Objective 1 status to a large part of the region. However, a commensurate commitment of resources has not been forthcoming from London. The absence of directly elected regional government was illustrated when Objective 1 status was also awarded to South Wales. The Welsh Assembly was able to press Whitehall and the Treasury in particular for additional resources to help provide the matched funding which would unlock the supranational funding. Yorkshire and the Humber did not possess the same facility and therefore faced the potential redistribution of public spending from other parts of the region into South Yorkshire to match its Objective 1 funding.

An evaluation of the new institutions – the response of key stakeholders

Any evaluation of Yorkshire and the Humber's new regional institutions cannot ignore their three fundamental weaknesses. First, none of them are directly elected or accountable on a regional basis, not least the RDAs which are themselves a major extension of the quango state. Second, none of them possess control over sufficient policy and resources to affect regional economic development at anything other than the margins of a plethora of centrally determined policies and initiatives. Third, the absence of regional accountability and control over resources has meant that policy has remained fragmented rather than 'joined-up' and integrated. That being said, these new regional institutions have attempted to embed themselves in the region's political culture and political economy with some success. However, one specific dilemma which the new regional institutions have only partly but not completely redressed is the diversity of designations of the region's multitude of unelected and appointed governance structures. The political and broader cultural identity of the region is Yorkshire. The administrative identity of the region is Yorkshire and Humberside or, latterly, as it has been subsequently designated by some parts of Whitehall, Yorkshire and (the) Humber. Perhaps more than most English regions, it has manifested the regional confusion over political and administrative boundaries characteristic of the broader longstanding and centralising British state tradition of technocratic pragmatism which has reduced the English regions to managerial and functionalist entities (Lee, 1999a, 1999b).

Yorkshire Forward (YF): Yorkshire and the Humber RDA

In its first Annual Report, YF sought to emphasise its capacity for pioneering innovations in RDA policy by noting that it had been the first RDA to sign a Strategic Alliance with the NHS, to ensure the incorporation of health improvement initiatives in the RDA's activities, and the first to launch a web-based interactive information system. YF was also the first RDA to establish a concordat between itself and the Regional Chamber. It also claimed to be the first RDA to launch a regional rebranding exercise by commissioning (with the Yorkshire Tourist Board) a Leeds-based consultancy, Out-Think, to develop "a new brand for the region demonstrating its commercial, cultural and characteristic strengths" (YF, 2000b, p 9). This £300,000 marketing campaign aims to rebrand Yorkshire by proving that the region is "Alive with Opportunity" (YF, 2000c). The RDA had sponsored research which had shown that "Yorkshire is not truly understood outside of the region and suffers from persistent stereotyping and misconception" for "At worst, it is relegated as the land of Yorkshire Pudding, cloth caps and whippets populated by blunt, unsophisticated folk" (YF, 2000c). The RDA has launched a Market Towns initiative as a national pilot scheme for establishing how market town communities may be enabled "to identify and deliver niche market opportunities for the towns themselves and their rural hinterland" (YF, 2000d). With One NorthEast and the Northwest Development Agency, YF has combined its US operations to create the North of England Inward Investment Agency, which was launched on the 28 February 2001. Among its more quantifiable achievements, YF claimed (2000b, pp 59-60):

- to have created or safeguarded more than 17,000 jobs;
- started 400 new businesses;
- trained 20,000 people in new skills;
- created or improved 210,000 square metres of commercial floorspace;
- built or improved 1,800 homes;
- provided direct support to 871 community groups.

To achieve these results, YF spent £153.7 million in its first full year of operation. Of this sum, £5.6 million was spent on the wages and salaries of its 211 staff (YF, 2000b, p 39).

The RDA has also acted as an advocate for regional issues, fulfilling the role which a directly elected regional assembly should be playing. For example, in the wake of the severe flooding experienced in North Yorkshire, Graham Hall, Yorkshire Forward Chairman, wrote to John Prescott pointing out that the 63% proposed increase in the flood defence levy would divert resources away from the region's capacity to tackle economic problems (YF, 2001d). In a similar vein, he wrote to the Chairman of Railtrack voicing concerns about the impact upon the business community in the region of the post-Hatfield rail crash repair work, pointing out that the community had been "hit hard by the ongoing transport problems" (YF, 2000e). Hall also wrote to the European Commission to support the £70 million subsidy which would secure the future of the UK's 17 remaining pits, including those within the Selby Coalfield. Had the subsidy not been approved, it had been estimated that two thirds of the pits would have shut (YF, 2000f). Hall has been among the most vocal of the RDA chairmen. His reward for having hosted the first dinner provided by an RDA for the Governor of the Bank of England – at which Hall called for a 0.5% cut in interest rates (a measure subsequently undertaken by the bank) because "We need to strike a balance in economic decision-making to recognise the needs of businesses across the northern regions as well as London and the south east" (YF, 2001e) – has been his appointment to the bank's Court of Directors (YF, 2001f). Whether this appointment is intended as a means of muzzling the chairman remains to be seen.

The RDA's most important funding stream remains the Single Regeneration Budget (SRB). Prior to the establishment of YF, the SRB had provided £650 million for 64 schemes within the region, which had created more than 14,500 jobs, 5,000 business start-ups, and funded nearly 4000 voluntary groups (YF, 1999b). During 1999-2000, the SRB provided £100 million to 67 ongoing schemes in the region. In July 2000, under SRB5, a further 14 schemes with a lifetime value of £98.5 million were approved. In August 2000, it announced that it was providing £230.2 million for bids which would help to deliver the RES and that an additional £141.8 million could be forthcoming from other YF programmes as its contribution towards a total of £1.34 billion of public and private investment (YF, 2000g). Yorkshire Forward has consolidated all its funding streams, including SRB funding, into a single YF Development Fund. However, the advantages of this consolidation for RDA autonomy will be offset by the prescriptive nature of the Public Service Agreements (PSAs), and the fact that much of the apparent significant real terms increases in RDA spending over the period of settlement devised by the 2000 Spending Review is accounted for by SRB funding which is already earmarked. The paucity of its resources means that YF's capacity to improve economic and social conditions in the region will remain vulnerable to the sudden impact of restructuring in the private sector, such as that which occurred in the summer of 2000 when more than 2,400 jobs were lost following redundancies at major employers in the region, notably BAe Systems at Brough and Corus steel in Rotherham.

The Regional Assembly for Yorkshire and Humberside

A distinctive feature of Yorkshire and the Humber as a region is that it anticipated the election of a Labour government committed to devolution by giving civic institutional form to its distinctive regional identity by creating the voluntaristic, non-statutory Regional Assembly for Yorkshire and Humberside in July 1996. Based at Wakefield, the assembly was created in the immediate aftermath of the Major government's ineffectual local government reorganisation which had abolished Humberside County Council and replaced it with four unitary authorities. The assembly is composed of 67 members who represent the region's 22 local authorities. Its purpose is "To act as a strategic body for local government and for the promotion of democratic locally elected community leadership in the Yorkshire and Humberside region" (RAYH, 1999, p 1). To this end, the assembly seeks to develop consensus and promote the economic, social and environmental interests of the region by adhering to "the principle of subsidiarity that regards local authorities as the principal unit of local governance". Thus, the assembly has sought to confine its attention to those matters requiring a regional approach (RAYH, 1999, p 1). The importance of effective coordination of the region's local authorities is demonstrated by the fact that they collectively invested £5.4 billion in economic, social and environmental well-being in 1999, vastly exceeding the resources at the disposal of either YF or the GO. The fact that the assembly has contributed to no fewer than 18 strategies for the region since its creation serves to demonstrate the degree of fragmentation in policy delivery within the region.

The assembly duly served as the vehicle for an extensive consultation process among the region's stakeholders which established regional priorities for economic regeneration and economic development. So effective was the assembly's work that the title and many of the priorities of its June 1998 strategic framework, *Yorkshire and Humberside: Advancing together into the millennium* (RAYH, 1998) were adopted by YF's RES (YF, 1999a). The assembly can point to a number of other successes. First, to overcome the potential fragmentation which might arise from the assembly having responsibility for preparing Regional Planning Guidance (RPG) and YF responsibility for drawing up the RES, in July 1999 the assembly and the RDA jointly launched their respective draft RPG and RES. This was the first instance of the joint launch of two key strategy documents in the English regions. The joint launch was indicative of the attempts to integrate the 15-20 year timeframe of the RPG with the shorter ten-year timeframe of the RES (YF, 1999c). It also revealed the value of the assembly, with its past track record of effective consultation in the preparation of regional economic strategies. However, it also demonstrated how much more accountable this process could yet be if the RES and RPG were drawn up between the RDA and a directly elected Regional Assembly. Second, the assembly has also delivered the first RPG to incorporate an integrated transport strategy developed with its partners in the Regional Chamber for Yorkshire and Humberside.

The Regional Chamber for Yorkshire and Humberside

In March 1998, Yorkshire and the Humber was the first English region to launch its own Regional Chamber, although it was also the very final chamber to receive official designation on the 27 July 1999. The early momentum was maintained when the chamber and the RDA agreed a joint voluntary concordat more than two months before the formal launch of YF. Since 22 of the chamber's 35 members are the same local authorities who comprise the Regional Assembly, the chamber and assembly have been able to work closely together – not least because they share the same base in Wakefield. Thus far, the chamber has established five commissions to carry forward the regional agenda first identified in the Regional Assembly's strategic framework (RAYH, 1998). Indeed, the themes of the five commissions, namely an Advanced Economy, Robust Infrastructure, Skilled and Flexible Workforce, Sustainability, and Quality of Life, are precisely those of *Yorkshire and Humberside: Advancing together into the millennium*. In relation to YF, the chamber's scrutiny of the draft RES led to significant amendments being incorporated, most notably:

- a stronger role for the health sector in economic development;
- use of the chamber's business support blueprint;
- an enhanced role for local authorities;
- better supply chain collaboration;
- greater recognition of the importance of a skilled workforce;
- the importance of RPG and consistency in the planning system;
- the need for effective economic, environmental and social indicators;
- a stronger, integrated approach to sustainability;
- a range of criteria which balanced GDP and jobs in the choice of key sectors (YF, 2000b, p 20).

Despite these useful contributions, the Regional Chamber, like the other new regional institutions, has remained virtually invisible to the broader population.

The Campaign for Yorkshire

In Yorkshire and the Humber, the quest for directly elected regional government has been led by the Campaign for Yorkshire. The campaign, whose president is the Archbishop of York, has in turn been led by its director, Jane Thomas, and managed by a 17-person Steering Group. In its Claim of Right, the campaign has welcomed the creation of both the RDA and the Regional Chamber, but has asserted "the right of the people of Yorkshire and the Humber to determine their own domestic affairs should it be their settled will to do so" (www.cfy.org.uk/claim.html). Therefore, the campaign has called upon the government "to bring forward legislation for accountable and representative regional government in Yorkshire and the Humber at the earliest possible opportunity" (www.cfy.org.uk/claim.html). The campaign held a Preliminary Constitutional Convention in York on 21 October 2000. The convention had three broad aims. First, "to explore issues about devolution and the possibilities for this region". Second, "to ensure that there is a participative approach to this and that the discussion is as broad and inclusive as possible". Third, "to try and identify some areas of agreement and a way forward" (www.cfy.org.uk/convention2000.html). In fulfilling the first and second objectives, the majority opinion at the convention was that the strongest argument for elected regional government lay with increasing the accountability of existing "remote" institutions within the regions. However, support for tax varying powers to be allocated within regional government was "not overwhelming". In terms of the third objective, following the convention, the campaign established a series of Working Parties to further explore some of the details and principles surrounding directly elected regional government. Particular attention has focused upon the powers which a putative assembly might possess, the nature of representation, and new ways of working which the assembly might embrace, and the financial powers it might seek. A Second Constitutional Convention was held in Wakefield on 30 June 2001, at which the findings of the Working Parties were discussed. In September 2001, the Campaign published its own White Paper on regional government, *Giving the people a voice*, which envisaged the creation of a directly elected regional assembly of "between 30 and 50 members" (CFY, 2001, p 21). The White Paper also suggested that regional government in England should operate "as a REGULATOR, as an imitator/ architect of STRATEGY and as a FUNDING body" (CFY, 200, p 11). On 9 March 2002, the Campaign organised a Commission on Regional Government that provided the opportunity for evidence to be submitted on the Campaign's White Paper. Given its limited resources, the biggest challenge confronting the campaign remains how to broaden its base so as to appeal to and mobilise the mass of the region's population. The answer would appear to lie in exploiting the electorate's concern with the provision of key public services, by highlighting the inequalities in funding for health, education and transport which continue to accentuate the competitive disadvantage of Yorkshire.

The main controversies: the emergence of distinctive regional policy issues

There have not yet been any major controversies which have assumed a high profile in the regional media. However, two distinctive regional policy issues have emerged which by their nature are applicable to other English regions. The first issue is the frustration felt at the RDAs' lack of effective powers and their lack of autonomy because of central prescription over policy resources. The second is the growing discontent surrounding the funding settlement for England which arises from the operation of the Barnett Formula. These issues were highlighted when Graham Hall was the only RDA chairman to contribute to the Smith Institute's *Towards a new regional policy* pamphlet (Hall, 2000), which has been interpreted in some quarters as having signalled the Chancellor of the Exchequer's genuine interest in devolution to the English regions. In his contribution, Hall noted that two problems with the capacity to deliver the RES were apparent to the RDA chairmen from the outset. First, that the RDAs "did not have the tools to do the job", not least because "The 11 different stovepipe funding streams, with a number of detailed strings attached, were not focused on the key issues identified in the strategies". Second, that the "RDAs were increasingly perceived as creatures of DETR, rather than agencies of economic growth and joined-up Government envisaged by their architects, John Prescott and Dick Caborn" (Hall, 2000, pp 24-5). Consequently, within four months of the RDAs' establishment, the RDA chairmen, with Hall playing the leading role, had sought six changes in the governance of the English regions in general and the RDAs in particular.

These changes had included the call for a single block grant for RDAs within two years, "an early discussion with Ministers on the Barnett formula", and "a review of outputs and assessment methods in key departmental funding streams" (Hall, 2000, pp 25-6). In response, the government had promised a single pot for RDA spending from April 2002, but a discussion with ministers on the Barnett Formula had merely found that "the Government's position was unchanged". On the question of resources, Hall argued that "The time has surely come to look again at the Barnett formula" because "A fair and equitable distribution of public spending per capita will be vital to ensure that the poorer English regions have a much greater chance of narrowing the gap with London and the South-East". The Spending Reviews could be used to redistribute resources for education, health and transport to poorer regions like Yorkshire (Hall, 2000, p 29). Hall has received support from the *Yorkshire Post* which has supported demands for a redistribution of public spending towards Yorkshire, contending that "This so-called Barnett formula is a blatant iniquity which has been reduced to absurdity following the Government's cack-handed attempts at devolution" ('Spotlight on "£2bn divide" as cash row grows', *Yorkshire Post*, 29 April 2001). Rather than supporting devolution for Yorkshire, the paper has asserted that a better policy would be to implement "a fairer allocation of resources, one which ends the nonsense of the Scots and Welsh being subsidised by the English" ('Spotlight on "£2bn divide" as cash row grows', *Yorkshire Post*, 29 April 2001).

Despite the government's commitment to a 'single pot', Hall expressed his exasperation that the concept was "so counter-cultural to the way Parliament votes money, the accountability mechanisms and the command and control nature of large parts of Whitehall" (Hall, 2000, p 27). He urged that the concept of a single pot would only work with "a clear corporate planning process, whereby the Government buys a single set of outcomes-one Public Service Agreement-from RDAs, and sensible monitoring and review arrangements". However, "It must not consist of separate corporate plans, prescriptive guidance, an excessive degree of detail in planning and reporting, mid-year initiatives involving RDA bidding and outputs so specific as to make any flexibility mythical. That is our biggest current challenge for Ministers" (Hall, 2000, p 27). Hall had just delivered a withering critique of the existing governance of the RDAs. He also proceeded to urge that the RES be given "real teeth" by ensuring that key delivery agencies for the RES, notably local authorities, Learning and Skills Councils, the Small Business Service, universities and local strategic partnerships, should be judged against the RES. Indeed, the RDAs could be given a "key role in measuring the performance of public agencies in delivering those national and regional targets" (Hall, 2000, p 27).

In May 2000, when a concordat had been signed between the RDAs and the Local Government Association, it had been Hall who had represented the RDA chairmen and called for both RDAs and local authorities to be given "as much flexibility as possible to deliver on local and regional concerns" (YF, 2000h). Hall's frustration at the overly prescriptive nature of central government policy has been evident. For example, he has urged that "Councils, communities and partnerships must be encouraged to evolve without over prescriptive guidance, if we are to see local strategic partnerships develop into the kind of partnerships we want" (YF, 2001g). The concordat had included the principle that "Sufficient tools need to be made available to tackle inequalities within and between regions and achieve the urban and rural renaissance desired by central government. This should include an examination of fiscal measures to supplement the grant programmes currently available" (YF, 2001g). Hall was also critical of the March 2000 Budget, expressing his disappointment that public transport had only received an additional £280 million. Prior to the Budget, Hall called for greater tax incentives for companies to invest in technology and research and development (R&D), and for the taxation on patents licensed in cluster-related geographical areas to be zero-rated (YF, 2001h). In June 2000, Hall had welcomed the prospect of greater flexibility within the RDAs' budgets that had emerged from a meeting between the RDA chairmen, John Prescott, Gordon Brown, Richard Caborn, David Blunkett and Hilary Armstrong. However, while welcoming the government's recognition of the RDAs' leadership and coordination roles, Hall stated that the RDAs needed "to be able to intervene on strategic issues". Furthermore, YF would be looking for "concrete examples" of funding increases for Yorkshire in the 2000 Spending Review, and had supported local authorities in their calls for more funding for education (YF, 2000i). Hall subsequently welcomed the Budget 2001 announcement of an increase of £130 million in YF's budget over the 2001-04 period covered by the 2000 Spending Review. However, he has continued to press for tax breaks on R&D to be extended beyond large companies to cluster-related geographic areas (YF, 2001i).

The response of social and political interests in the regions to the prospect of elected regional government

Yorkshire-based politicians have been prominent among those seeking both to extend and to oppose elected regional government in England. John Prescott and Richard Caborn have been the two most vocal and frequent advocates of English devolution, while William Hague has led the Conservative Party's opposition to directly elected English regional government and its advocacy of the abolition of the RDAs. However, the debate has not been confined to Yorkshire's national political figures. For example, in his contribution to a Fabian Society debate on 'The English Question', Austin Mitchell, the most vocal backbench Labour MP within the region, defined a "Manifesto for the North". In articulating the Manifesto, Mitchell claimed that "The North is developing a regional political life but lacks the same stage as Scotland to put it on" (Mitchell, 2000, p 48). However, he dismissed the notion of an English Parliament as "An elephant in a cuckoo's nest" which would merely entrench the dominance of London (p 50). Mitchell lamented the "culture of dependency and grant-surfing" which had turned local government into "lobbyists not doers" and "latter day Jarrow marchers" for whom "The pilgrimage to Brussels had joined the begging bowl visit to London" (pp 50, 52). As an alternative, Mitchell has advocated regional government in England with "similar powers and roles to Scotland". Regional Assemblies, with a maximum of 100 members and a three-year term, should be elected by proportional representation. In addition, regional government should be funded through block grants, the capacity to raise local income tax and the power to borrow (Mitchell, 2000, p 56).

What evidence is there of genuine civic interest in the new regionalism?

There is little evidence of genuine civic interest in the new regionalism. Yorkshire appears to express opinions consistent with those in other regions of the North. For example, in the October 2000 ICM 'State of the Nation' Poll (ICM Research/Joseph Rowntree Reform Trust, 2000, Q 10), 34% of those questioned in Yorkshire thought that an elected assembly for the region was the best way of deciding how "to generate new jobs, develop major roads and public transport, and other similar issues". This was above the average for England (32%) but below that for the North as a whole (43%). In Yorkshire, 31% of those questioned thought that the answer lay with appointed business and local government representatives from the region (compared to an English average of 29%). A further 15% favoured decisions being taken by government officials meeting at the regional level, but only 10% agreed that ministers in Whitehall should decide Yorkshire's fate, taking into account the needs of the country as a whole. An earlier MORI opinion survey for *The Economist* had found that there was net agreement of +51% with the proposition that a Regional Assembly would look after the interests of the region better than central government. However, there was also +41% net agreement with the notion that a Regional Assembly would lead to more bureaucracy than the present system of government (*The Economist*, 27 March 1999, p 26).

At the General Election, not one of the region's 56 seats changed hands. New Labour dominates the region with 47 seats and a 48.6% share of the vote. The Conservatives won 7 seats and 30.2% of the vote, and the Liberal Democrats retained their 2 seats with a 4.1% share of the vote. However, the most damning statistic was the turnout which, at only 56.7%, was down 11.6% on the 1997 General Election. As one of Labour's 'heartlands', and in the absence of a nationalist party to provide voters with a credible alternative location for their vote, New Labour could take retention of the overwhelming majority of seats in Yorkshire and the Humber for granted and target its efforts on more marginal seats in 'Middle England'. Against the context of an extremely low-key campaign, in terms of political activism rather than media-led and focus-group driven politics, the notion of a politically active citizenry is an extremely challenging one to sustain.

The regional media

For those campaigning for devolution to Yorkshire, one of the most frustrating barriers to mobilising popular support behind the campaign for Yorkshire has been the obdurate opposition of the region's only daily newspaper, the *Yorkshire Post*, to the possibility of directly elected regional government. Indeed, in its editorials during the recent General Election campaign, the paper aligned itself more closely with William Hague's 'English Votes for English Laws' agenda. For example, the paper wrote of "the self-appointed apostles of regional democracy" and dismissed the economic case for regional government as "globaloney". The paper's alternative agenda for remedying the region's democratic deficit has been the reform of local government, "not inventing yet another tier of bureaucracy". It has advocated the restoration of the powers which Thatcher "rightly stripped from irresponsible, loony-Left councils in the 1980s" in the belief that "Institutions which once embodied the civic pride of Yorkshire towns and cities could once again flourish if they were given greater control over their budgets and the ability to raise more of their own revenues" ('Regions of the Heart', *Yorkshire Post*, 29 May 2001). In a thinly veiled assault on the Deputy Prime Minister, the paper had previously suggested that "Those within Ministerial circles who favour English devolution are no great political thinkers and their reasons for wanting regional assemblies are poorly thought out" ('Assembled voices', *Yorkshire Post*, 12 April 2001). Indeed, the paper claimed that a 150,000 or 5% threshold for a petition of Yorkshire's three million voters to trigger a plebiscite on a Regional Assembly "is much too low", and would neither be a sufficient demonstration of demand for "so radical a constitutional change" nor a sufficient argument for "a fully-blown regional parliament" to be regarded as the sole means to rectify the region's democratic deficit ('Assembled voices', *Yorkshire Post*, 12 April 2001). In a parliamentary debate on devolution, Denis MacShane, the Labour MP for Rotherham, expressed his regret that the *Yorkshire Post* "supports entirely the Tory view that everything should be centralised in London and that devolution to Yorkshire should not be on the political agenda". Austin Mitchell, the Labour MP for Great Grimsby and the most vocal backbench Labour advocate of devolution within the region, described this situation as "a tragedy and a betrayal", and noted that the newspaper "used to be part of the Yorkshire Conservative Newspaper Company Ltd, which is no doubt why it takes such a position" (*Official Record*, 17 January 2001, cWH96).

Conclusion

An Opinion Research Business (ORB) opinion poll, commissioned by the BBC in March 2002, has offered some encouragement to those campaigning for devolution for Yorkshire and the Humber. No fewer than 72% of those questioned in the region supported the creation of Regional Assemblies. In addition, 45% were willing to pay additional taxes to finance the assemblies, with 41% against. While opponents of devolution, not least the *Yorkshire Post*, have identified the potential abolition of North Yorkshire County Council as a rallying point for opposition to devolution, the ORB poll found that no fewer than 59% of respondents in the region were not concerned about this prospect.

   In the aftermath of the rioting in the Harehills district of Leeds in June 2001 and the more widespread riots in Bradford in July 2001, perhaps the most disappointing aspect of the devolution debate in Yorkshire and the Humber is that it remains trapped within a discourse that can see no further than the functional management of territory and questions of economic development (eg YF, 2002). Although these questions are themselves vital, it is hard to see how the populations of the poorer inner urban core of West and South Yorkshire will benefit from regeneration (as opposed to the renovation of the physical environment which they inhabit) until devolution extends to questions of citizenship and the identity of multicultural and ethnically diverse communities. If it was large enough in membership and sufficiently empowered, a directly elected Parliament for Yorkshire could yet play a vital role in the identification of a more inclusive and civic English regional identity.

References

Cabinet Office (1999) *Sharing the nation's prosperity: Variation in economic and social conditions across the UK*, London: The Cabinet Office.

CFY (Campaign for Yorkshire) (2001) *Giving the people a voice: Campaign for Yorkshire's White Paper on Regional Government*, Sheffield: CFY, www.cfy.org.uk/cfywhitepaper01.pdf

Government Office for Yorkshire and the Humber (GOYH) (2000) *Annual Report 1999/2000. Government Office for Yorkshire and the Humber*, Leeds: GOYH.

Hall, G. (2000) 'Rising to the challenge: The changing agenda for RDAs and government in building world class regions', in E. Balls and J. Healey (eds) *Towards a new regional policy: Delivering growth and full employment*, London: The Smith Institute, pp 24-30.

Hazell, R. (2000) 'Conclusion: the State and the nations after one year' in R. Hazell (ed) *The State and the nations: The first year of devolution in the United Kingdom*, London: University of London Constitution Unit, pp 269-81.

Her Majesty's Treasury (HMT) (2000) 'Gordon Brown calls for enterprise for all: New figures show differences in small business creation around the country', HMT Press Release 80/00, 23 June.

HMT/Department of Trade and Industry (DTI) (2001) *Enterprise and productivity. The Government's strategy for the next parliament*, London: HMT/DTI.

Huggins, R. (2000) *An index of competitiveness in the UK: Local, regional and global analysis*, Cardiff: Centre for Advanced Studies.

ICM/Joseph Rowntree Reform Trust (2000) *State of the nation poll*, (www.icmresearch.co.uk/2000/state-of-the-nation-2000.html).

Lee, S. (1999a) 'Yorkshire forward or backwards? The Limits of "New Regionalism" in the governance of Yorkshire', in *New Regional Strategies: Devolution, RDAs and Regional Chambers. Conference Proceedings of the Regional Studies Association Annual Conference*, London: Regional Studies Association, pp 57-60.

Lee, S. (1999b) 'The competitive disadvantage of England' in K. Cowling (ed) *Industrial policy in Europe*, London: Routledge, pp 88-117.

Mitchell, A. (2000) 'A Manifesto for the North' in S. Chen and T. Wright (eds) *The English Question*, London: The Fabian Society, pp 45-62.

Office for National Statistics (ONS) (2001) *Regional Economic Indicators: May*, London: ONS.

Regional Assembly for Yorkshire and Humberside (RAYH) (1998) *Yorkshire and Humberside: Advancing together into the millennium: A strategic framework*, Wakefield: RAYH.

RAYH (1999) *Regional Assembly for Yorkshire and Humberside Constitution*, Wakefield: RAYH, (www.rayh.gov.uk).

Select Committee on Trade and Industry (TISC) (2001), *Enterprise policy in the regions*, Thirteenth report from the TISC, Session 2000-2001, HC 815, (www.parliament.the-statione...01/cmselect/cmtrdind/513/51304.htm).

Yorkshire Forward (YF) (1999a) 'Major new Board appointment', YF Press Release, 15 December.

YF (1999b) *Advancing together: The regional economic strategy for Yorkshire & Humber*, Leeds: YF.

YF (1999c) '£91million regeneration programme announced for South Yorkshire', YF Press Release, 14 July.

YF (2000a) 'Yorkshire Forward unveils boost to cluster development', YF Press Release, 12 September.

YF (2000b) *Yorkshire Forward Annual Report and Accounts 1999-2000*, Leeds: YF.

YF (2000c) 'Has Yorkshire gone soft?', YF Press Release, 29 September.

YF (2000d) 'Yorkshire Forward and Regional Chamber's vision of regeneration', YF Press Release, 28 November.

YF (2000e) 'Yorkshire Forward Chairman calls for answers over rail crisis', YF Press Release, 18 December.

YF (2000f) 'Yorkshire Forward joins calls for state aid for coal industry', YF Press Release, 5 April.

YF (2000g) 'Yorkshire Forward unveils £100 million regeneration', YF Press Release, 2 August.

YF (2000h) 'Yorkshire Forward's pioneering agreement with local authorities', YF Press Release, 25 May.

YF (2000i) 'Yorkshire Forward welcomes extra responsibilities', YF Press Release, 23 June.

YF (2001a) 'Yorkshire Forward identifies key industries to drive economy', YF Press Release, 12 June.

YF (2001b) 'Businesses set to benefit from £25m venture capital fund', YF Press Release, 14 June.

YF (2001c) 'Yorkshire Forward welcomes two major European announcements', YF Press Release, 2 March

YF (2001d) 'Government cash in response to flood', YF Press Release, 12 January.

YF (2001e) 'Yorkshire Forward Chairman calls for interest rate cut', YF Press Release, 16 January.

YF (2001f) 'Chairman given prestigious Bank of England appointment', YF Press Release, 3 May.

YF (2001g) 'Yorkshire Forward calls for freedom for region's partnerships', YF Press Release, 18 January.

YF (2001h) 'Yorkshire Forward Chairman calls for innovative budget', YF Press Release, 22 February.

YF (2001i) 'Yorkshire Forward chairman welcomes budget regeneration measures', YF Press Release, 7 March.

YF (2002) 'White Paper establishes RDAS as economic powerhouses', YF Press Release, 9 May.

FIVE

Institutional collaboration in the West Midlands region

Sarah Ayres, John Mawson and Graham Pearce

Introduction

Approaches to governance in each of the English regions during the postwar period have followed different trajectories, a consequence of historical, economic and geographical circumstances and shifts in institutional structures. In some, rivalry between local authorities constrained the emergence of a genuine commitment to regional working. In this respect the history of postwar collaboration between authorities in the West Midlands is distinct from many other English regions. Indeed, it is the only region, apart from the South East, that can claim a strong unbroken tradition of strategic planning associations since the 1960s, and which are regional rather than metropolitan or city-regional (Thomas, 1999).

A key explanation for this collaboration may lie in the region's geographical and administrative boundaries. The West Midland conurbation – Birmingham, the Black Country towns, Solihull and Coventry – dominates the region, and accommodates nearly half the region's population of over 5.3 million. The only comparable urban centre is on the northern edge of the region – around Stoke-on-Trent and Newcastle – with a population of some 0.3 million. The administrative boundaries of the metropolitan authorities are tightly drawn, separating the conurbation from the surrounding shire counties – Herefordshire, Shropshire, Staffordshire, Warwickshire and Worcestershire – rural areas with both country and new, expanding towns, many of which have gained rapid population from the dispersion of population from the metropolitan area.

Drewett's account of early postwar planning in the region showed how the conurbation and shire authorities were encouraged to collaborate by the need to find regionally based solutions to the population, housing and industrial growth of Birmingham (Hall et al, 1973). Given the economic downturn beginning in the mid-1970s, it might have been expected that the need for urban–rural cooperation would have become less urgent. However, there was a recognition among political leaders across the region that urban regeneration should be *the key objective* and that a failure to tackle the problems arising from economic and social decline in the conurbation would have serious implications for the wider region (Marshall and Mawson, 1987).

For much of the postwar period, regional working relied on generally dependable relations between various central government departments in the region and local authorities. Since the mid-1990s, however, the institutional context has been subject to profound change as the government's reform agenda for the regions has begun to take effect. In some respects the presence of an established platform of collaboration has assisted this transition, but the emergence of the new institutional architecture has brought new challenges and has by no means been trouble free.

Regional working in the West Midlands has, therefore, followed several distinct phases. This chapter reviews them chronologically, and begins by briefly outlining the key socio-economic features of the region. Second, it assesses developments in regional working during the early postwar period through to the election of New Labour in 1997. Third, it describes recent developments in regional governance, focussing on the four key regional institutions. Fourth, it considers tensions between them, in particular the role of the Regional Development Agency (RDA). Fifth, an account is presented of the emerging debate surrounding the prospects of an elected Regional Assembly. Finally, this chapter offers a perspective on the key policy issues confronting the region, and assesses the extent to which the present institutional structures are capable of responding to these.

West Midlands regional socio-economic context

The long postwar boom saw rapid economic and population growth in the West Midlands. However, its reliance on manufacturing industry – particularly car production – left it exposed to growing foreign competition and the shift to service employment. The transition from a traditional to an advanced industrial economy proved difficult, and during the 1970s and 1980s the region suffered rapid employment loss, particularly in those areas most dependent on manufacturing – the conurbation and the medium size towns (Spencer et al, 1986). From being ranked second only to the South East in terms of per capita GDP during the early 1970s, ten years later it had become the poorest region in England. This was accompanied by increased economic and social polarisation between the major urban areas and the shire counties. Between 1981 and 2000 the shire counties experienced a population increase of 10%, while the former West Midlands County declined by 7% (ONS, 2001).

The West Midlands' relative economic performance improved throughout the 1990s, but per capita GDP in 1998 was still only 92% of the UK average. However, this masked wide variations within the region. Analysis of 2000 wage rates shows that average male weekly earnings in Herefordshire and Stoke-on-Trent were only £352 and £378 respectively, compared with £467 in Warwickshire and £439 in the conurbation (ONS, 2001). There are concentrations of poverty and underemployment in the metropolitan area, parts of North Staffordshire, Telford, Redditch, North Warwickshire and Herefordshire. Regional unemployment declined from 7.2% in 1996 to 3.8% in 2001 but in parts of the conurbation remained well above 5%, with a high proportion of long-term unemployed. The West Midlands contains some of the most deprived wards in the country, and Birmingham is the most deprived district in terms of residents experiencing income and employment deprivation (ONS, 2001). Poverty is also an issue in some of the region's more peripheral rural areas.

In comparative terms manufacturing remains a significant but declining component of the regional economy, accounting for 29% of regional GDP in 1998, compared with 21% in the UK. Employment in manufacturing is high – 23% – compared with less than 16% in the UK in 1999. By contrast only 15% of regional employment was in financial and business services, compared with 19% nationally, and in parts of the west of the region the proportion was below 12%. Engineering and motor vehicle companies, including Rover and their suppliers, still dominate manufacturing. In 2000 the automotive sector accounted for almost 5% of regional GDP and regional employment and "has also been a major catalyst for inward investment into the region in the last 10 years with almost 40% of jobs created coming from the automotive sector or related industries" (Rover Task Force, 2000). The region has a significant presence of foreign direct investment companies and there has been a rapid growth in financial and business services, hotels and catering.

As elsewhere in the UK, employment growth has frequently been associated with information and communications technologies (ICT) including business services. The growth of services has largely, but not entirely, been associated with the growth of central Birmingham as a regional and international business centre, built around the National Exhibition and International Convention Centres. Driven by a powerful elite, the city centre has been revitalised as part of a strategy to establish Birmingham as a leading European centre (Martin, 1995). That process is continuing with major new phases of regeneration in the Bull Ring and the city's 'East Side'. However, within walking distance are some of the most deprived wards in the country containing a concentration of disadvantaged ethnic minority communities.

The legacy of regional working

The tradition of regional institution building, notably in the form of regional planning structures, can be traced back to at least 1945. This longevity can partly be attributed to the boundaries of the planning region which remained fixed throughout this period, helping to secure consistency and elite engagement with the regional agenda. For instance, the Cadbury family was involved in successive regional initiatives throughout the 20th century, and the Cadbury Trust currently supports the activities of the West Midland Constitutional Convention, a body concerned with promoting the case for elected regional government.

Arrangements for local authority collaboration have been continuously adapted and shaped by the changing regional context (Mawson and Skelcher, 1980). In 1968, for example, the West Midlands Planning Authorities Conference was established to oversee the preparation of a regional land use strategy. Similarly, recognition of the growing importance of regional planning issues led to the creation of the West Midlands Forum of County Councils, membership of which was subsequently extended to include District Councils (WMRF, 1993a). Serviced by a small technical officer team – the West Midlands Regional Study – the significance of the forum lay in the political legitimacy and the organisational framework it provided for coordination between the conurbation and shire authorities, for example Strategic Planning Guidance (SPG) in 1987, and Regional Planning Guidance (RPG) (WMRF, 1993b). The forum also took the lead in preparing the first European Strategy for the region in 1993, signalling the capacity of local authorities to collaborate in this emerging policy area (WMRF, 1993b; Martin and Pearce, 1994).

In the early 1990s regional strategic planning took a further step forward with the establishment of the West Midlands Regional Economic Consortium (WMREC), comprising representatives of the Training and Enterprise Councils, business community, trades unions and local government, each of which recognised the need for a single cohesive voice for the region in promoting its economic interests at national and European levels. WMREC was serviced by the local authority funded West Midlands Regional Study team and their collective efforts included the preparation of various regional strategies/studies in partnership with the forum.

Through its activities, WMREC developed a close working relationship with the Government Office for the West Midlands (GOWM) which was established in 1994 to coordinate central government activities in the region concerned with the environment, transport, employment and industry. A Regional Director was charged with oversight of these programmes, providing a single clear voice for central government and its policies in the region and articulating regional interests in Whitehall. The GOWM also played a key role in fostering the development of various regional and subregional partnerships and the management of new regionally based programmes, in particular the Single Regeneration Budget and the EU structural funds. In recognition of the growing importance of European funding, the forum and WMREC established an office in Brussels in 1996 to promote the interests of the region.

New Labour's regional agenda: continuity and change

Like other English regions, the period since 1997 has seen significant changes in the formal arrangements for the governance of the West Midlands: a strengthened GOWM, the creation of an RDA – Advantage West Midlands (AWM) – and the establishment of a West Midlands Regional Chamber.

In the West Midlands these changes were accompanied by:

- the creation of a regional office of the West Midland Local Government Association (WMLGA);
- an agreement – in the form of a regional concordat – between GOWM, AWM, the Regional Chamber and the WMLGA;
- the creation of a West Midlands in Europe partnership.

The immediate impact of these developments has been to make the regional institutional landscape far more complex than it was in 1997, with overlapping spheres of influence and functions involving different tiers of government – EU, central and local – and private and voluntary agencies. A recent 'audit' of governance structures in the West Midlands has provided a snapshot of the organisations that currently contribute to the region's 'governance capacity' (Ayres and Pearce, 2002). It revealed both the large number of organisations (50+) involved in setting policies and delivering services in the region and the extent of their expenditure, which (excluding local government) amounted to some £8 billion annually. The need to impose some order on these 'jigsaw' arrangements has fostered collaborative approaches and the participation of a wide range of regional and local organisations in the preparation of regional strategies dealing with the economy, spatial planning, environmental sustainability, transport and the EU structural funds.

The Government Office for the West Midlands (GOWM)

The role of the GOWM has been greatly strengthened since 1994 and currently embraces elements of the work of many of the key domestic government departments. Its key objectives include:

- supporting and promoting a coherent regional approach to competitiveness, sustainable development, regeneration and social inclusion, both through the government programmes over which the office has direct control, and by influencing the action of partners/partnerships;
- managing the government's relationship with regional partners, by promoting and supporting effective partnership working and in particular through sponsorship of AWM and supporting it in the development of its strategy;
- representing and communicating parent departments' national policy at local levels and providing a channel to inform national policy with local views and issues.

Although GOWM has lost some functions and staff to AWM, it still has more than 350 staff and an annual budget of £923 million (2000-01), and remains a major force in regional governance.

Advantage West Midlands (AWM) – the Regional Development Agency

Advantage West Midlands was established in April 1999 with a board of 14 directors, chaired by Alex Stephenson, and is responsible for establishing regional development priorities with local partners, and bringing to bear AWM's own economic development programmes and budgets. It is business led, but includes other regional stakeholders drawn from local government, education, trade unions, community and voluntary organisations, environmental groups and the private sector. With a staff of 164 it receives an annual budget of £183 million (2000-01) from central government, funded through the Department of Trade and Industry (DTI), the Department of Transport, Local Government and the Regions (DTLR), the Department for Education and Skills (DfES), and the EU's structural programmes. Its key funding streams are the Single Regeneration Budget, Land and Property Programme, Rural Programme, Skills Development Fund and the Regional Innovation Fund.

AWM's initial task was to rapidly prepare a Regional Economic Strategy (RES) entitled *Creating Advantage* to meet a tight timetable dictated by central government (AWM, 1999). The focus was on achieving 'sustainable economic regeneration', which AWM would seek to promote through its roles, as regional champion – an advocate for the region, working on its behalf to secure funding and investment and to influence policy and external perceptions of the region. At the same time it sought to bring others together to deliver actions of regional significance or to work together better, and, as regional catalyst, using its funding and strategic overview to align strategies and programmes of others with the RES.

Arising out of *Creating Advantage* a more detailed action plan document *Agenda for Action* (AWM, 2001) was prepared which set out 60 actions over ten years which were to be undertaken by AWM and its partners to implement the RES. For example, in drawing up *Agenda for Action*, links were made with other key regional-level strategies and action plans, including an early draft of RPG and the related Regional Transport Strategy, the Regional Sustainability Framework, Innovation Strategy and Action Plan and the region's £500 million Objective 2 programme.

West Midlands Regional Assembly

The West Midlands Chamber was formed in 1999 to fulfil a scrutiny role in relation to AWM's economic development activities and specifically the RES. It was renamed the West Midlands Regional Assembly in 2001. Following the outcome of a review of the chamber's activities a decision was taken in December 2000 to broaden its role beyond the scrutiny of AWM's economic development activities to a wider remit facilitating the development of economic, social and environmental priorities and partnerships across the region (Mawson and Saunders, 2000). The principal governing body is the Assembly Council, with a voting membership of 100 nominees comprising 68 local authority representatives, 16 business sector representatives and 16 other economic and social partners.

The West Midlands Local Government Association (WMLGA) is responsible for local government representation on the assembly which is designed to reflect the region's political and geographical balance. The coordinating body for the business community is the West Midlands Business Policy Group (WMBPG), which nominates from within its ranks business representatives on to the chamber. A third category of chamber members – 'Other economic and social partners' – comprise a heterogeneous grouping including higher and further education, black and minority ethnic communities, faith communities and voluntary and community organisations in which each 'sector' has its own nominating body.

There are three elected assembly officers, the chair (a local authority representative) and two vice-chairs (representing the business sector and the other economic and social partners). Since completion of the Chamber Review, the assembly has instituted policy forums and other task groups to help take forward work set out in its annual work plan. The full Assembly Council meets quarterly and an Annual Conference is held, open to all regional interests, whether or not they are directly represented in the assembly structure.

Following the review of its roles and responsibilities (Mawson and Saunders, 2000) the assembly redefined and broadened its purpose as follows:

- to articulate a single, coherent voice on important issues and events affecting the region;
- to provide a lobbying authority to protect and advance the social and economic interests of the region;
- to provide for the coordination, oversight and endorsement of regional strategies;
- to be the principal consultative mechanism for activity and the arbiter of partner inclusiveness in regional structures;
- to contribute to and scrutinise the work of AWM;
- to make regional policies more transparent to the public.

In the past, the main sources of funding for the assembly (in both cash and kind) have been its constituent sectors, particularly local government. However, in March 2001, central government announced further finance of up to £0.5 million per annum, initially for a three-year period, to enable the expansion of the assembly's work and to enhance its scrutiny role of AWM (DTLR, 2001).

West Midlands Local Government Association (WMLGA)

The increasing attention being given to the regional dimension in public policy, New Labour's commitment to devolution and the prospect of a unified national Local Government Association all pointed to the need to forge a strengthened and fully representative voice for local government in the region. In the spring of 1997 it was decided to change the constitution of the Regional Forum to give every local council in the region representation in its decision making through an indirectly nominated assembly – the West Midlands Local Government Association. A structure of committees was established to service the assembly, which broadly reflected that of the national LGA (WMLGA, 1997).

The objective of the WMLGA was to create a body to represent the wide range of local government interests at regional level and, in particular:

- to secure a strong regional voice for the West Midlands in relation to regional, national and international issues;
- to act as the regional link to the national LGA and determine and promote a regional perspective on national issues affecting local government;

- to undertake regional collaboration in policy areas where regional working will add value.

The WMLGA has a Member Council on which all authorities are represented. It also has a Regeneration Conference (dealing with planning, transport and economic development), and a Provincial Council (representing authorities as employers to interface with Trade Unions). The detailed business of the WMLGA is managed by an Executive Committee and through small 'portfolio management groups' responsible for particular policy areas. The WMLGA has an annual budget of £1.8 million (2000-01) – 60% from subscriptions from constituent authorities and 40% from other sources. It is supported by a secretariat of 40 full-time staff based in Birmingham and by numerous voluntary officer networks and other 'support in kind' by constituent authorities.

As the regional planning body for the region, the WMLGA has a specific responsibility for preparing Draft RPG and the Regional Transport Strategy, which it incorporates. As a spatial strategy, it will also inform the development of strategies and programmes of other public agencies and service providers, including health and education, and will provide the longer-term planning and land use framework for the region's economic and cultural strategies and Sustainability Development Framework. The Draft will be the subject of a formal consultation exercise and a public examination in 2002, following which the RPG will be approved by the Secretary of State at the DTLR in 2003.

The West Midlands in Europe partnership

In 2000 the West Midlands established a new regional partnership to develop the European dimension of regional policies and activities. Its objective is to enable "regional partners to engage with evolving EU legislation, policy and future funding programmes and provide a collective benefit for the region in these matters" (West Midlands in Europe, 2001). The partnership includes AWM and the WMLGA, jointly responsible for directing the Brussels office, and higher and further education institutions, business culture/arts and the voluntary sector.

The partnership budget is £0.51 million (2001-02) of which the WMLGA and AWM contribute 70% and the region's universities about 10%. This supports a Brussels office, comprising a team of seven permanent staff, which aims to assist in "unlocking the wide range of existing expertise in the partnership through the following objectives":

- regional representation with key decision makers in the EU institutions;
- providing advance information and intelligence on EU policy, funding and legislation;
- raising the profile and marketing the region in Europe;
- facilitating networking and exchanging best practice with other regions and international bodies.

The current policy priorities of the partnership include arts, audio-visual/ media, Birmingham's bid to become European City of Culture in 2008, e-commerce and ICT, the debate leading up to the 2004 IGC structural funds and the post-2006 agenda, and EU policies on inclusion/poverty, gender, ethnicity and disability.

The regional concordat

The complex nature of the emerging institutional structures has given rise to anxieties about the clarity of roles and relationships and duplication and overlap in the preparation of various regional strategies. In responding to these concerns, collaboration between the four key regional institutions – GOWM, AWM, the assembly, WMLGA – is being facilitated via a voluntary concordat, agreed in 2001, to provide a framework to clarify the multitude of territorial boundaries and organisational remits and assist in integrating of regional strategies (see Figure 5.1).

Figure 5.1: Key institutions participating in the West Midland regional concordat

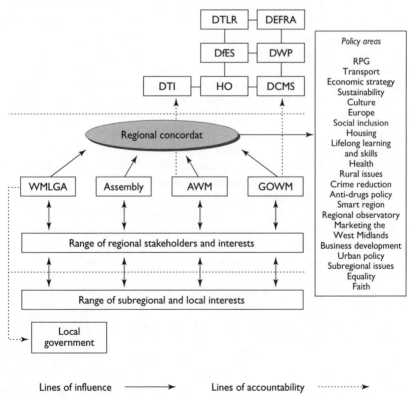

The formal objectives of the concordat include clarifying and rationalising the roles and responsibilities of organisations engaged in regional work, promoting more effective integration of interrelated activities, enshrining cross-sector partnership working and committing the principal agencies to be open and accountable to regional interests.

The concordat sets out activities in progress, and proposes roles and responsibilities in relation to the prosecution of the work. Lead responsibilities are identified to show the organisations/groups charged with ensuring the activity is completed. It reveals the breadth and depth of regional work currently being undertaken, and underlines the commitment of the key regional organisations to joint working. As such the concordat can be regarded as an important step towards achieving the level of sophistication and quality of partnership working required to tackle the challenges facing the region.

Institutional tensions

The new regional institutions had a legacy of regional working to draw on, but this did not prevent them from being embroiled in controversy at an early stage, in particular around the preparation and development of the RES.

Establishing the RDA and Chamber

The prospect of an RDA was widely welcomed in the region. Expectations were high, reflecting longstanding frustrations over what was perceived to be underinvestment and the long list of initiatives waiting to be implemented (WMREC, 1997). In advance of the establishment of the RDA (Advantage West Midlands), considerable preparatory work was undertaken by regional stakeholders in the public, private and voluntary sectors and coordinated by WMLGA. In March 1998 WMLGA organised a conference to identify key issues and views on the way forward. The subsequent report laid out a strategic framework for the RDA and Chamber and how the RES should be developed and delivered (WMLGA, 1998). It emphasised a bottom-up, fully inclusive approach, building on existing partnerships and regional working.

However, this enthusiasm had begun to evaporate by the time the RDA was formally constituted in April 1999. There was increasing suspicion about the dominant role of the GOWM during the start-up phase. Many regional stakeholders were anticipating meeting AWM's new board members, the chair and chief executive, but GOWM resisted such engagement. This led to suspicion among some stakeholders that GOWM was exerting far too much influence over the new agency and that, once set up, AWM would merely operate as an arms-length agency for the GOWM.

There was also disquiet about the substantial staff transfers from GOWM to AWM which would serve to establish a 'civil service' culture within AWM, judged not conducive to partnership working. The business sector, in particular, was seeking a new, dynamic, business-led organisation and viewed the transfers with apprehension. There was also concern that staff were being placed in positions where they had limited competencies. Concerns were also raised about the process surrounding the appointment of AWM board members. Many viewed it with scepticism, accusing GOWM of 'corridor deals'. The business and community sectors felt excluded because their 'preferred candidates' were not appointed, leaving them to question the criteria used in selection.

The Regional Economic Strategy (RES) and Action Plan

These tensions came to a head around the preparation of AWM's economic strategy. The requirement to prepare a regional economic strategy within a year of AWM's establishment placed considerable pressures on AWM staff and board members. The idea that AWM would provide a strategic leadership and coordination role through the preparation of a regional economic strategy was a novel one for all parties concerned, particularly given the agency itself had a comparatively small budget and limited range of responsibilities for implementation. Initially the process of preparing the RES was widely criticised as being limited in scope, timescale, inclusivity and based on inadequate information and limited analysis.

The chairman of AWM, Alex Stephenson, and chief executive, Tony Cassidy, had been appointed in the autumn of 1998 and the board members in the spring of 1999. While the board itself was not formally constituted until April 1999, work had already started on the development of the regional strategy. The Regional Competitiveness Action Plan and work previously undertaken for the WMREC on the regional economy strongly influenced the approach. The board reached an agreed vision for the region early in the process which was presented at the first meeting of the Regional Chamber in January 1999.

In April 1999, AWM engaged in a subregional consultation exercise organised by local partnerships and the draft strategy was presented to the annual meeting of the Regional Chamber in July 1999, attended by over 400 people. The launch was seen by the WMLGA as a "summer of consultation". However, at the beginning of September the Regional Chamber heard that AWM was intending to process the results of the consultation exercise, make revisions and submit the revised RES to the GOWM and the DTI independently of the chamber. A chance meeting between the chairs of AWM and the chamber led to a rethink in which it was agreed that the chamber would have the opportunity to comment on the final document. The chamber formally endorsed the strategy, *Creating Advantage*, and it was submitted to government in October 1999.

The vision underpinning the WMRES was that "within ten years the West Midlands will be recognised as a premier European location in which to live, work, invest and to visit, regarded internationally as world class and the most successful region in creating wealth to benefit everyone who lives in the area" (AWM, 1999, p 10).

The strategic framework for delivering the vision comprised two major themes and four main policy foci, or Pillars, which were intended to provide the link between the aims of WMRES and the associated Action Plans and four cross-cutting policy frameworks.

The two main themes were 'Creating Wealth Through Enterprise' and 'Providing Opportunity'. The four Pillars were:

1. Developing a diverse and dynamic business base
2. Promoting a learning and skilful region
3. Creating conditions for growth
4. Regenerating communities in the West Midlands.

The four cross-cutting policy frameworks covered were:

1. Building a sustainable future
2. Developing a new and creative cultural framework
3. Developing links between urban and rural areas
4. Valuing equal opportunities.

The strategy was approved by the Secretary of State in December 1999. Overall the view in the region was that AWM had responded to the consultation feedback and created a broad strategic framework which gave sufficient flexibility to enable where necessary more specific detail or differences to be resolved later. Others were disappointed with the lack of depth and clarity of the policies and the absence of priorities.

In April 2000 AWM produced a draft Action Plan for the period 2000-03 which was prepared by working groups drawn from the ranks of the RDA, board, chamber, and other relevant stakeholders and supported in their work by a consultancy company. A month later the chamber produced a commentary on the draft Action Plan based on feedback from all the sectors represented in the chamber. As far as the process as a whole was concerned there was a widespread feeling that AWM lacked an understanding of partnership working, and had failed to secure ownership and commitment to the action planning process. Procedurally there were complaints about the short notice and poor organisation of the meetings and specifically the lack of time to consider draft papers and gain the views of relevant constituencies. For many partners the approach to developing the plans was complex and difficult to understand. All too frequently the individual Action Plans did not deal with the practicalities of delivery, timescale and resources.

It was against this background of difficult working relationships with key regional partners that there was an increasing demand for a change in style and approach. In June 2000 the chief executive stepped down following pressures on central government from certain RDA board members, the business community and other stakeholders (O'Brien, 2000). His successor John Edwards, a former chief executive of the Rural Development Commission, was seen as somebody who was sympathetic to and understood the need for a more positive approach to partnership working. At the Annual Meeting of the Regional Chamber and AWM in July 2000, a decision was taken to put on hold the Action Plan process while it was subject to review by external consultants.

There was recognition on all sides that there had been a number of difficulties surrounding the preparation of WMRES and the Action Plan process. Other partners explicitly acknowledged the time pressures, staffing difficulties and other problems which AWM had faced. Equally AWM acknowledged that mistakes had been made, and was anxious to learn lessons and move forward as quickly as possible.

In the autumn of 2000 AWM and the Regional Chamber agreed to a consultative process with regional partners which led to the production of *Agenda for Action*. This Action Plan was completed and approved in the spring of 2001 (AWM, 2001). It was deliberately not 'all encompassing' but focused rather on major actions of regional significance. Altogether 60 main actions were identified with each having a single organisation designated as 'lead partner' with overall strategic responsibility for the action and accountability for progress.

While progress was being made with the action planning process, an internal review of the chamber's role and constitution was also carried out in the summer and autumn of 2000 (Mawson and Saunders, 2000). At the December meeting of the chamber, it was decided to increase the size of the chamber so that the 'private' and 'other sectors' categories of membership were able to more properly represent their wide range of interests and constituencies. There was a commitment to develop a regional concordat in partnership with AWM and GOWM. With funding now available from central government to support chamber activities, a decision was also taken to establish an independent Secretariat of four staff (DTLR, 2001). This decision had the active support of the 'business and other sectors' grouping of the chamber who wished to see the assembly displaying a clear independence from the WMLGA.

The politics of regionalism

One of the factors underlying the decision to undertake the Chamber Review was a recognition that the Labour administration might in due course bring forward proposals to establish elected Regional Assemblies. In that situation it was felt that the region should have in place a body capable of bringing together the various public, private and voluntary sector interests in the region and facilitating a debate about the options.

Prior to the establishment of the chamber there had been no popular groundswell of opinion calling for elected regional government in the West Midlands. The region's major political parties did not regard the issue as of any great significance in election campaigning or policy development nor was there much active interest in the issue among the region's MPs and MEPs. Not surprisingly the local media rarely covered the issue. Following the launch of the RDA and assembly however, there was a 'sea change' with an increasing awareness of the region's unfavourable position in powers and resources relative to the new devolved administrations of Scotland, Wales and Northern Ireland, and the Greater London Assembly and Mayor. The *Birmingham Post* began to adopt a less hostile position towards regional government and to consider the issues and options in a more constructive and objective manner than had hitherto been the case (Dale, 2001). This shift was also reflected in the voluntary sector and business community's willingness to engage with the new regional structures. However, these groups remained concerned about a move from an appointed to an elected Regional Assembly fearing that they might lose their seat at the table. There were also some tensions between grass roots membership and regional coordination bodies such as the Business Policy Group and Regional Action West Midlands (RAWM), on the basis that they were far too 'top down' and in search of roles to play. Such tensions were also evident among the region's 38 local authorities with those at county level tending to oppose elected assemblies on the grounds that the second tier already provided strategic planning while some district and unitary authorities took the alternative view that there should be a single tier of local government following the establishment of a Regional Assembly.

Nationally, New Labour's regional agenda led to the emergence of a campaigning group to advocate the establishment of elected regional authorities. Following the launching of the Campaign for the English Regions (CFER) in 1998, the West Midlands Constitutional Convention was formally constituted on 1 March 2000. Initially a steering group prepared the ground by securing a grant from a local charitable body, the Cadbury Barrow Trust to employ an administrator/campaigner. Further funding came from CFER to support the public launch of the convention and its community outreach work.

The steering group was chaired by the Bishop of Birmingham and included senior politicians from all three major political parties across the region. Running in parallel, an independent group of academics from the region's universities was established. This group issued a prospectus inviting interested parties to participate in an action research programme addressing key issues surrounding the creation of a more democratic form of regional government. With the support of the Regional Assembly an audit of the region's existing governance structures was undertaken together with the production of a paper setting out various alternative models of elected regional government (Ayres and Pearce, 2002). A series of local meetings was held around the region to discuss the research findings and promote a debate on the way forward. Further funding was made available to the group to undertake a more systematic assessment of public opinion based on a series of polls and focus group meetings.

Survey evidence suggests that there may be more interest in changing the present regional governance arrangements than sceptics in the region would be prepared to admit. An ICM poll undertaken in October 2000, for example, found that in response to the question "Which is the most appropriate form of government to generate new jobs, develop road and public transport and other similar issues?", only 11% opted for government ministers in Whitehall, and a mere 15% for government officials in the region. In contrast, 32% favoured an elected assembly, while 28% felt that appointed business and local government representatives from the region should take the decisions (ICM, 2000). A subsequent BBC opinion poll in March 2002 found that 76% of West Midlanders favoured an elected assembly for the region, the highest figure across the country. It remains to be seen whether such sympathies would be sufficiently strong to

---

be translated into a significant positive turnout in the event of a referendum on regional government.

Achievements and prospects

In retrospect, the two years following the creation of the new regional institutions in 1999 can be seen as a lacuna in the history of postwar institutional relations in the region. However, the affect was to create unpredictable alliances. At the beginning of 1999 it was the RDA that was seen as offering the best opportunity to develop an innovative approach to regional working, but only a few months later much of that confidence had dissipated.

West Midlands Local Government Association (WMLGA)

One of the beneficiaries was the WMLGA, which quickly came to be regarded as a productive and responsive partner. This view was held particularly among the business sector through its new and unforeseen alliance with the Regional Chamber. The WMLGA's role, as Secretariat to the Chamber, provided the opportunity for it to engage with the majority of organisations and interests in the region. It also began to enjoy a productive relationship with the WMBPG, providing an encouraging example of new cross-sector ties. Long-standing interpersonal relationships and information exchange lubricated the building of organisational relationships between the WMLGA and other agencies, and many regional partners came to depend on informal channels of communication afforded by the WMLGA's Secretariat. The WMLGA therefore played a crucial role in facilitating the process of consultation and collaboration during a time of turmoil and uncertainty.

Business and voluntary sector reorganisation

Since 1999, the business and voluntary sectors have continued to strengthen their regional presence. The growth of the regional agenda and the prospect of an elected Regional Assembly are driving these changes. Acting on a request from AWM, the business sector is seeking to ensure representation of a wide range of business interests which will be vital in the advent of an elected Regional Assembly. In mid-2002, the WMBPG will reorganise its activities around two new bodies – the Confederation of West Midlands Chambers of Commerce, and a West Midlands Business Council (or Forum) – which will relate closely to the Regional Assembly's business sector members. The reorganisation of the business sector is widely welcomed as a means for solving some of the representational and coordination inadequacies it currently suffers. In addition, there is some recognition in the business community of the need to encourage the region's 'big businesses' – the CBI, Rover, British Telecom and Price Waterhouse Coopers – to participate more fully in the process of regional policy formation.

As with business, so with the voluntary organisations, steps have been taken to establish an effective voice for the sector. Regional Action West Midlands

(RAWM) is a strategic network organisation working on behalf of the voluntary and community sector in the region which has been funded by substantial grants from the Home Office, National Lottery and Single Regeneration Budget over the past three years. It was established in part as a response to the increasing demands from various central government departments and agencies for a view from the sector on policy developments and implementation.

Relationship between AWM and the Regional Assembly

Since 2000 the assembly and AWM have worked hard to improve their working relationships. In particular, there is now a more constructive approach to the assembly's scrutiny role. Both sides view scrutiny in a positive light as a form of positive partnership working, rather than an exercise in negative commentary. This progress has required imagination and commitment. The advent of the regional concordat is seen as helpful in this regard and AWM staff and board members now regard assembly meetings as far more productive than they once were.

Considerable progress has also been made in working relationships between AWM and regional partners arising from collaborative working on various regional issues. For example, work is proceeding on RPG, efforts have been made to build a consensus around regional transport objectives to assist in lobbying Westminster and Whitehall, a West Midlands Rural Affairs Forum met for the first time in March 2002, and AWM and the assembly have recently submitted an Innovative Actions bid to the EU to help develop the process styles and competencies of the two institutions. The support given by AWM to the Rover and North Staffordshire Task Forces and to rural businesses following the recent Foot and Mouth episode are also evidence of increased regional capacity.

Progress has been made in developing a more collaborative approach but some anxieties remain. Some fear that the recent reorganisation of government departments and the placing of RDAs under the jurisdiction of the DTI may result in AWM adopting a more 'hard nosed' economic development perspective at the expense of a more balanced sustainable development agenda. However, AWM has recently provided the voluntary sector with considerable additional funds through the SRB and has promoted initiatives to develop social enterprises suggesting that its commitment to the inclusion and the active engagement of social interests in the region remains in place.

There are also concerns that AWM's RES should be set firmly within the overall framework of the RPG. AWM should have a social and economic agenda that is consistent with the forthcoming RPG strategy. A failure to resolve potential conflicts between RES and RPG would be interpreted as a failure to coordinate cross-cutting regional policies and serve to rekindle tensions between the region's institutions.

The introduction of a regional tier of governance in the West Midlands has presented a new set of collaborative challenges to existing local institutions. Faced with an array of interrelated economic, social and environmental issues partners have sought to promote cross-sector collaboration and present a coherent regional voice. The emphasis is clearly on increased 'joined-up' thinking – building "institutional thickness" (Amin and Thrift, 1994). The establishment of the new regional institutions and processes to enhance partnership working (for example, the concordat), have been pivotal in this regard. Along with their regional partners, each has experienced a 'bedding in process'. Other stakeholders have often responded, as best they can, to the regional agenda. Some organisations, like AWM and GOWM, have sought to orchestrate the emerging arrangements while other partners have simply sought to keep pace and secure influence when the opportunity arises. Evidence of mismanagement can be found alongside encouraging signs of Best Practice and entrepreneurship. Problems of policy coordination are ever present, and it remains to be seen whether the present arrangements will be sufficiently robust to reconcile competing interests and provide the independence, powers and resources necessary to effectively tackle the long-term problems facing the region.

References

AWM (Advantage West Midlands) (1999) *Creating Advantage*, Birmingham: AWM.

AWM (2001) *Agenda for Action*, Birmingham: AWM.

Amin, A. and Thrift, N. (1994) 'Living in the global', in A. Amin and N. Thrift (eds) *Globalisation, institutions and regional development in Europe*, Buckingham: Open University Press.

Ayres, S. and Pearce, G. (2002) *Devolved approaches to regional governance in the West Midlands: A briefing paper*, Birmingham: West Midlands Governance Action Research Group, West Midlands Regional Assembly and West Midlands Constitutional Convention.

Dale, P. (2001) 'Accounting for ourselves', *Birmingham Post*, 29 June.

DTLR (Department of Transport, Local Government and the Regions) (2001) *Strengthening regional accountability*, London: DTLR.

Gregory, D. (1987) *West Midlands unitary development plans: Advice on strategic guidance. Report by the chairman of the main conference*, Birmingham: Aston Business School.

Hall, P., Gracey, H., Drewett, R. and Thomas, R. (1973) *The containment of urban England*, London: PEP/Allen and Unwin.

ICM (2000) *Joseph Rowntree Trust State of the Nation opinion poll*, 28 October.

O'Brien, J. (2000) 'New leadership crisis hits enterprise agency', *Birmingham Post*, 26 October.

Martin, S. (1995) 'From workshop to meeting place? The Birmingham economy in transition', in R. Logan Turner (ed) *From the old to the new: The UK economy in transition*, London: Routledge.

Marshall, M. and Mawson, J. (1987) 'The West Midlands', in P. Damesick and P. Wood (eds) *Regional problems, problem regions and public policy in the UK*, Oxford: Oxford University Press, pp 95-124.

Mawson, J. and Skelcher, C. (1980) 'Updating the West Midlands Regional Strategy. A review of inter-authority relationships', *Town Planning Review*, vol 2, pp 152-170.

Mawson, J. and Saunders, W. (2000) *Review of the West Midlands Regional Chamber. Report of the Members Review Task Group*, Birmingham: WMLGA.

Martin, S. and Pearce, G. (1994) 'European regional development strategies: strengthening meso government in the UK', *Regional Studies*, vol 27, no 7, pp 499-503.

ONS (Office of National Statistics) (2001) *Regions in figures: The West Midlands*, London: ONS.

Rover Task Force (2000) *Final report by the Rover Task Force: Conclusions and recommendations to the Secretary of State*, Birmingham: AWM.

Spencer, K., Taylor, A., Smith, B., Mawson, J., Flynn, N. and Batley, R. (1986) *Crisis in the industrial heartland. A study of the West Midlands*, London: Oxford University Press.

Thomas, K. (1999) 'The metropolitan planning experience', in P. Roberts, K. Thomas and G. Williams, *Metropolitan planning in Britain: A comparative study*, London: Jessica Kingsley.

West Midlands in Europe (2001) *West Midlands in Europe: Business Plan*, Birmingham: West Midlands in Europe.

WMLGA (West Midlands Local Government Association) (1997) 'New Local government Association for the West Midlands Launched', *Regional LGA Matters*, Birmingham: WMLGA, p 1.

WMLGA (1998) *Making the West Midlands work. A Regional Chamber for the West Midlands*, Consultation Paper, Birmingham: WMLGA.

WMREC (West Midlands Regional Economic Consortium) and other regional interests (1997) *A response to government's consultation on proposals to establish Regional Development Agencies in the English regions. A West Midlands regional perspective*, Birmingham: WMREC.

WMRF (West Midlands Regional Forum of Local Authorities) (1993a) *Advice on regional planning guidance for the West Midlands: 1991-2011*, Stafford: WMRF.

WMRF (1993b) *Partners in Europe: West Midlands European regional development strategy (1994-99)*, Stafford: WMRF.

West Midlands Regional Chamber (2001) *West Midlands Regional Concordat*, Birmingham: West Midlands Regional Chamber.

SIX

England's North West

Benito Giordano

Introduction – a fragmented region?

The North West is England's second largest region with a population of seven million, or 12% of the total UK population. This means that it is comparable in size to Scotland and Wales combined, and has more inhabitants than four European Union (EU) member states – Denmark, Finland, Ireland and Luxembourg (Jarvis and McNamara, 1999). Due to its size, therefore, the North West clearly occupies an important position in the regional landscape of England. As this chapter explores, from the 1980s onwards there was a crystallisation of public and private sector interests at the regional level in the North West, which saw the creation of various institutions aimed at promoting regional coherence. More recently, of course, with the creation of the North West Development Agency (NWDA) and the North West Regional Assembly (NWRA), the region has been able to build upon these earlier developments. However, as this chapter goes on to discuss, it would seem there is still a degree of ambivalence, within the region, about its role in what is the emerging mosaic of English regional devolution.

There are several reasons for this. Firstly, the North West region, which stretches from Crewe in the south to Carlisle in the north, is probably one of the most fragmented in England (Bristow, 1987). Of course, this is certainly not unique to the North West, since the majority of the English regions have (at least for the moment) distinctly artificial boundaries. However, it must be said that in the North West this problem is accentuated because of its particular geographical location, which includes the counties of Cheshire, Greater Manchester, Merseyside, Lancashire and Cumbria. In particular, the 'Cumbrian Question' is a particularly intractable one for the region because of its proximity and its historical allegiance to the North East and Scotland. Put simply, Carlisle is much closer to both Newcastle and Glasgow than it is to either Manchester or Liverpool. Similarly, there is a strong case for including the district of High Peak which, administratively speaking, lies in Derbyshire but is clearly a part of the Greater Manchester travel-to-work area (Burch and Holliday, 1993).

Secondly, alongside the North West's fragmented geography, the region is beset by the problems of uneven economic development. On the one hand, the two cities of Manchester and Liverpool, and their respective conurbations, have undergone fairly severe processes of deindustrialisation; the same can certainly be said for some of the towns in Lancashire such as Burnley and Blackburn. On the other hand, parts of Cheshire, especially the so-called 'southern crescent' have undergone significant economic development in recent years based mainly on the growth of financial services and hi-tech industries (Deas and Ward, 2000; Hebbert and Deas, 2000). Consequently, the North West, probably more than any other region outside London, has marked disparities between its affluent and relatively poorer areas.

Thirdly, in terms of the political culture of the region, it is clear that up until the 1990s there was very little cooperation to try to promote a regional response that could ameliorate the problems of economic decline. Most notably, there was considerable hostility between the principal cities of Manchester and Liverpool, and a culture of parochiality prevailed (Bristow, 1987, Burch and Holliday, 1993). However, as will be explored later in the chapter, it would seem that recently this has changed because both cities have developed a much better working relationship which, in part at least, is thanks to the introduction of a regional tier in the North West.

This chapter is divided into three parts. The first discusses in more detail some of the main social and economic challenges facing the North West region. The second explores how the new regional institutions have settled, which is followed by a discussion of the ways in which the evolving regional strategies are meeting the challenges facing the North West. Finally, the third part focuses upon the future prospects for elected regional government in the North West and explores the extent to which regionalism is permeating further out into civil society.

Main social and economic challenges facing the region

Like the other northern English regions, by far the biggest challenge facing the North West is that of overcoming economic decline. The North West has undergone a process of massive deindustrialisation, which began in the 1970s, intensified in the 1980s, and continued into the 1990s. From 1993 to 1999 for example, the region lost some 80,000 manufacturing jobs. Of course, the recent past is not only a tale of decline, because the region witnessed an increase in employment in services by over 100,000 jobs during the same period (Jarvis and McNamara, 1999). By March 2001, the region's unemployment stood at 4% (unadjusted claimant basis) compared to the UK average of 3.5%. The International Labour Organization figure for the region, from December 2000 to February 2001, was slightly higher at 5.2%, which was identical to the UK figure and compared with an EU average of 8.0%. For the same period, according to the Labour Force Survey, the North West's proportion of those of working age and economically active was 76.9%, compared to 78.9% in the UK (*Economic Bulletin for NW England*, 2001).

In terms of GDP, the North West lags behind the southern regions of England. Most notably, although the North West's GDP per capita increased from £7,775 in 1990 to £10,990 in 1998 – a 41% increase in the eight-year period – the region was still only ranked above the North East and Yorkshire and the Humber in the league table of English regions. Compared to the South East and London regions, which in 1998 had GDP per capita figures of £14,529 and £16,245 respectively, the North West clearly performs badly. In fact, the North West (along with the North East) had the lowest net increase in GDP per capita between 1990 and 1998. Overall, the sobering trend is that the gap between the northern and southern regions of England actually widened in the 1990s (Robson and Deas, 2000).

At the subregional level, the scenario is one of mixed fortunes with certain districts in the North West doing badly while others are doing relatively well, even compared to the south of England. The so-called 'southern crescent' is conspicuous because it is an area of considerable economic growth, based on financial services and hi-tech jobs, which spans from the south of the Manchester Ship Canal and Warrington, to Manchester Airport and the M56 corridor down to Chester (NWDA, 2001b). Without a doubt, the subregional economy of Cheshire, with a population of one million people, is by far the most prosperous part of the North West. For example, in 1996 its GDP per capita (as a percentage of the EU average) was 111% compared to 90% for Greater Manchester, 86% for Lancashire and 73% for Merseyside (Jarvis and McNamara, 1999).

On the other hand, the North West has a disproportionately high number of districts that have the highest levels of deprivation in England. For example, of the 30 worst districts in the Index of Multiple Deprivation 2000, 12 were located in the North West, including Liverpool and Manchester. By comparison, the next highest was the North East region, which had eight of the 30 worst districts. Similarly, in 1997, of the percentage of houses selling for less than £20,000, the North West again had 12 of the 30 worst districts – the highest number in all of the English regions. Furthermore, the North West had 11 of the 30 worst districts on the indicator of Standardised Mortality Rates (1997) – the highest number yet again. Lastly, in terms of percentage unemployed (1997), the North West had eight of the worst 30 districts (Robson and Deas, 2000). Clearly this constitutes a miserable picture for a number of the North West's districts, such as Manchester and Liverpool, which consistently perform badly on most indicators of deprivation and (un)employment change.

Amidst this scenario of decline, both Manchester and Liverpool have suffered badly from the processes of deindustrialisation which have beset the region in recent decades. Indeed, conventional accounts of the economic histories of Liverpool and Manchester suggest that both cities have shared similar experiences. Both emerged from the industrial revolution, and both were simultaneously characterised by some of the most extreme manifestations of Victorian opulence and squalor. Both cities experienced protracted periods of economic decline during much of the 20th century, spawning attendant social problems of similar scale and type. In addition, both cities were characterised by local politics frequently at odds with national norms, most strikingly during the early 1980s as city leaders adopted confrontational stances towards central government (Giordano and Twomey, 1999).

Standard narratives of economic and political change in the two cities also emphasise their divergent fortunes from the late 1980s onwards. Manchester is generally regarded to have been at the forefront of recent changes in local governance in UK cities, where the redrawing of the institutional landscape arguably proceeded more rapidly and more comprehensively than any other English city, transforming a national reputation for minoritarian, oppositional politics to one based on 'can do' pragmatism and flexibility, coupled with a marked aptitude for deal making to secure funds, events and publicity (Hebbert and Deas, 2000). And according to conventional understandings of the recent histories of the two cities, this transition from a city in which the political agenda was dominated by the welfarist concerns of "defending jobs, improving services" (in the words of the then slogan) to one which aspires to be "up and going" is held to contrast with Liverpool's experience, with stereotypes of trade union militancy, crime and deprivation persisting into the 1990s (Giordano and Twomey, 1999; Hebbert and Deas, 2000).

If one considers the statistical contours of employment change, however, it becomes apparent that both cities, in spite of the claims about Manchester's 'entrepreneurial turn', have been beset by similar trajectories of decline (see Table 6.1). For example, between 1971 and 1996, Manchester lost just over 130,000 jobs, which was a decline of almost one third. Liverpool, during the same period, lost 192,000 jobs, which was over a 50% decline. In terms of the two respective conurbations, total employment in Greater Manchester, on the one hand, dropped by 139,311 in 1996, representing a decline of 12% on the 1971 total. Merseyside, on the other hand, lost 237,281 jobs (or 35%) during

Table 6.1: Change in the numbers of male and female jobs in England, Greater Manchester, Manchester, Merseyside and Liverpool (1971-96)

	Male	Female	1971-96
England			
1971-96	−2,005,836	2,413,466	407,630
% change	−17.3	34.0	2.2
Greater Manchester			
1971-96	−199,419	60,108	−139,311
% change	−28.6	13.1	−12.1
Manchester			
1971-96	−83,377	−20,337	−103,714
% change	−41.5	−14.2	−30.1
Merseyside			
1971-96	−202,451	−34,830	−237,281
% change	−50.0	−13.1	−35.4
Liverpool			
1971-96	−142,607	−49,954	−192,561
% change	−64.6	−34.9	−52.9

Source: NOMIS

the same 25-year period. The scale of these losses is reinforced by corresponding data for England which show that between 1971 and 1996, total employment increased to 19,081,148 – a 2.2% increase of 407,630 jobs (Giordano and Twomey, 1999).

Overall then, Liverpool's decline has been broader and considerably deeper than any other city in the UK. Furthermore, even though Manchester has generally fared better than Liverpool, comparison with other cities across the country suggests that Manchester can be grouped alongside Sheffield, Glasgow and Birmingham as cities that have lost between 12% and 19% of their total employment between 1981 and 1996. In actual fact, the contrast between 'core' decline and 'outer' growth in employment has been more acute in Greater Manchester than any other conurbation in Britain: core employment fell by 19% while the number of jobs in the outer areas increased by 5% (Turok and Edge, 1999).

In spite of their relative declines, however, both Manchester and Liverpool obviously play an important role as the drivers of economic dynamism in the North West. Firstly, they constitute the region's key employment centres, providing 450,000 jobs between them, which means that the two cities have an extensive geographical spread and influence in terms of travel-to-work areas (Harding et al, 2001). Furthermore, the two cities have the highest concentration of the region's largest firms between them, and, of course, both are important nodes in the region's transport, social-cultural and knowledge-based infrastructure (Harding et al, 2001). In fact, the two cities are increasingly working together, partly as a consequence of the emerging regional agenda in the North West.

How have the new regional institutions settled in each region?

There were various 'regional initiatives' in the North West prior to the recent developments. For instance, in the 1960s the North West Industrial Development Agency (NORWIDA) was set up, which was one of the earliest attempts in the UK to try to coordinate and promote regional economic development. However, this institution proved to be largely ineffective and lost creditability both within and outside the North West (Burch and Holliday, 1993). In the late 1980s, however, certain institutions argued for the need for greater regional coherence in the North West. For example, in 1987 the North West Civic Trust published a document, which advocated the development of a strategy for the North West (Burch and Holliday, 1993).

In 1988, an important institution, the North West Business Leadership Team (NWBLT) was created, which involved influential figures from the leading 28 businesses that had headquarters in the region (Burch and Holliday, 1993). The NWBLT's aim was to provide a forum for the region's business elite to develop solutions to economic problems as well as improve regional coherence. In actual fact, the NWBLT continues to play a leading role in the region, representing the interests of the private sector and helping to promote a regional coherence on economic issues (Hebbert and Deas, 2000).

In 1992, building on from the creation of the NWBLT, a significant step forward was made when the North West Regional Association was established. For the first time the North West regional elite had unified with the precise aim of developing a regional economic strategy (Burch and Holliday, 1993). All 46 local authorities in the North West agreed to join the association, and more importantly they also agreed to contribute a quarter of the overall £200,000 budget that was needed to fund the production of a regional strategy. The NWBLT agreed to fund another quarter and the other half was provided by the European Community. From the outset, the association involved other partners in the development of its strategy, such as the Confederation of British Industry, the Trades Unions Congress, Training and Enterprise Councils and chambers of commerce. The aim was to involve a broad spectrum of regional interests (Burch and Holliday, 1993; NWRA, 1993).

There were several reasons behind the creation of the North West Regional Association (which in 1995 became known as the North West Partnership). Firstly, there was a prevailing view, which was partly influenced by Graham Meadows who was the then Head of the European Commission DG XVI (responsible for EU Structural Funds), that, unless the North West could prove that it had a political and economic coherence, it was likely to lose out on attracting EU funding. This obviously helped to mobilise support for the regional agenda. Secondly and obviously linked to the first point, the association was borne out of an increasing realisation on the part of the North West's business and political elite that economic problems required a coherent response and a regional strategy would help to provide that (Burch and Holliday, 1993; Hebbert and Deas, 2000).

The association's regional strategy covered the period 1994-1999 and did provide a number of direct benefits, such as coordinating the North West's voice in Brussels and Whitehall. Of course, the problems of parochialism and fragmentation did not go away, and in actual fact the rivalry between Liverpool and Manchester resurfaced over the issue of airport development in the latter (Burch and Holliday, 1993; Hebbert and Deas, 2000). However, the crucial point was that there was an increased interaction between key regional players from the private and public sectors, which helped to forge effective networks and longer lasting relationships. This regional elite cohesion, as the next section discusses, has significantly enhanced the way in which the 'new' regional institutions have been able to embed themselves in the region.

The North West Regional Assembly (NWRA), and North West Constitutional Convention (NWCC)

In 1998 the NWRA was created, its mission being "to promote the well-being of the region in economic, environmental and social terms" (NWRA, 1999). The NWRA is a partnership between a number of different bodies including local government, business, public sector and voluntary organisations, and many of its members were part of the North West Regional Association and hence have already considerable experience of working at the regional level. The NWRA has a Policy Unit and Secretariat that it is taking the lead on coordinating the three-year programme that it has in place, which is based around five Regional Key Priority Groups – economic development, skills and competitiveness, European affairs, innovation, information and technology, and lastly planning, environmental and transport issues (NWRA, 1999).

It is in the area of regional planning that the NWRA has been particularly active. It took the lead in the preparation and writing of the North West's Regional Planning Guidance (RPG) document. This outlined the contours of the region's future planning needs, which are based upon six key objectives, including achieving greater competitiveness, securing an urban renaissance, sustaining rural and coastal communities, prudent management of environmental and cultural assets, securing environmental quality, and creating an accessible region (NWRA, 2000). The general view of the planning guidelines document presented by the NWRA, however, was not completely favourable, which can in part be explained by a lack of necessary resources.

Linked to the NWRA, the NWCC was formed in July 1999, and is chaired by the Bishop of Liverpool. The main aim of the NWCC is to "decide whether there was a case to be made for regional devolution for the North West" (NWCC, 2000, p 1). Moreover, its other aims include:

- developing the role of the NWRA;
- establishing a clear, written national constitutional agreement;
- developing a fair regional voting system with links to a national second chamber;
- securing independent budgets for the North West;
- building a strong relationship with other regions in Europe (NWCC, 2000).

The NWCC has cross-party membership, and as such aims to promote a consensus view about the future regional structures for the North West. This makes it somewhat of an anomaly, especially when compared to the other regional constitutional conventions which have developed into 'campaigns' for regional government for their respective English regions. Indeed, the NWCC is the only region to remain an associate member of the Campaign for the English Regions (CFER). In autumn 2000, after a period of widespread consultation with the key regional players in the North West, the NWCC produced its Final Report, which was entitled *New way forward – No way back* (NWCC, 2000). In summary, this report provided an interesting overview of the main issues but it clearly failed to establish a consistent line about the North West's demands for regional government.

The North West Development Agency (NWDA)

The NWDA, with a staff of over 220 and a budget of £250 million, is one of the largest development agencies in England (NWDA, 2001a). By far the most important piece of work that the NWDA has carried out has been the formulation of the North West's Regional Strategy, which is entitled '2020: A vision for England's North West'. This was again developed in consultation with the other regional players from the public, private and voluntary sectors. In terms of content, the strategy is set out into four key themes or areas in which investment needs to take place in the region. Perhaps not surprisingly, these are:

- *business and ideas:* with the aim of accelerating new business development;
- *people and communities:* with the aim of developing skills and to deliver an urban renaissance;
- *infrastructure:* with the aim of strengthening strategic communications;
- *image and environment:* with the aim of projecting a positive image for the region (NWDA, 2001a).

The NWDA's role is to oversee and coordinate the implementation of the various projects within each of the themes. For example, the NWDA's Regeneration Directorate is responsible for spending £220 million to facilitate the socio-economic regeneration of specific areas in the region. Secondly, the Business Development Directorate is responsible for the operational delivery of the business and ideas theme of the Regional Strategy. In particular, 14 'established' and 'embryonic' target economic sectors were identified in the Regional Strategy that will receive specific investment in order to try to stimulate economic development. A Regional Intelligence Unit has also been set up with the aim of providing an effective regional information collection and dissemination point (NWDA, 2001a). As the next section discusses, however, there are certain tensions and issues surrounding the Regional Strategy as well as more generally, with the emergence of the regional tier in the North West.

Meeting the challenges in the North West

Overall, the NWDA's Regional Strategy has been welcomed and has received fairly widespread support. However, it clearly remains to be seen whether it will really have any significant impact. In addition, there are certain inherent tensions within the Strategy. For example, on the one hand, there is a strong emphasis on sectoral issues, which try to promote clustering in certain key sectors, such as biotechnology. However, this is obviously insensitive to territorial differences, and may even exacerbate the unevenness of development in the region by benefiting certain areas more than others. Yet, on the other hand, perhaps to try to counter this, there is an increased trend within the NWDA towards the development of subregional strategies, which will focus on the five main conurbations within the region. The danger is that, in effect, five smaller development agencies may be created and this will most probably increase the tensions and fragmentation between the respective subregions. This, however, is precisely what the NWDA is trying to overcome.

On the one hand, it is clear that the development of the regional tier has had wide-ranging benefits in the North West. The fairly long history of regional elite cohesion and interaction has, on the other hand, helped to get the various institutions off the ground very quickly. It is fair to say that a regional tier of sorts already existed before the changes of 1998; obviously this helped, and ensured that the NWRA, in particular, was able to make a positive impact after its inception. Indeed, the NWRA has been successful in encouraging and promoting further cooperation and networking among regional elites and the signing of the Regional Concordat between the NWRA, the NWDA, and the Government Office (GO) for the North West was clearly testimony to that. This formalised the working relationships between the various institutions in a tripartite structure within the region.

In terms of policy areas, it seems that the NWDA has had a positive impact upon the coordination of responsibilities for inward investment. This has been an area of particular conflict because it was a crowded institutional stage in which different agencies, located in different parts of the region competed for inward investment. Similarly, in terms of the North West's representation and 'voice' in Brussels, it seems that there is at least a willingness for the respective subregions to work with the NWDA's regional representative there. However, tensions in these areas, as well as others, will not disappear overnight.

By far the most important development in terms of the emerging regional agenda has been the coming together of Manchester and Liverpool. The commissioning of the Liverpool-Manchester Vision Study, by the two respective districts as well as the NWDA (funded by the EC), represented somewhat of a sea change in relations between the cities, which have traditionally been seen as adversaries. The aim was to explore ways in which Liverpool and Manchester could work together in order to enhance their joint development. The study was important because it actually stated that:

> Manchester acts as the regional capital, hosting a wide variety of specialist business functions while Liverpool is a crucially important regional centre for many other functions and services. While there is inevitably some competition between the two cities, it is less intense than that with other cities in the UK and abroad. (Harding et al, 2001, p 2)

This is a very significant statement because it gives credence to the argument that Manchester is the regional economic capital, which is something that has long been disputed.

The culmination of the Vision Study resulted in the symbolic signing, on 26 September 2001 in Manchester's Bridgewater Hall, of the so-called 'Liverpool-Manchester Joint City Concordat' by the respective leaders of the two councils, as well as the chair of the NWDA. Not surprisingly the signing of the concordat received a certain amount of media attention in the region even though it must be said that it is a very brief statement, containing five rather terse points:

1. "Competition is healthy and natural";
2. The two cities will "recognise distinctiveness" in terms of strengths and specialisations;
3. The two cities will "concentrate on areas of mutual benefit";
4. The two cities will "work on building linkages";
5. The two cities recognise the need for an "inclusive approach" (Harding et al, 2001, p 4).

Of course it clearly remains to be seen whether the warm words will amount to much.

Already, however, certain trends point in the right direction. For example, the two cities are coming together in a number of areas, such as the development of a 'biotechnology corridor' that links the Universities of Manchester and Liverpool. Of course, Manchester's staging of the Commonwealth Games is an important event not just for the city but (potentially at least) for Merseyside and the North West region as a whole. Indeed, Liverpool's bid to be the European City of Culture in 2008 is likely to benefit from exchanging ideas with Manchester on its successful bid for the Games. Of course, this coming together is partly to do with changes in personnel in the two cities as well as Liverpool's recent turnaround in economic fortunes. Undoubtedly, however, the development of a regional tier has clearly had an impact upon the two cities and helped to facilitate the development of closer ties. Nevertheless, as the next section discusses, it still remains unclear whether or not such successes will mean that the North West will choose to have an elected regional government.

The prospects for elected regional government, and civic interest in regionalism?

Certainly, the development of the regional tier in the North West has created certain benefits – not least promoting greater links between Liverpool and Manchester. However, an ambivalent attitude still prevails in the North West about the future direction in which the regional agenda should go. This is partly exemplified by the stance of the NWCC, which remains reluctant to commit fully to the CFER. Patently, there is a 'wait and see' tendency that dominates some of the regional elite discourses, which stress that the North West will follow the developments that take place in the other English regions, and in particular in the North East, but that it certainly will not be taking the lead role in instigating any changes.

In addition, given the fragmented geography of the region and the continued importance of subregional structures and identities, it seems possible that the regional agenda will be usurped by the latent political demand for a redrawing of metropolitan or city-regional structures in the North West. For example, the creation of five city-regions (defined as broad travel-to-work areas) for Greater Manchester, Greater Merseyside, Greater Chester, Greater Preston and Greater Carlisle would perhaps provide far more meaningful entities for strategic planning and transport, for promoting economic competitiveness, and for resolving labour market issues, than the current North West regional structure can (Robson and Deas, 2000). There is some interest, especially in Manchester City Council, in the potential for the development of such city-regional administrative structures.

This point is made even more problematic when one considers that regionalism in the North West remains very much confined to the elites involved in the various institutions. This is partly because of the continued strength of subregional identities in, say, Manchester or Liverpool, but also precisely because the region remains an artificial construct that is somewhat far removed from popular culture. This is in contrast to the North East, it would seem, where regional identity is on the increase. However, that is not to argue that a North West regional identity cannot, or indeed will not, emerge in due course, because certainly that must not be ruled out. Moreover, as the example of Spain and Italy shows, having city-regional structures does not preclude the development of effective and indeed powerful regional government (Giordano and Roller, 2001; Stoker, 2001).

Conclusion

On the one hand, it is too early to tell whether the regional strategies have been able to make a significant difference to the North West's economy and society. Yet, on the other hand, a common sentiment expressed by certain key actors is that the 'region has grown up'. In other words, it would seem that the regional agenda has helped the North West to start to (slowly) move away from the 'politics of parochialism', which previously beset it. In addition, there has been a further coalescence of elite interests at the regional level, which have, on the one hand, helped to benefit the functioning of the nascent regional institutions while, on the other, have been enhanced through greater interaction precisely within these institutions.

On the contrary, there has been very little diffusion of interest and indeed awareness of regional issues into the realms of civil society in the North West. This means that it is very difficult to gauge the extent to which public opinion in the region views the work of the regional institutions favourably (or not). Furthermore, it is almost impossible to say whether the people of the region would vote for or against the creation of regional government in the North West. The relative lack of popular interest in regionalism is partly, but not solely, due to the lack of attention given to the issue by the media in the region. Again this is partly to do with the North West's size and fragmented nature, which makes it very difficult to talk of a 'regional media'. However, for regionalism in the North West to fully take-off there needs to be a concerted effort on the part of the regional institutions (and media) to champion the issue of spreading the debate out into the public realm.

Of course, the artificiality of the North West's regional boundaries directly weaken and hinder any sense of regional identity. That is not to say, however, that a regional identity will not develop as the institutions become more and more embedded in the region's political, economic and social fabric. Nonetheless, the issue of fragmentation remains an important one as tensions and animosity still exist between different parts of the region as well as between different tiers of authority. These will not go away with the creation of regional government in the North West, however, in theory it will be at the regional level where such disputes and tensions are resolved and not in Whitehall or Westminster. At the moment, it is outside the region where the future of regionalism in the North West is decided, or dictated by national government policy. However, this may indeed change because the North West's regionalist 'genie' is most certainly out of its bottle and it seems likely that it will gain increased force over the coming years.

References

Bristow, M.R. (1987) 'The North West', in P.J. Damesick and P.A. Woods (eds) *Regional problems, problem regions and public policy in the United Kingdom*, Oxford: Clarendon Press.

Burch, M. and Holliday, I. (1993) 'Institutional emergence; the case of the North West region of England', *Regional Politics and Policy*, vol 3, no 2, pp 29-50.

Deas, I. and Ward, K. (2000) 'From the new localism to the new regionalism? The implications of Regional Development Agencies for city-regional relations', *Political Geography*, vol 19, no 3, 55-75.

Economic Bulletin for NW England (2001) *North West regeneration in practice*, winter 2000 to spring 2001, GO of the North West.

Giordano, B. and Roller, E. (2001) *A comparison of city-region dynamics in the UK, Spain and Italy*, Manchester: University of Manchester.

Giordano, B. and Twomey, L. (1999) *The economic fortunes of Manchester and Liverpool: assessing the conventional wisdom*, Working Paper no 1, ESRC Cities Programme, Liverpool-Manchester Integrated Case Study, May 1999.

Harding, A. and Wilks-Heeg, S. (2001) *The Liverpool-Manchester Vision Study: Key findings*, Manchester: SURF Centre, University of Salford.

Hebbert, M. and Deas, I. (2000) 'Greater Manchester – up and going?', *Policy and Politics*, vol 28, no 1, pp 79-92.

Jarvis, C. and McNamara, T. (1999) *An English region in the European Union – the North West*, EC Representation in the United Kingdom, London.

North West Constitutional Convention (NWCC) (2000) *New way forward – No way back*, Final Report, NWCC.

North West Development Agency (NWDA) (2001a) *An essential guide to the North West Development Agency*, Warrington: NWDA.

NWDA (2001b) *Investing in infrastructure, North West Development Agency clarifies position in response to CPRE criticism*, (www.nwda.co.uk/inside/ PressRelease.asp?PressID=187).

NWRA (North West Regional Assembly) (1993) *Regional economic strategy for North West England*, Wigan: NWRA.

NWRA (1999) *A bold new North West*, Wigan: NWRA.

NWRA (2000) *People, places and prosperity*, Draft RPG for the North West, July.

Robson, B.T.R. and Deas, I. (2000) *Slim picking for the cities of the North*, Manchester: University of Manchester.

Stoker, G. (2001) 'Top Heavies: An elected mayor confronting a regional assembly in a battle of wills: is this the future of local government in England?', *The Guardian*, June 13.

Turok, I. and Edge, N. (1999) *The jobs gap in Britain's cities: Employment loss and labour market consequences*, Bristol/York: The Policy Press/Joseph Rowntree Foundation.

SEVEN

The South West

Tom Bridges[1]

Introduction

The South West is one of the largest and most diverse English regions. Until recently there was neither a strong track record nor well-established networks of partnership and interagency working at the regional level. The regionalisation experience in the South West is instructive, with some important issues and lessons for the wider processes and timescales for regionalisation across the different English regions.

This chapter sets out a brief profile of the region and the main regional strategies. It then considers the 'institutional inheritance' for the Regional Development Agency (RDA) and the regional institutions, and the process and partnership working issues in relation to the development of the Regional Strategy and Action Plans. The following section outlines the main features of the progress so far in the development of the regional institutions, regional stakeholder fora, and subregional partnerships. Some next steps for the regional bodies are then discussed, followed by the setting out of some conclusions and issues for the wider process of regionalisation in other regions.

The regional context

The nature of the region and the main social and economic challenges

The South West covers the largest geographical area of all the English regions, stretching from Lands End in the far south west to Gloucestershire in the north, and Swindon, Wiltshire and Dorset in the east. From the northern edge of Gloucestershire, it is as far to the Scottish border as it is to the western tip of Cornwall. While some parts of the region such as Bristol and the M4 corridor have good access to the rest of the country, peripherality and lack of accessibility are important issues for many other areas. In economic terms, the region has in recent years underperformed in comparison to the rest of the UK. GDP per capita is below the UK and European Union averages, although unemployment has fallen relative to the UK average (and in absolute terms). It is a highly diverse region in terms of economic structure, with significant differences between the nature of problems and opportunities of different subregional areas. The M4 corridor and Bristol and its northern fringes have been relatively successful in attracting hi-tech businesses, and investment and employment in corporate 'head office' functions, and business and financial services. Much of the region has historically been dependent on defence industries, and in recent years has faced the difficulties from the consequences of restructuring in both the aviation (particularly Bristol – where aviation remains an important sector – and Somerset) and marine defence (particularly Plymouth) sectors.

There are several areas in particular need of regeneration. Cornwall has underperformed in economic terms for many years, and has generally failed to overcome the long-term effects of the decline in the minerals extraction, tourism, and fishing industries. This has led to the county being designated as eligible for EU Objective 1 funding. The major cities of Bristol and Plymouth also have economic problems associated with industrial restructuring and the decline of port-related industries. Areas of these cities suffer from severe problems of deprivation and social exclusion, and are eligible for Objective 2 funding. There are also pockets of deprivation in the other principle urban areas in the region. There are also significant problems of rural deprivation.

Large areas of the region are predominately rural in character, and agriculture and tourism are important sectors (tourism accounts for around 10% of the region's GDP). The region has therefore suffered disproportionately from the long-term restructuring of tourism and the more recent restructuring in the agricultural sector. These problems have been exacerbated by the outbreaks of Foot and Mouth Disease (FMD) in the summer of 2001.

The response in the main regional strategies

The South West Regional Development Agency (SWRDA) Regional Strategy was published in October 1999 (SWRDA, 1999). The strategy focussed on setting out the broad vision, themes, principles and objectives for the region. It did not include detailed proposals, or outline priorities and actions on a spatially specific basis. While the strategy was certainly difficult to argue with, it was not particularly distinctive to the region, and did not demonstrate foundations in a detailed analysis of the issues facing the regional economy. In some areas it could be argued that the strengths and the potential of the regional economy were overestimated. Themes such as the 'environment' as a 'key driver' for the economy, or the importance attached to hi-tech industries, were not always fully justified and supported by the (limited) analysis in the document. To a large extent, these features of the strategy reflected the political reality faced by the RDA, and the limited base of background research and analysis. A conscious decision was taken to use the strategy process to build consensus around broad principles for the region, rather than to focus on difficult issues of priorities and implementation.

The current Regional Planning Guidance (RPG) for the South West was published in its final form in September 2001 (GOSW, 2001). This followed the production of a draft by the Regional Planning Body (RPB), South West Regional Planning Conference (SWRPC), and a Public Examination. The RPG aims to focus development within or close to the eleven Principal Urban

Areas[2], with development that cannot be accommodated in these areas to be located in other substantial towns. In short, the spatial strategy is based on the existing settlement pattern. A policy of 'sustainable growth' is outlined for the *Northern subregion* (including Bristol, Bath, Swindon, Gloucester and Cheltenham). This is recognised as an area of economic strength, where continued economic growth is likely to be to the benefit (not the detriment) of the rest of the region.

In the *South Eastern subregion*, the Bournemouth and Poole conurbation area is recognised as offering good potential for economic growth, and there are also policies to assist the more disadvantaged coastal areas, including Weymouth and Portland. In the *Central subregion*, RPG sets out policies to promote economic growth (particularly in Exeter and Taunton), economic diversification (particularly in Torbay), and to locate development elsewhere to reduce social exclusion and need in rural areas. For the *Western subregion* (including Plymouth, its West Devon hinterland, Cornwall, and the Isles of Scilly). The RPG outlines policies to alleviate remoteness through investment in transport and communications infrastructure, promote economic development, tourism and environmental improvements.

The poor regional institutional inheritance

At the time of the formation of the RDA, in comparison to other regions, regional structures for partnership working were in the early stages of development.

The Government Office (GO) for the South West (GOSW) had been in operation since 1994, although it was split between the main offices in Bristol and Plymouth (covering different parts of the region). The GO had worked hard to promote effective region-wide partnership structures and networks. In fact, until 1999, it was the only strategic regional organisation able to do so. For instance, prior to the formation of the RDA, there was no single regional strategic partnership in the South West. Instead, there was one partnership covering Devon and Cornwall, and another (the West of England Partnership) covering the remainder of the region.

The South West Regional Assembly was designated as the formal Regional Chamber in 1998. However, at this stage, and throughout the critical stage in 1999 when the RDA was producing the Regional Strategy, the assembly was very much in its early stages of development with extremely limited staff resources. It was not until mid-2000 that the assembly secured a full-time secretariat. As indicated above, the lack of any region-wide strategic partnership meant that the assembly did not have strong and well-established regional networks, or a wide body of expertise on regional issues (outside the GO) on which to build. The region's local authorities had worked together on Regional Planning issues under the auspices of the SWRPC.

In addition to this underdeveloped set of regional institutions and partnership working, there was (and to an extent still is) a low level of regional identity. There was, initially, some opposition to the concept of a single RDA for the

South West. Many indicated that they would have preferred the region to be divided into two, with one RDA for Devon and Cornwall and one for the rest of the region. Partners in some areas close to the region's boundary stated they felt more affinity with neighbouring regions than they did with the South West (for example, Bournemouth and Poole). In fact, a subregional partnership that cuts across the regional boundary in the Bournemouth and Poole area has been formed to this effect (the Central Southern England Regional Alliance).

At the subregional level, partnership structures and capacity were highly varied across the region. In Cornwall, a major catalyst for interagency working and capacity building had been (and continues to be) the availability of Objective 1 funding. In Devon, a well-established partnership had played a leading role in developing strategic priorities for the new Objective 2 region (which includes parts of Plymouth and also parts of Bristol). In other subregions, small partnerships existed focussing mainly on promotion and retention of business investment. Examples included the West of England Development Agency covering the former Avon area. Strong city-area partnerships existed in areas such as Bristol and Plymouth where the availability of Objective 2 funding, and the importance of other regeneration programmes, provided a strong incentive for partnership working.

The SWRDA therefore began work in an extremely challenging position. The lack of any previous region-wide strategic partnership or economic development and inward investment agency meant that there was a limited framework of relevant strategy documents and associated background research on which to build. Furthermore, because there had been relatively limited work on strategy development at the regional level, the SWRDA also had a difficult starting point in terms of the 'political' and partnership context. Partners had an underdeveloped understanding of and engagement in regional issues.

Despite this challenging context, SWRDA was required to develop its Regional Strategy and Action Plans in its first few months. It formed a Strategy Steering Group and a series of working groups to draft the Regional Strategy. A draft strategy was launched at a region-wide conference in June 1999, and this was followed by three months of extensive consultation. There were a series of 'roadshow' consultation events throughout the region (seven events in each of the seven subregions defined by the SWRDA, making 49 events in all).

The SWRDA's task in developing a regional strategy within the tight timescale set by government was widely recognised as extremely challenging. The Final Regional Strategy commanded the general support of partners in the region. The strategy was considered to set out a clear (if not particularly distinctive) vision for the region and a basis for moving forward. The development process was successful, within a short timescale, in bringing partners together and fulfilling the necessary objective of developing a high profile for the SWRDA in the region.

However, the process and the SWRDA were not without critics. Partners' expectations were very high and, in many cases, unrealistic. There was a general lack of awareness of the constraints that the SWRDA was operating under: its limited financial and staff resources, and the technically, logistically and 'politically' onerous task in developing the strategy. There were a number of criticisms. Unlike in several other regions, no major consultation was undertaken at the outset of the process on the main principles, themes and structure for the strategy. The first opportunity to comment for many partners was on publication of the draft strategy when the document was already fairly well developed. It was felt by many that the quantity of consultation events had been to the detriment of the quality of consultation and genuine partner engagement. Limited available staff resources were spread far too thinly. As a result, some high profile consultation events were led by fairly junior staff. Staff pressures also hindered the ability of senior personnel to build relationships with key partners outside the formal consultation mechanisms. There were also organisational teething problems stemming from the difficulties in undertaking a logistically burdensome task of developing the strategy with many key staff new to their posts and when the organisation was still very much in its start-up phase.

The SWRDA drew up draft Action Plans and launched them alongside the RES in October 1999. It then went on to develop more detailed plans (with little consultation). These were widely seen as overly prescriptive by partners who felt that they represented a simplistic, prescriptive approach to implementation that was not based on consensus. Part of the problem was that guidance from the government on Action Plans was limited and unclear, and the SWRDA felt under pressure from the government (as well as partners) to develop detailed documents within a short timescale.

In response to these criticisms, SWRDA modified its approach, and reverted to a less detailed format for the documents, which were retitled *Frameworks for Action*. This approach enabled the development of some more detailed Action Plans where the SWRDA or other partners had the lead role in implementation and were able to proceed straightaway, while at the same time allowing others to indicate a general intent but enabling partners to develop plans at the pace which they desired. An 18-month review period and standard template was specified. Most partners recognised that in the circumstances and within the short timescale available, the *Frameworks for Action* approach represented a pragmatic and appropriate way forward.

The Development of the main Regional Institutions

Following this challenging first few months for the SWRDA, steady progress has been made in the evolution and development of the main regional institutions. Following the development of the Regional Strategy, SWRDA underwent a period of consolidation. In particular, it undertook effective delivery of physical regeneration projects, ensuring these were closely aligned with wider strategic priorities. SWRDA has also developed a proactive and productive involvement in the management of EU funding programmes in the region. Changes in the corporate structure (such as creating subregional lead staff, or an account management system for major businesses) have led to far more effective relationship management and joint working with partners 'on the ground'.

The South West England Regional Assembly, despite capacity and resource constraints at the time, played an effective role in supporting, as well as scrutinising, the production of the SWRDA Regional Strategy. Since then, the assembly has raised its profile significantly, and has secured increasingly active and widespread engagement of partners. The expansion of the staff team has also helped develop capacity and expertise in specific policy areas. The focus for the assembly has very much been to support and assist in the development of the new regional institutions, and has developed productive and close working relationships with the SWRDA, GO, and other new regional bodies. A priority for the assembly is developing mechanisms for improving integration and coordination between the strategic activity in the region and the various regional strategies. Following publication of the RPG, the assembly has taken on the role of the Regional Planning Body, and is recruiting a land-use planning team.

The GOSW has played a vital role in supporting and guiding the development of the new institutions. The roles and priorities of the GO have also been changing as a result of the Cabinet Office *Reaching Out* report (PIU, 2000) and the work of the Regional Coordination Unit, which has outlined a more 'crosscutting' role for GOs in coordinating policies and programmes at the regional level. In response, GOSW has adopted a matrix-management structure whereby key staff have a functional role (that is, planning, skills, regeneration) as well as subregional responsibilities. The 'crosscutting' subregional focus has proved successful in other regions (Arup Economics and Planning, 1999) in enabling government staff to develop closer relationships with partners, as well as to improve the integration of policy and services at the subregional level between different functional areas.

In terms of wider stakeholder interests there has been a significant raising of awareness, and engagement in, regional networks and issues. In the arts and culture sector, this is the first time many partners have become engaged in a meaningful sense in regional issues and regional networks. The regional cultural consortium, Culture South West (CSW), has been established, and the Regional Cultural Strategy was published in July 2001 (CSW, 2001). Organisations and groups with an interest in sustainable development have developed the forum of Sustainability South West (SSW). SSW has played an active role in working with the SWRDA, and influencing the development of RPG, to ensure that sustainable development concerns were addressed by the main regional strategies. This group published the *Regional Sustainable Development Framework* in 2001 (SSW, 2001).

Within the private sector, there has been close joint working with the SWRDA by the main business organisations. In the voluntary and community sectors, capacity building has been undertaken to develop the engagement of regional representative organisations with the new regional structures. At the subregional level, an early decision by the SWRDA was to identify seven Sub-Regional Partnerships (SRPs). The rationale was to take account of the diversity and distinctiveness of the different subregions, and to be a sensible and practical framework for delivery and partner liaison in such a large region. The SRP boundaries were based on the geographical areas of (former) counties. As indicated in the previous section, the track record and existing structures for partnership working varied between subregions.

In practice there has been confusion in relation to the roles and purpose of the SRPs. It was not envisaged that the SRPs would be involved in direct implementation activities, instead, they would be strategic, consultative bodies and conduits to partners in their areas. However, there have been cases where SRPs have been encouraged to undertake tasks more associated with implementation (such as developing Single Regeneration Budget [SRB bids]). This has led to concerns that the limited capacity and resources of the SRPs have not always been commensurate with the roles they have been expected to undertake.

Next steps – the main issues to be addressed

As was indicated, since production of the SWRDA Regional Strategy, the new regional institutions have become well-established, and have raised their capacity and profile over time. A framework of regional strategies has now been developed and finalised. This represents significant progress, and the South West has gone a long way in 'catching up' with other regions, in terms of the profile and capabilities of the new regional institutions. The move to 'single pot' funding for RDAs will pose challenges and opportunities for the SWRDA. This will inevitably lead to a shift away from competitive funding regimes of fragmented programmes and to a more selective and joined-up approach.

The full implications remain to be seen of the ending of SRB funding and the increased role of the GO in managing neighbourhood renewal initiatives. This may lead to the SWRDA moving more towards a physical infrastructure, and business competitiveness focus for its regeneration work. SWRDA will also be required to review and update the Regional Strategy. This process should benefit from the significant amount of background economic research and analysis commissioned by the SWRDA over the past two years.

There are also three particular policy issues where it is recognised that improvements are needed in the coordination of action and integration of strategies at the regional level: rural development, transport, and 'regional coordination'.

Rural development

In a region that has such large areas of countryside and economic dependence on agriculture and tourism in rural areas, rural development has been an important regional development theme.

In its early period, the SWRDA was criticised for not outlining rural development as a specific or distinctive policy area in the strategy, or for specific senior staff/board level responsibility. This was done with the best of intentions:

the view was that rural issues were relevant to all aspects of the SWRDA's work and should not be 'compartmentalised'. However this was unpopular with partners, especially those with a predominately rural remit (for example, the Ministry of Agriculture, Fisheries and Food [MAFF], and the Countryside Agency). In response to these criticisms, the SWRDA developed rural board and staff leads. Research has been commissioned on the economy and regional policies for rural areas (DTZ Pieda, 2000). The SWRDA has developed a Rural Action Plan, and has undertaken a series of specific rural development initiatives.

The outbreaks of FMD in summer 2000 led to a significant increase in the importance of rural development issues. The FMD crisis was a major catalyst for the SWRDA to adopt a high profile role in lobbying government and coordinating the economic and policy response in the region. This was combined with the institutional and policy changes resulting from the Rural White Paper, which has led to the RDA developing a more active, leading and coordination role for RDAs on rural issues.

Prior to May 2001, the SWRDA had a difficult task in attempting to develop a coordinated regional approach to rural development. As Figure 7.1 shows, the SWRDA was placed in a complex and fragmented network of separate government departments, regional offices, executive agencies, and strategies and programmes all relating to rural development in the region. The changes in Whitehall and the GO (GOSW inherited a large contingent of former MAFF staff) in May 2001 simplified this framework to an extent. However,

Figure 7.1: Rural development in the South West: the complex institutional and policy framework (pre changes in Whitehall in May 2001)

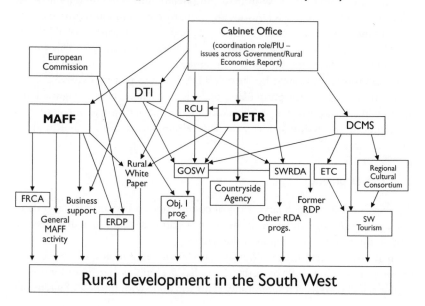

confusion and tensions exist in relation to the respective roles and responsibilities of specific organisations (for example, between the SWRDA and the Countryside Agency).

The priorities for the SWRDA are to resolve these issues, and to address more effectively key rural development issues, such as tourism development and promotion, business support and assistance, agricultural diversification, and CAP reform.

Transport

Improving transport to address economic and spatial development needs is a priority of the main Regional Strategies as well as the Objective 1 programme for Cornwall. A Regional Transport Strategy (RTS) was developed as part of the RPG that was published in September 2001. The RTSs should form an integral part of RPG providing a long-term strategic framework that informs development plans and Local Transport Plans (LTPs), as well as outlining a wider strategy for transport in the region. A review of the RTS will need to be undertaken by 2003 in order to bring the strategy up to date and to inform the next round of LTPs, on which local authorities will need to begin work in 2004.

A problem with the current RTS is that it is not sufficiently integrated with the wider spatial policies of RPG. There is scope for greater analysis of the nature of the existing transport network, and its ability to support new development and the transport implications of the spatial strategy. A major problem was that the draft RTS was largely prepared separately to the rest of RPG. The RTS working group comprised mainly of local authority transport offices, with only limited engagement of land-use planning expertise or wider stakeholder interests.

A major difficulty in developing the current RTS was the absence of outputs from the Multi Modal Studies (MMSs) in the region. These MMSs have assessed and appraised the options for transport investment across different modes in main transport corridors or areas. Most of the South West region is covered by a major MMS, which will report in 2002.

An important priority for the RTS is to improve the long-distance rail network. However there are concerns about the targets set by ministers for the Strategic Rail Authority. These are national targets, focused on increasing total passenger miles and freight tonnes. This could potentially disadvantage the South West, where the case for investment is based primarily on wider impacts on tourism and economic development, rather than increasing passenger numbers in absolute terms.

Regional coordination

The proliferation in strategic activity at the regional level poses challenges to ensure that the various regional strategies and the work of the regional institutions are consistent, integrated, and collectively address shared priorities.

The Regional Assembly is considering how best to develop an 'Integrated Regional Strategy' framework to formally outline the processes and interrelationships between the various regional strategies.

There is a need to oversee the development of the main regional institutions (for example, the RDA's move to 'single pot' funding, or the increasing 'coordination' role of the GO) to ensure their respective roles, responsibilities and programmes are integrated and clearly defined. There is also scope for developing greater clarity regarding structures and roles at the subregional level, between SRPs, other city-based partnerships, the new Local Strategic Partnerships, local authorities and the subregional teams of GOSW.

Attitudes towards elected regional government

There is genuine enthusiasm among many partners for the new regional networks and institutions, but there also remains some scepticism among those (particularly some in the private sector) of their real added value. There is, however, only limited wider support and interest for the potential of elected regional government among the public in the region. There is a general perception that the priority is for the regional institutions to become more firmly established and 'prove themselves' first.

A regional 'movement' has emerged – the South West Constitutional Convention (SWCC) – led by Michael Langrish, Bishop of Exeter. However, even among the SWCC's supporters there is debate about whether elected regional government should constitute a greater devolution of powers, or focus on introducing mechanisms to improve accountability of the existing regional bodies (see the quotes below). There is also still opposition to the concept of a South West region on the basis of its current boundaries. For instance there is a formal regional movement for Cornwall, the Cornwall Constitutional Convention (CCC).

There is also opposition to greater devolution from Conservative MPs and councillors in the region, many of whom equate 'regionalism' with greater integration with Europe. Also, the government has indicated that elected regional government will be taken forward in the first instance in areas where there is enthusiasm for the concept and also a predominately single tier structure to local government. This has caused a degree of concern among some in the region's county councils. Political leaders have begun to articulate the regional interest:

> "We are seeking to democratise powers that have already been devolved to the West by way of the Government Office for the South West and the RDA." (Ian White, former Bristol MEP, Labour)

> "It fits very neatly into a federal Europe of the regions. Tewkesbury has very different needs from Devon and Cornwall. We have nothing in common with them." (Laurence Robertson, Conservative MP for Tewksbury)

"This isn't a Brussels plot, this is a South West plot." (Graham Watson Lib Dem, MEP)[3]

But there is also a Cornish dimension to these developments, as evidenced by the establishment of the CCC:

"The Cornish Constitutional Convention welcomes the stimulation of debate concerning regional assemblies, but maintains that a monolithic approach to democratising 'standard regions' is not the way ahead in South-West Britain." (Stephen Horscroft, CCC)[4]

Conclusions

The South West is unlikely to be one of the regions to move to elected regional government. While good progress has been made from the poor 'regional institutional inheritance' in 1999, the regional institutions and partnership networks remain underdeveloped in comparison to their counterparts elsewhere. The focus in the region is likely to be one of continued consolidation and development of the regional organisations and strategies within the existing statutory frameworks for regional governance.

The next stage of the regionalisation in the South West is likely to focus on issues such as the transition to 'single pot' funding for RDAs, improving coordination of strategic activity, or addressing more effectively at the regional level priorities for rural areas or transport. These issues will pose significant challenges for the RDA, assembly, GO and their partners, as they continue to improve their capacity and effectiveness.

The progress and processes of regionalisation in the South West to date raise some important wider issues and conclusions for consideration.

Firstly, there is the need for appropriate timescales and formats for regionalisation and regional strategies. A problem in the South West has been that, while often working to arbitrary timetables set by the government, there have been attempts to move forward regional strategies and implementation frameworks too fast. The lack of experience or structures of partnership working, consensus building and strategy development placed the RDA and assembly at a serious disadvantage to their counterparts in other regions.

Despite this, the same timetable as in other regions was set for the development of the SWRDA. As a result, the SWRDA developed its strategy in the absence of necessary background research and initial consultation. This meant that there had been no opportunity to develop a region-wide shared understanding and consensus on the main issues facing the region. This led to an (over ambitious) attempt to undertake a huge quantity of consultation on the strategy, which was to the detriment of the quality of consultation and partner engagement.

Secondly, and partly in response to arbitrary government timetables and pressure (both real and perceived) from government and partners, overly prescriptive Action Plan documents were produced quickly and without adequate consultation and discussion. The revised approach of the *Frameworks for Action* developed over a longer timescale, represented a far more appropriate and pragmatic way forward.

Thirdly, the development of the regional strategies and the work of the regional institutions has been demanding in a technical sense, particularly as there was relatively little previous expertise or experience in dealing with regional issues. The RDA strategy was weakened by the lack of supporting technical background analysis on the regional economy. The RTS has been developed in the absence of important technical inputs from the MMSs, and limited regional (as opposed to local authority) and wider policy expertise in the SWRPC. In some of the subregional partnerships, there has been limited policy expertise beyond business competitiveness issues.

The 'organisational' issues for regionalisation.

Organisational issues have been central to the success, or problems associated with the development, of the regional organisations and their strategies.

Staffing and resourcing issues had a significant bearing on the strategy development process for the SWRDA. The experience demonstrated the importance of ensuring an appropriate balance between the quantity and quality of consultation, and ensuring the clarity and transparency of the process, and the accessibility of senior staff. Since then, the SWRDA has undertaken far more effective partnership working as a direct result of new organisational structures and processes for management of external relationships.

Problems have often been caused by capacity and staff constraints in the RDA, assembly, RPB, or at subregional level. Strategy development has been shown to be a logistically onerous task, particularly in such a large and complex region, and it is vital that it is adequately resourced. In terms of implementation and action, it is also essential that the roles and responsibilities of organisations are commensurate with the capacity and resources at their disposal. For instance, it will be important to ensure that the SWRDA has the relevant staff resources and expertise to adopt a more active role in the field of rural development.

The move to 'single pot' funding for the RDA, and the increasing focus of the GO on a 'crosscutting' policy and programme coordination role, will also have important organisational implications. It will also require the development of staff competencies that may not have had the same importance when individuals were in their previous programme management roles.

Some of the main challenges and priorities for the regional bodies have been and will continue to be improving the coordination and integration of the different strategies, policy initiatives, and programmes in the region. As has been shown by the example of rural development, the plethora of activities and initiatives stemming from different government departments, their executive agencies and regional bodies, present a major challenge to ensuring effective and joined-up approach, to addressing strategic objectives and priorities for the region. Many of these problems are not of the making of those in the regions. They stem from a lack of integration and 'joined-upness' between (and sometimes within) departments and agencies of central government.

The experience in the South West demonstrates the importance of building high-level genuine stakeholder and partner engagement, involvement, and dialogue. This is an essential prerequisite to the development of strategy and Action Plan documents whose effectiveness and success depends on the level of partner 'buy-in' and commitment.

In the absence of directly elected regional government, regional strategies need to be based on consensus, and as such need to represent a series of 'political settlements' or consensus that has emerged through the dialogue of main stakeholder interests[5]. The regional bodies in the South West started work in 1999 in the context of underdeveloped involvement and focus at the regional level of main stakeholder interests.

In this respect, significant progress has been made over the past two to three years. The next challenge for the regional institutions is to build on this and move forward in a way and at a pace appropriate to the region. This is unlikely to include elected regional government in the short- to medium-term. In outlining the way forward for the English regions, the government must avoid imposing on the South West a timescale and structure designed for regions with far different and more well-established structures and experience of regional partnership and joint working. The South West is likely to require a steady and sensitive approach to regionalisation.

Notes

[1] Tom Bridges writes this chapter in a personal capacity.

[2] Bristol, Bath, Weston-super-Mare, Swindon, Gloucester, Cheltenham, Bournemouth/ Poole, Exeter, Taunton, Plymouth, and Torbay.

[3] 'Devolution for the west – is this the beginning?', *Western Daily Press*, 19 May 2001.

[4] 'Way Forward for the South West', Campaign for the English Regions Winter, 2000 Newsletter. See also 'Cornwall Wants to Go it Alone', *The Guardian*, 12 January 2001.

[5] See *Strategy Development and Partnership Working in the RDAs*, Arup Economics and Planning with Aston Business School and Associates for DETR, 200.

References

Arup Economics and Planning (1999) *Government Office for the South West Partner Satisfaction Survey*, Report for GOSW, London: Arup Economics and Planning.

Performance and Innovation Unit (PIU) (2000) *Reaching out – the role of central government at regional and local level*, London: Cabinet Office.

CSW (Culture South West) (2001) *In search of chunky dunsters. ... A cultural strategy for the South West*, Bristol: CSW.

DTZ Pieda (2000) *The South West of England. Regional policy in a rural region*, Exeter: SWRDA.

GOSW (Government Office South West) (2001) *Regional Planning Guidance for the South West (RPG 10)*, Bristol: GOSW.

SWS (Sustainability South West) (2001) *A sustainable future for the South West. The Regional Sustainable Development Framework for the South West of England*, Bristol: SWS.

SWRDA (South West Regional Development Agency) (1999) *Regional Strategy for the South West of England 2000-2010*, Exeter: SWRDA.

EIGHT

Regionalism in the East of England

Neil Ward and John Tomaney

The East of England and recent institution building

The region in context

The East of England is a relatively new geographical construct. Its geography results from the merging of the East Anglia standard planning region (which comprised the counties of Norfolk, Suffolk and Cambridgeshire) with the counties of Essex, Hertfordshire and Bedfordshire, that formerly made up part of the South East Regional Planning (SERPLAN) region. Together, the six counties of the East of England have been among the fastest growing in terms of population and economic activity in the UK. In per capita terms, the output of the region ranks 35th out of 77 regions in the European Union (EU) – a position higher than all other UK regions, apart from London and the South East. Between 1993 and 1998, the economy of the region grew by 3.5% per annum compared with the UK average rate of 2.5%, and the official rate of unemployment for the region in 1999 was 3.5% compared to a national figure of 4.8% (Townroe and Moore, 1999). Prosperity has been both followed and driven by strong population growth since the 1960s. The current population of some 5.3 million residents has grown as a result of marked net in-migration, with net population growth in the region of 9.0% between 1981 and 1996.

The region's economic and industrial structure resembles that of the UK as a whole. Although East Anglia in particular has an image as a rural and agricultural region, only 2.1% of the East of England's workforce are employed in agriculture, fishing and forestry, and the proportion employed in manufacturing closely matches the national average of 18.2%. The manufacturing sector is characterised by a relatively large proportion of medium-sized companies and a high rate of growth in new companies. In contrast to the rural character of Norfolk and Suffolk, the regional economy of the East of England is being increasingly represented as hi-tech. The region has the highest research and development employment per capita of all UK regions – not least as a result of the influence of Cambridge – and has strengths in electronics, telecommunications and biotechnology sectors.

The Government Office for the East of England (GO-East) has offices in both Cambridge and Bedford and has been working on this geographical basis since its establishment in 1994. The period 1994-99 also saw the region's first experience of regional programming under the EU Structural Funds with the East Anglia Objective 5(b) Programme (Ward and Woodward, 1998). Regional institution building has gained new momentum since 1997, however, with the establishment in 1999 of the new RDA for the region, the East of England Development Agency (EEDA), and the new regional chamber, the East of England Regional Assembly (EERA). EEDA has the smallest budget of any Regional Development Agency (RDA) in England, reflecting the relative lack of designations for economic development assistance and the general perception of the East of England as a prosperous region. This is not to say, however, that the region is without its development problems.

A conundrum for regional strategists is the spatial imbalance in economic development opportunities within the region. The southern parts of the region – from Bedfordshire, through the Cambridge city region, to Hertfordshire and South Essex – are better integrated into the growth patterns and trajectories of London and Cambridge. London dominates the labour market for much of the south of the region, and Cambridge is the UK's archetypal case of a high-growth hi-tech cluster based on new information technologies and biosciences. Those parts of the region facing the greatest economic development challenges tend to be more geographically peripheral from these growth zones, and include the Norfolk and Cambridgeshire Fens, Great Yarmouth and Lowestoft. EEDA's strategy is to seek to maintain the momentum of innovation and investment in the growth sectors of the region, particularly information technologies and the biosciences, and to foster economic clusters such as that which has become known as 'the Cambridge phenomenon' (EEDA, 1999, 2001a). The economically weaker localities will continue to receive assistance under various regeneration schemes, including EU Structural Funds.

Politically, the region has been dominated by the Conservative Party. Several senior cabinet ministers of the 1992-97 Conservative administration had their constituencies in the region, including the Prime Minister (John Major, Huntington), secretaries of state for the environment (John Gummer, Suffolk Coastal), agriculture (Gillian Shephard, Norfolk South West), transport (John McGregor, Norfolk South), the party chairman (Brian Mawhinney, Cambridgeshire North West) and the chief whip (Richard Ryder, Norfolk North). Indeed, political commentators spoke of John Major's "East Anglian Mafia". However, the Labour Party took control of several local councils from the Tories in the mid-1990s, and gained an 11% swing in the region in the 1997 General Election.

Geographical boundaries and regional identity

There is a sense for some in the region that the East of England's boundaries have been imposed from above. The composition of the region, however, has less to do with any attempt to forge a coherent and meaningful regional territorial identity than with simple administrative expediency. In this sense, what now constitutes the East of England region is almost an accident of history. Since its establishment in the early 1970s, the Department of the

Environment (DoE) has had a regional office structure. This included the six counties of the current East of England region, plus Buckinghamshire. Even though the DoE was responsible for planning issues, the standard planning regions did not correspond with DoE regions – the current East of England counties coming under both East Anglia and SERPLAN. Nor did the regional structures of the Department of Trade and Industry (DTI) or the Department of Transport (DoT) regions equate with those of the DoE. When the government Regional Offices, then known as the Integrated Regional Offices, were established in 1993-94, the issue was one of aligning the boundaries of the three component government departments (DoE, DoT and DTI). The result was a region of six counties. There was little consideration at this time of the likelihood of the region attaining some constitutional status as a region of the UK, with a Regional Assembly and RDA.

The effects of the decision to use existing regional boundaries on the development of regionalism in England remain to be seen. In other regions, such as Yorkshire and the Humber, the boundary issue is relatively uncontroversial. For the East of England, however, the question of the definition of the region remains an important contest for some.

For those concerned about the definition of the East of England, the main issue is the perceived lack of coherence of the region both as a territorial entity and as a regional identity. Tables 8.1 and 8.2 show how opinion polling illustrates that the level of regional identification is generally low among people in the East of England. For example, when asked which type of locality they identified most with, 50% of Britons mentioned their region, but the proportion was just

Table 8.1: Identification with different spatial scales of locality in Britain and the East of England

Q:*Which two or three of these, if any, would you say you most identify with and least identify with?*

	Most		Least	
	Respondents in British sample	**Respondents in East of England**	**Respondents in British sample**	**Respondents in East of England**
This local community	41	49	5	2
This (GOR) region	50	17	9	29
England/Scotland/Wales	45	28	4	7
Britain	40	43	3	0
Europe	16	24	35	33
The Commonwealth	9	23	45	36
The global community	8	20	55	43
None of these	*	0	3	8
Don't know	2	2	6	3

* denotes a value of less than 0.5% but not 0%.

Base: 923 British adults aged 18+ (24-27 September 1999)

Source: MORI/*The Economist*:'British Identity'

Table 8.2: Identification with the regional level in British regions

Q: Which two or three of these, if any, would you say you most identify with and least identify with?

	% identifying with (GOR) region	
	Most	Least
All	50	9
North East	83	0
North West	70	2
Scotland	62	1
South West	58	7
West Midlands	55	7
Yorkshire and Humberside	52	7
Wales	50	0
London	43	10
South East	41	18
East Midlands	31	9
East of England	17	29

Base: 923 British adults aged 18+ (24-27 September 1999)

Source: MORI/*The Economist*: 'British Identity'

17% in the East of England, where far more people identified more strongly with their local community or with 'Britain' as a nation (Table 8.1). While 83% of North Easterners identified most with their region, far fewer people did so in the East of England. Notably, the proportion of people identifying *least* with their region is also highest in the East of England (29%) – more than three times the proportion found nationally (Table 8.2).

It is argued by sceptics in the region, such a local journalists, that the constituted East of England "makes no sense" as a geographical entity, stretching as it does from Lowestoft in the east to Tring in the west, from Cromer in the north to inside the M25 in the south. One regional journalist talked of the component parts of the region having "no commonality of purpose at all". Another described the region as "forced" and "not natural". Various dualisms are invoked, some of which overlap. Some parts of the region "look to London" while others "look to East Anglia". Some parts of the region are "more rural" while others are "more metropolitan". Some parts of the region are more comfortable with regional working; others are cast as far more reluctant players.

One regional official from the local authority sector explained the difficulty in the following terms:

> "One of the big challenges for us is simply to get people to accept that the new regional maps are durable, and it's not possible for people in, say, Hertfordshire to opt out. They either play on the basis of the regional map as it exists now, or they don't play, and that they lose out on something by not playing. The acceptance of the East of England region is greatest in East

Anglia, because their sense of regional identity has been established for many years. Where we have problems ... is on the boundaries of other regions. So in South Essex and Hertfordshire there's issues about London. In the very westerly fringes there are issues of cross-boundary activity with Milton Keynes.... Most of these issues are in the west. We speak about 'having trouble on the western front', by which we mean Hertfordshire and Bedfordshire." (Interview, local authority officer)

Others, particularly in East Anglian parts of the region, see little sense in having Hertfordshire and Bedfordshire included in the regional structure, or areas in the south of the region that form part of the London Green Belt. East Anglia is felt to have a reasonably coherent identity, and an even stronger sense of attachment to county identities, particularly in Norfolk and Suffolk. The editor of the region's largest selling newspaper, the *Eastern Daily Press*, put it like this:

"I cannot see the synergy between Norfolk and Hertfordshire. I can see a synergy between Norfolk, Suffolk and Cambridgeshire, which is traditional East Anglia.... I can see that those three counties hang together. But, you know, trying to include Essex in this, trying to include Hertfordshire, to me is just nonsense." (Interview)

The rural-versus-metropolitan dualism is one that many people recognise as having some influence upon the nature of regional working. One interviewee explained:

"There is this stereotyping going on. If you're in Hertfordshire, where you can jump on a tube train and be in the centre of London in three-quarters of an hour, the image of East Anglia you have is pheasants, tweed hats, cream teas and Norwich, and people speaking with funny accents, and Bernard Matthews turkeys and stuff like that. Very unfairly. And equally, the East Anglian people are maybe a little suspicious about, you know, 'what do we have in common with the ethnic diversity of Luton, or the south Essex stereotypes of XR3i's?'... It's very unfair that people have these stereotypical perceptions and that it tends to reinforce their sense of place." (Interview, regional official)

The editor of the *Eastern Daily Press* was keen to reinforce this point about differences within the region, however. He saw it as not just an issue of stereotyping, but of communities with essentially differing values in different parts of the East of England:

"I suppose the problem is that Norfolk, Suffolk and Cambridge, by and large, are rural communities underpinned by farming, with not very good road links, but with a kind of unspoken comfortableness with each other. As soon as you start to plug in Essex and Hertfordshire and Bedfordshire, you think 'hang on, these people have not got the same values.... They are much more attached to London and the suburbs. They are not rural.... It is a different culture." (Interview)

Those who think about regional identity can give a strong narrative about the nature of East Anglian identity:

> "It's strongly agricultural. The industrial revolution to a large extent passed it by. So there was not the huge growth followed by collapse that there has been elsewhere.... It's a very European facing part of the world.... It has close sea connections to Europe. The nearest capital city to Norwich is Amsterdam, not London – it's physically nearer. There is a feeling of separateness. Geographically it is a bulge. You don't go through the region en route.... You could go back further and point out that is was a stronghold of the republican movement during the English civil war, that it has a history of Methodism and dissent. Many of the founding fathers of America came from here for this reason.... That's where the feeling comes from. 'Do different' is a Norwich slogan that applies in East Anglia ... dissenting, cussedness and agricultural tradition, rather than a manufacturing one." (Interview, Managing Director, Anglia TV)

This sense of the separateness of East Anglia, alongside proximity to London, is a recurring theme in commentary about it. Writing in the 1960s, Hadfield (1965, p 7) could claim:

> As one crosses the Stour into Suffolk one quickly realizes that London, though only seventy minutes away from Ipswich by train, is as far in every other sense as it is from, say, Bristol, Exeter, or Hull. Is there any other region so near to the capital that has its own daily morning newspaper? I think not: and that surely is a symptom of cultural independence.

Indeed, a strong case could be made for the distinctiveness of a historical East Anglian identity, which has important contemporary legacies. This would focus on being a separate part of the south (not the Home Counties). Until relatively recently, its industries were founded on its distinctive agricultural and maritime practices, which have left a set of distinctive environmental problems, reflecting the fact that much of the region lies at or below sea-level. This is the 'Waterland' evoked in Graham Swift's eponymous novel. The region's landscape and environment speak of its historical links with the Low Countries. This legacy can be found in the Fens – drained by the Dutchman Vermuyden – and in the built environment. The perpendicular churches of the region and market squares of Norwich, Great Yarmouth and Kings Lynn are reminiscent of Flemish towns (see British Association, 1961). The Norwich School of Painters, perhaps the foremost provincial school of artists, which existed for 30 years at the beginning of the 19th century, reasserted these historic links. The paintings of Cotman and Crome, were directly inspired by the work of the 17th-century Dutch masters. Coastal scenes, flat landscapes, vast skies and frequent windmills of the region were the central theme of the school's work (Moore, 1985). The dissenting, Protestant traditions of the region marked it out from other parts of the south. Cromwell's Eastern Association speaks for itself, but arguably Thetford's Thomas Paine was a product of this distinctive regional culture.

All of this has little resonance in other parts of the region. For those on the periphery of London, the East of England concept seems remote from the concerns of metropolitan suburbs, as the leader of Watford Council explained:

> "We are, in Watford, on the extreme edge of the Eastern region and ... that's a region that goes out as far as Hunstanton and we don't have a lot in common with Hunstanton. And I have to say sitting through East of England meetings of over an hour of discussion on coastal protection, hasn't exactly been our top priority or a good use of our time, and we are probably critical that congestion on the M25 never seems to be mentioned." (Interview)

Watford's character is more akin to that of a London borough, most notably reflected in its ethnic mix. Region building here has less immediate political significance than the fact that it was the first locality in Britain to elect a mayor in 2001. Political leaders in Watford place a priority on issues such as extending the London Underground Metropolitan Line to Watford Junction – issues which are more to do with the governance of Greater London than the East of England.

Among those responsible for administering new regional institutions, and among other opinion formers in the media and local government in the region, there are different schools of thought on the significance of the boundary issue and the questions it raises about issues of regional identity. While some who are sceptical about the regional devolution agenda raise the definition of the East of England as a fundamental problem, those who are already engaged in regional working tend to see the definitional issues as a simple inconvenience which, over time, is likely to fade. For these latter actors, the definition of the region is considered to be a closed issue and is no longer 'up for debate'.

The question of regional identity nevertheless has exercised the minds of the region builders. For example, in the spring of 2000, EEDA commissioned MORI to conduct a programme of research "to *help develop* an image and identity for the East of England" (MORI, 2000, p 1, emphasis added). The research employed public opinion polling, as well as qualitative research through discussion groups and personal interviews, to elicit perceptions of the East of England among people currently living and working there, and among opinion formers and national and international business interests.

The study revealed relatively low levels of identification with the East of England (Table 8.3). Fewer than one in ten of the 1,023 residents polled correctly identified the East of England as the government administrative region they lived in. Over half those living in Norfolk, Suffolk and Cambridgeshire believed that they lived in East Anglia, while residents in Essex and Hertfordshire were more likely to think that they were in the South East (41% and 38% respectively). Stronger attachments to local identities were expressed, rather

Table 8.3: Spontaneous living awareness in the East of England by residents of the region's component counties

Q: Which region do you think you are in?

	East Anglia	South East	East of England	Others	Don't know
Bedfordshire	40	14	4	12	30
Cambridgeshire	52	3	7	24	14
Essex	21	41	7	11	19
Hertfordshire	10	38	5	17	31
Norfolk	56	5	12	19	9
Suffolk	55	6	11	13	15
Total	**35**	**23**	**8**	**15**	**20**

Base: 1,023 East of England residents aged 16+ (10-31 March 2000)

Source: MORI (2000)

than a regional identity, with attachment to the county being strongest in Norfolk (78%) and attachment to towns being strongest in Essex (81%) (Table 8.4).

This loose sense of regional attachment, which itself is differentially experienced across the region, is not seen as a problem by some regional officials. One explained:

> "East Anglia is an established region. East Anglia has got its own media – *Eastern Daily Press, East Anglian Daily Times* and so on. It's got the two television channels based in Norwich. Their coverage doesn't cover the whole region. As you come closer to London, you get London Weekend, and Meridian.... So I doubt if most people in Essex or Hertfordshire have any particular concept

Table 8.4: Strength of belonging to types of areas in the East of England

Q: How strongly do you feel that you belong to each of the following areas?

	% very/fairly strongly						
	Beds	Cambs	Essex	Herts	Suffolk	Norfolk	Total
Neighbourhood, this village or nearest village	81	67	78	72	82	73	76
This town or nearest town	76	70	81	71	74	76	75
Local borough/district/city/area	61	71	73	58	64	75	68
County	59	67	76	65	75	78	71
East of England region	50	63	57	46	67	61	57
London	30	9	24	40	10	16	23

Base: 1,023 East of England residents aged 16+ (10-31 March 2000)

Source: MORI (2000)

of living in the East of England. They see themselves as Home Counties. Now I don't think that necessarily matters. And perhaps over a long period of time, the perception will change." (Interview, regional official)

Similarly, Vincent Watts, Chair of the Board of EEDA, and responsible for promoting the economic development of the region, accepted the relatively weak sense of identity with the East of England region among the people of the former SERPLAN areas. Comparing the sense of 'the region' in Hertfordshire and Essex with that in the North East of England, he explained:

"When you have a very successful world city on your doorstep, it obviously changes things. And people who live in Watford, St Albans, whatever, commute into London everyday. What have they got to do with Norwich? Absolutely nothing. And they're never likely to have. And I don't really think that we should ever expect them to feel part of a region in the way [people] probably do in the North East." (Interview, Vincent Watts, Chair EEDA)

Yet EEDA is working to develop a greater sense of identity, especially in terms of 'branding' the region for inward investment purposes. The rationale for thinking about the East of England *as a region* is spelt out in a section of EEDA's new economic strategy, *East of England 2010: Prosperity and opportunity for all*, dealing with image and identity:

The eight new English regions are here to stay. As they get established the clear sense of belonging and pride in place that they instill is important. That's what gives a region confidence in itself, and makes it attractive to those who live or want to start businesses here. (EEDA, 2001a, p 144)

The strategy goes on to explain:

Our goal is for the East of England to be seen as a successful, strong, confident and cohesive region, which is an excellent place to live, work, visit and invest. This depends on a clear and consistent identity and image for the East of England – in the region itself, in the rest of the UK and internationally. (p 145)

Living East, the regional cultural consortium, charged with producing a strategy for the region's cultural industries, has had to struggle with the identity issue in a direct way. Its chair, Graham Greelman, while acknowledging the historic claims of East Anglia, argued this could not be given a central role in the new East of England structures. Instead, it fell into line with the hi-tech image of the region:

"We have avoided a heritage based view of the region. There is an enormous concentration of heritage in the region. But what we were trying to develop, I suppose, is a kind of 'Californian' image – high quality of life, good access to cultural facilities, clean air, fine cities and buildings. A good place to come and settle with your family." (Interview)

Therefore, cultural policy has been put at the service of region building. East of England Arts, the regional arts board, launched a new arts magazine, *East Life*, in 2002 with the strapline 'East of England – the new European region'.

Part of the remit of the MORI study was to understand how the region was perceived by businesses outside the region and overseas. Perhaps unsurprisingly, respondents from the world of international business had heard of Cambridge and saw it as a key strength of the region. An international branding consultancy was commissioned to develop a brand for the region, and recommended "the spirit of ingenuity" as the overall branding concept, with "The East of England – space for ideas" (EEDA, 2001b) as the main marketing strapline. A consultant explained: "We want to capture the region's unbroken relationship with ingenious ideas – from draining the Fens in the 1600s, to the basis for modern fibre-optics developed at Nortel Networks' Harlow laboratories in 1966, to pioneering research taking place in and around BT's research centre at Adastral Park, Suffolk" (quoted in EEDA, 2001b). Although explicit reference to Cambridge has been downplayed within this branding exercise, the linking of ideas and innovation to the regional brand clearly plays on the Cambridge phenomenon.

Cambridge is also gradually becoming the centre of the region's institutions of governance. GO-East, the RDA and East of England Arts all have their headquarters in Cambridge. The National Health Service Regional HQ has also recently moved there, and other private sector organisations, such as Barclay's Bank, have altered their regional structures in response to the emerging regional set-up centred on Cambridge. Perhaps paradoxically, one of the region's more pressing planning problems is how to manage the growth pressures in and around Cambridge (GO-East, 2000). Yet the very process of region building is fuelling the demand for office space in the city as various government agencies relocate there too.

Political and administrative regionalism: government and governance

If regionalism is understood as the quest for greater powers and discretion in policy making at the regional level, then it is useful to distinguish between two different strands in this movement. The first is what might be termed a democratic or political regionalism and is based on the potential role of regional government in adding accountability and democratic legitimacy to policy making (see Marquand and Tomaney, 2000). The second is a more technocratic or administrative regionalism, which is based on the view that the regional level is more propitious to efficient and effective policy making. Administrative regionalism is also often closely related to arguments about the spatial scale for the coordination of economic strategies or imperatives resulting from the increasing importance of the regional level within the EU (DETR, 2000).

Table 8.5: Percentage of respondents supporting or opposing their own region of England getting an Elected Regional Assembly

Q: Would you support or oppose your region of England (name of region), getting its own elected assembly?

	Support (%)	Oppose (%)	Don't know (%)	Net support (%)
All	45	38	17	+7
London	60	21	19	+39
North East	51	29	20	+22
West Midlands	46	37	17	+9
South West	47	39	13	+8
East Midlands	40	35	24	+5
East of England	43	42	15	+1
Yorkshire and the Humber	42	42	16	0
North West	42	44	14	−2
South East	37	47	16	−10

Base: 1,810 British residents aged 15+ (5-8 March 1999)

Source: MORI/The Economist: 'Attitudes to Regional Government'

An administrative rather than a democratic or political imperative has driven recent events in the East of England. The East of England is not among those regions with the strongest public support for elected Regional Assemblies (Table 8.5). Nevertheless, the need for regional *governance*, if not government, is generally accepted not only among opinion formers in the East of England, but even those who are more sceptical of the case for regional government. Indeed, among the officials in GO-East, the RDA, local government and various development quangos there is enthusiasm for working at the regional level and recognition of the benefits regional working can bring.

A brief survey of recent regional initiatives underlines the growth of regional working since 1998:

1. EEDA produced its economic strategy for the region during 1999, with much of the work being carried out, including consultation with stakeholder organisations, in just a six-month period. A revised strategy was published in July 2001 (EEDA, 2001a).
2. The new EU Structural Fund programmes for the 2000-06 programming period were required, under Objective 2, to be combined in a Single Programming Document for the region as a whole. Improved regional working enabled more effective prioritising of bids from within the region, with the effect that the region secured an increased proportion of structural fund monies within England at the time of a shrinking national allocation.
3. The East of England region was required to draft a regional chapter of the England Rural Development Plan under the new, post-Agenda 2000 arrangements for administering the Common Agricultural Policy. This required the new regional bodies (such as EEDA and the new Countryside

Agency) to contribute to a strategy led by the then Ministry of Agriculture, Fisheries and Food (MAFF).

4. The Regional Planning Guidance (RPG) for the East Anglia region for the period to 2016 was agreed in November 2000, and regional planners have begun to assess how to combine the RPG for the three East Anglian counties with the guidance being produced for the SERPLAN region to produce a single RPG for the whole East of England region.

5. Joining the growing family of regional plans and strategy documents is the new Regional Cultural Strategy, drawn up by a consortium led by the Department of Culture, Media and Sport (Living East, 2001).

Collectively, these initiatives are reinforcing the profile of regional working among public sector agencies and stakeholder organisations. Irrespective of the debate about political decentralisation a new imperative for regional working is being established.

Although regionalism has a relatively low profile in the East of England, its Regional Assembly was, paradoxically, the first to call its RDA to account. In April 2001, EERA refused to endorse the new regional economic strategy. Assembly members were reportedly concerned about the environmental impact of its 3.2% growth target, its alleged failure to take account of subregional differences, and the arrangements for partnership working and that questions of social inclusion had not been properly dealt with (*Local Government Chronicle*, 12 April 2001). EEDA agreed to revise its first version after EERA had voiced what its chair, John Kent, described as "severe reservations". Concerns raised by Sub-Regional Partnerships (SRPs) prompted the assembly to reject the strategy, and Mr Kent accused EEDA of "ducking the difficult decisions" needed to stimulate development.

The RDA reacted angrily. EEDA's Chief Executive, Bill Samuel, said:

> EERA's lack of endorsement is an indication that some members of the regional assembly are reluctant to commit to firm and positive action to move the region's economy forward.... It is disappointing that, despite significant time and effort on EEDA's part, some regional assembly members still did not buy into EEDA's recommendations for creating more prosperity, better opportunities and an increased quality of life for all who live and work in the region. (EEDA, 2001c)

According to the *Local Government Chronicle*, EEDA officials and board members were prepared to push ahead with the strategy without the endorsement of EERA, but ministers intervened to insist that the two bodies reach agreement.

These events represent the most public flexing of muscle by a Regional Chamber to date. Of course, the assembly has no right of veto over the RES, as EEDA is answerable to the Secretary of State. However, as the *Local Government Chronicle* put it, this "eastern insurrection" highlighted some of the democratic tensions around the new regional governance, and it may serve as a "dress rehearsal for future battles".

Conclusions

It is clear that a process of regionalisation is underway in the administrative structures of governance in the East of England. From the perspective of English regionalism and the 'English Question', however, an important unresolved issue is whether or not this process will, over time, generate greater calls for democratic accountability over these institutions of regional governance – the regional quango-state – by means of a directly elected Regional Assembly.

For those opposed to the idea of a directly elected Regional Assembly in the East of England, the defence of the status quo is likely to emphasise the appeal of county-based identities in the region. For example, the editor of the *Eastern Daily Press* talked of the paper being "fiercely opposed to Norfolk becoming submerged into a greater being". Sceptical local politicians, particularly in the Conservative Party, will probably present regionalism as a threat to county councils and county identities. However, even in what might be considered to be among the most unpropitious of conditions, tendencies can be identified in the East of England that may yet generate a greater propensity for regional working, and even possibly political devolution in the longer-term.

In this chapter's analysis, distinguishing between technocratic and democratic regionalism helps to pinpoint the nature of the regional project in newly created regions such as the East of England. The argument here is that there are circumstances in which strengthening one could fuel the development of the other. The technocratic elite running the regional institutions of the East of England is not having to respond to a clamour for regional institutions from the people of their region. Rather they are living with the effects of others' calls for devolution elsewhere in England. Some officials and politicians are embracing the opportunities that the new institutions bring with them and adding impetus to the process of region building.

As a conceptual conclusion, this analysis of the case of the East of England would reinforce the argument that there is no simple and inexorable logic behind the rise of the 'new regionalism', which is sometimes the conclusion drawn from the literature on economic restructuring and regional competitiveness (see Tomaney and Ward, 2000). Building new regional institutions is a politically contested process, and the national political scene crucially shapes the parameters of this struggle.

Yet if regionalism is conceptualised in relational terms then we can see from cases such as the East of England that the current situation is far from stable. Increased regional powers and responsibilities for other regions such as the North East, the North West, Yorkshire and the Humber would be likely to raise the profile of the question of regional devolution in the East of England. Moreover, the higher profile and scope for action of those nascent bodies who are already engaged in the region building project could also prompt calls for increased democratic accountability and new, democratically elected regional institutions.

Acknowledgement

The authors acknowledge the support of the Leverhulme Trust, ESRC and the University of Newcastle upon Tyne. John Tomaney would like to acknowledge those who participated in the seminar, *East Anglia and regional devolution*, Norwich City Hall, 12 April 2002.

References

British Association (1961) *Norwich and its region*, Norwich: British Association for the Advancement of Science.

DETR (Department of the Environment, Transport and the Regions) (2000) *Regional government in England: A preliminary review of literature and research findings*, London: DETR (Local and Regional Government Research Unit).

EEDA (East of England Development Agency) (1999) *Moving forward: Regional Economic Strategy for the East of England*, Cambridge: EEDA.

EEDA (2001a) *East of England 2010: Prosperity and opportunity for all*, Cambridge: EEDA.

EEDA (2001b) 'The East of England – space for ideas', *EEDA Press Release*, 18 June.

EEDA (2001c) 'EEDA disappointed at Regional Assembly reluctance to sign up to prosperity', *EEDA Press Release*, 18 June.

GO-East (Government Office for the East of England) (2000) *Regional Planning Guidance note 6: Regional Planning Guidance for East Anglia to 2016*, London: The Stationery Office.

Hadfield, J., Scarfe, N., Lowe, M.E., Dewes, S., Jobson, A. and Watkins, M. (1964) *East Anglian heritage*, Ipswich: Anglian Publications Ltd.

Living East (2001) *Culture: A catalyst for change – A strategy for cultural development for the East of England*, Cambridge: GO-East.

Marquand, D. and Tomaney, J. (2000) *Democratising England*, London: Regional Policy Forum.

Moore, A. (1985) *The Norwich School of Artists, 1803-1833*, London: HMSO.

MORI (2000) *Perceptions of the East of England*, Research report to the EEDA, London: MORI.

Tomaney, J. (1999) 'In search of English regionalism: the case of the North East', *Scottish Affairs*, vol 28, pp 62-82.

Tomaney, J. and Ward, N. (2000) 'England and the "New Regionalism"', *Regional Studies* vol 34, pp 471-8.

Townroe, P. and Moore, B. (1999) 'The East of England', in M. Breheny (ed) *The people: Where will they work?*, London: Town and Country Planning Association, pp 51-64.

Ward, N. and Woodward, R. (1998) *The Europeanisation of Rural Development Policy in the UK: The case of East Anglia*, Centre for Rural Economy Working Paper Series no 31, Newcastle upon Tyne: University of Newcastle upon Tyne.

NINE

The South East region?

Peter John, Steve Musson and Adam Tickell

The South East of England is the region that no one seems to love. Central government civil servants created its boundaries to ensure there was a region in the parts of England which lie outside London, south of the Midlands and before the 'west country' begins. It serves to complete the map rather than act as an equivalent entity to regions like the North East. Moreover, it is easy to invoke some fairly straightforward stereotypes which seem to confirm the South East's 'peripheral' status within the regional project, something shared by the current government which sees regional government emerging first in the north of England.

The elements to the story of the South East are:

- the absence of a campaign for the region, indicating minimal elite and organisational mobilisation;
- the low level of support among the public for regional reforms – 58% disagree with the statement: 'regional politicians would be more trustworthy than members of parliament' (cited in Harding, 2000, pp 32-3)[1];
- fragmentation into competing subregions, which stymies attempts to build regional-level partnerships;
- the high level of prosperity, which limits interest in institutions that have their prime role in economic development.

The previous dominance of the South East by the Conservative Party has imprinted free market ideas on the mindset of political elites and the general public, predisposing them against regional government and regional coordination and policy making. The pre-existence of the networks and partnerships, which extend outside the region to other regions and countries, suggests the region has no cohesiveness (John, 1997). The lack of a centre or even a large 'capital city' does not offer a focus for political leadership, since most cities in the region have less than 100,000 inhabitants. Attractive as Guildford may be, it lacks something of the sweep and verve needed in a regional capital, which could compete with Bordeaux, Milan or Barcelona (although the lack of a dominant metropolitan centre could avoid the scenario of regional government becoming the project of its large city, such as Manchester in the North West and Birmingham in the West Midlands). Most of all, the existence of London as a region in its own right removes the natural centre of the South East in terms of its economy, polity and cultural life as it often has to feed through London to make sense of its problems and potentialities.

We argue elsewhere (Tickell and John, 2001) that the path of dependence of institutional patterns and political cultures will perpetuate the weakness of political regionalism in the South East. Such an outcome may be reinforced by criticisms of the costs of regional government and fear of the political power of northern Labour baronies, which are better able to access resources from the centre. It makes sense for the South East regional elites to rely on their 'luck' on having macro-economic policy designed in their favour (cf Dowding, 1996); they do not need regional institutions because they get all the economic policy outcomes they desire without trying. The anticipated reactions of policy makers in London and the standard operating procedures of institutions like the Bank of England may automatically produce policies that favour the South East.

Nonetheless, there is more mobilisation and institutional formation than implied by the stereotype. Any region has its share of both common and distinct economic and social problems, and the South East is no exception. It is possible to find each region crying out that it is unique, but yet to observe similar economic development strategies being put together by regional elites. Moreover, most English regions are artificial creations. Regional governance depends on the orientations of local political and administrative elites, and how they respond to government incentives, in the form of regional agencies, grants and representative mechanisms. In some senses there is not much difference in any part of England between a local authority chief executive or political leader responding to central government policies. Just like local authority or chamber-led economic development strategies, regional mobilisation is professionalised with South East public bodies drawing on the same corpus of economic development professionals who peruse *The Guardian's* job supplement on Wednesdays, as elsewhere. Moreover, whatever the initial level of regional mobilisation, the course of regionalisation in other European countries suggests that, once the boundaries have been drawn up and functions have been allocated to regional level institutions, especially when there is an element of direct election, elites and publics start to organise at that level, and are able to rediscover or even invent regional identities (John, 2001). With these comparative factors in mind, it is possible to overstate the lack of development of a 'laggard' region, such as the South East.

The social and economic challenges of the South East

The South East region – Berkshire, Buckinghamshire, East and West Sussex, Hampshire and the Isle of Wight, Kent, Oxfordshire and Surrey – is in some ways a socially and economically diverse region. It contains pockets of deprivation and affluence, frequently in close proximity, and distinct local economies ranging from those of north Kent and east Surrey, which lie on the outskirts of the Greater London conurbation, to rural east Sussex and west Oxfordshire. It is easy to contend that the region shares as limited an economic and social coherence as its regional identity. However, this is untrue. A broad range of issues, including economic competitiveness, the region's overstressed transport and infrastructure network, the quality and availability of commercial and residential land and property and, to a lesser extent, the quality of the environment and issues of social exclusion, are being recognised by local policy makers as regional and subregional issues that cannot be addressed by individual organisations or small-scale coalitions.

The South East region is, relative to the rest of the UK economy, in a strong economic position. It has a high level of research and development spending in strategically desirable growth industries such as biotechnology, pharmaceuticals and IT, and an associated large scientific and engineering labour force. Unemployment across the region is, with the exception of a number of areas, low. Many of the problems in the region are the results of economic success: labour shortages (particularly of those with basic skills), a congested and inefficient transport network, a lack of suitable premises for business start-up and expansion, and a lack of affordable residential housing. As such, in some parts of the region, policy makers are concerned that previous rounds of economic success could hinder competitiveness in the future.

The economic performance of the South East region is, in terms of both absolute and per capita GDP, second only to that of London. The region accounts for 16% of English GDP (ONS, 1998). Between 1990 and 1999, average annual GDP growth of 6.2% in the South East was greater than in any other English region. In comparison to other regions in the European Union (EU), the South East is less well placed, ranking 23rd in terms of GDP, and being far outperformed by comparable, non-city regions such as Baden-Wuerttemberg. For the South East England Development Agency (SEEDA), the main challenge is to improve the region's international standing. As such, the regional economic development strategy of the South East is characterised by an international, rather than inter-regional, outlook.

The main economic problem for the region is that, despite full use being made of the region's labour market, infrastructure, technical and environmental resources, productivity remains poor by international comparison. The challenge for the region is to find new ways of working, to make more effective use of the region's resources, and to compete with other 'world class' regions. Such an approach is not necessarily detrimental to other UK regions, and indeed the more effective use of the South East labour force can be seen as a way of limiting the drain on skilled employees from other regions (SEEDA, 1999b).

The regional labour market is one that is characterised by inequalities. In some places, the labour market is operating at near full capacity. For example, in Mole Valley, east Surrey, male unemployment is at 0.6%, while in neighbouring Guildford it is 1% (NOMIS, May 2001). In the 'core' areas of Surrey, former Berkshire and Oxfordshire, labour shortages and wage inflation hinder economic performance. Elsewhere in the region, however, Hastings has male unemployment of 7.2% and Brighton 6.8% (NOMIS, May 2001). Table 9.1 shows the male claimant rate for unitary and upper tier authorities in May 2001, the rate 12 months previously, and the percentage change. The first point

Table 9.1: Male claimant rate in the South East region (May 2000-May 2001)

Authority	May 2000 rate	May 2001 rate	% change
Bracknell Forest	1.2	1.1	-8.0
Brighton and Hove	7.6	5.9	-23.0
Buckinghamshire	1.8	1.6	-13.2
East Sussex	4.0	3.4	-15.9
Hampshire	1.9	1.5	-21.0
Isle of Wight	7.8	6.5	-15.9
Kent	4.1	3.5	-16.0
Medway	5.3	4.5	-14.5
Milton Keynes	2.3	2.1	-8.4
Oxfordshire	1.6	1.3	-15.5
Portsmouth	3.8	3.2	-16.3
Reading	2.3	2.0	-14.4
Slough	2.8	2.6	-6.4
Southampton	5.0	4.0	-20.7
Surrey	1.1	0.9	-22.4
West Berkshire	1.o	0.8	-16.0
West Sussex	1.8	1.5	-20.0
Windsor and Maidenhead	1.6	1.4	-13.5
Wokingham	1.1	0.9	-18.4
South East total	**2.6**	**2.2**	**-17.3**
England total	**4.9**	**4.3**	**-12.0**

Source: NOMIS

to note is that, compared to England as a whole, the South East labour market is increasingly buoyant. The second point is that, proportionally, those areas with a higher rate of unemployment in May 2000 did not follow a markedly different trajectory from those with lower rates. The apparent inability of market forces to strike a balance that incorporates more peripheral areas and relieves pressure on the overheated labour markets of the Thames Valley can be seen as two halves of the same regional problem. The introduction of regional strategies to incorporate all parts of the region into the prosperity is as much about sustaining growth in the most prosperous parts as it is about relieving deprivation in peripheral areas.

The labour market of the South East is commonly portrayed as one dominated by scientific and financial employment. Certainly, these have been major areas of growth, and they remain the most desirable sectors to regional institutions. However, as Table 9.2 shows, the structure of employment in the South East is diverse and, although a greater proportion of people are employed in real estate, renting and business activities, and fewer in manufacturing, the region's employment structure is broadly in line with the rest of the UK.

Although the economic performance of the South East appears to be strong, by UK standards, the main challenge for the region is to improve its performance

Table 9.2: Employment by standard industrial classification (1992) division in England and the South East (Government Office) region (1999)

SIC (1992) Division	England %	SE Region %
Agriculture, hunting and forestry	1.0	1.2
Fishing	0.0	0.0
Mining and quarrying	0.2	0.1
Manufacturing	15.7	12.2
Electricity, gas and water supply	0.5	0.4
Construction	4.4	4.2
Wholesale/retail trade, repair, etc.	17.9	19.2
Hotels and restaurants	6.4	6.2
Transport, storage and communication	6.2	6.8
Financial intermediation	4.5	4.1
Real estate, renting, business activities	15.3	18.7
Public admin/defence, social security	5.2	4.5
Education	8.0	8.2
Health and social work	10.1	9.3
Other community, social/personal service	4.9	4.7

Source: NOMIS

relative to its international competitors. In part, this improvement involves raising the region's profile as a 'world class' location for high value added business. In part, however, it also means addressing the sources of relative weakness in its corporate base. These weaknesses are low levels of entrepreneurship (measured through VAT registration) and relatively few incidences of collaboration and network development among companies.

The South East lags considerably behind London in VAT registrations, and is broadly comparable with the UK average (Table 9.3). New VAT registrations and a strong base of small and medium sized enterprises (SMEs) in the region are important for two reasons. Firstly, they provide the most likely route to establishing future high value added, high growth companies in the region (the 'Microsoft of the future'). Secondly, the establishment of an entrepreneurial corporate base across the region emphasises cohesiveness as well as a corporate separation from London. The desire to develop a base of small, specialised companies with growth potential is one that unites policy makers and economic development agencies at all levels across the region.

Regional institutions wish to encourage the development of knowledge dependent, and high technology corporate sectors with high added value. This aim is, of course, not new or unique to the South East. Unlike many other places, the South East starts from a good base: there are already a number of these companies in the region and several important clusters, which include aerospace in Hampshire and biotechnology in Oxfordshire. These locations have great potential, including high levels of local expertise in private companies and higher education institutions and access to capital and technology. However,

Table 9.3: VAT registrations as a percentage of total corporate base (1999)

Government Office – region	VAT registrations 1999 %
East Midlands	10.1
Eastern	10.5
London	13.8
North East	10.1
North West	11.3
South East	11.2
South West	10.1
West Midlands	10.6
Yorkshire and the Humber	9.9
England	**10.8**

Source: NOMIS

these are presently less well interconnected and less productive than other comparable regions in Europe.

The region has good infrastructure links with continental Europe and the rest of the world. The south coast has well-developed port facilities for both passengers (for example, Dover in the east of the region and Portsmouth in the west), and for cargo (for example, Southampton). The South East handles 80% of UK air traffic at Gatwick in West Sussex and Heathrow, immediately adjacent to the region, while the Channel Tunnel rail link passes through Kent with one existing terminal at Ashford and another planned in Gravesend. The region portrays itself as the 'Gateway to Britain' with some justification.

However, the transport and infrastructure within the region does not complement its external connections. The infrastructure is extensive but has suffered from low investment. Although the region contains 24% of the national motorway network and 12% of trunk roads, congestion is a serious problem in the economic 'core' of the region, Surrey, north Hampshire and the Thames Valley. This overload is compounded by heavy reliance on cars for travel to work and an underdeveloped and underused public transport system. For example, in Wokingham, where 79% of the local labour force travel to work by car, the severity of road congestion is such that unpredictable journey times are seen to deter potential inward investors (Wokingham District Council, 1999). In other parts of the region, the lack of infrastructure is the problem. For example, East Sussex has only 11 miles of dual carriageway. Although train travel from Brighton to London takes only 50 minutes, the travel time from Hastings is almost two hours (SEEDA, 1999b). The contrast between international and internal infrastructure quality generates inequalities. Almost all of the local authorities in the north west of the region (Surrey, Oxon, Berks) emphasise the requirement for better transport links to Heathrow, even those such as Wokingham and Slough that are only a short distance away. For those areas that are peripheral to these nodes of communication, overstressed regional infrastructure prevents them from sharing fully in the economic development.

The region's environment is under similar strain. Although large areas are protected as places of outstanding natural beauty, sites of special scientific interest and greenbelt, the intensity of traffic volume, waste production, water use and energy consumption in the region compromise environmental quality. In the region where greenbelt is 19% as a proportion of total land area (England 12%) and areas of outstanding natural beauty 32% (England 19%), the water supply is a constraint on development in many areas, and the region is barely self-sufficient. The shape of development in the region is in part dictated by these environmental concerns. Environmental quality can be seen as an important economic asset. Part of the appeal of the region as a residential area is in its natural beauty. In addition, tourism is big business in some areas, most notably in the towns – employment black-spots – on the south coast such as Hastings and Brighton, and on the Isle of Wight where the hotel and catering industry accounts for 38% of employment.

The main challenge for the new regional institutions in the South East is to use the region's resources more effectively. Even with its overstretched infrastructure, environmental resources and a labour market operating at near full capacity still leave it down the league table of Europe's most productive regions. What seems to be required is a more effective strategy that links the region as a whole, which channels investment from the overheated core areas to those places with underused capacity, and which recognises the need for infrastructure improvements in peripheral areas. The small-scale coalitions of local authorities and partnerships that still dominate economic development in the region are less capable of enabling this type of development than those institutions with a broader scale.

The new regional institutions

In January 1999, the government established a Regional Assembly for the South East. In terms of financing and structure, it does not differ from the bodies in other regions. Politically, however, it is different, as its chair, Councillor David Shakespeare, is a Conservative, making the assembly the only Conservative-led one up until June 2001, although the assembly's executive is composed of all the main parties. Another interesting development is that the assembly takes a role for areas outside its region. In April 2001, it took over an existing regional planning body, the South East Regional Planning Body (SERPLAN), which has members in London and beyond the borders of the region. SEEDA is also taking the leading role in developing the 'Thames Gateway' area, which incorporates the South East, East and London regions. The final unique feature is that subregional representative institutions have remained in place. Bodies such as the assembly claim to speak for the whole region but wish to work 'flexibly' to ensure that subregional sensitivities and political interests are not overridden.

The other institution is the Regional Development Agency (RDA), SEEDA, which came into operation on 1 April 1999, having the same structure as in other regions. In their first two years, SEEDA has invested £150 million in urban and rural regeneration schemes, and in initiatives to promote the development of skills, business competitiveness, investment and innovation.

The regional economic development strategy has an almost paternal recognition of the dominance of the South East region in the economy of the UK. In the main, it emphasises the importance of regional competitiveness on a European and international scale:

> The South East of England has the potential to be a World Class Region. A successful South East will also stimulate wealth creation in neighbouring regions and hence across the country. We should be one of the top 10 regions in Europe – perhaps the world. (SEEDA, 1999a, p 1)

Economic development policy in the South East does not aim to maintain institutional balance within the UK, or to boost competitiveness relative to other English regions. Rather, the South East is portrayed as a driver of economic development for the UK. The development of a more competitive South East is seen as an important requirement for improved national economic performance. As such, the success of the South East is rarely measured in terms of its position within the UK.

It is debatable whether the emphasis placed on the relatively poor performance of the South East region to its international competitors reflects a genuine concern to improve the 'league table' position of the region, or whether it is defensive rhetoric aimed at deflecting the claims of other English regions to the privileged wealth and prosperity of the South East.

The response of social and political interests

The articulation of interests takes a special form in the South East because of the place of the region in the hierarchy of prosperity. The assembly has been quick to argue that the South East has a special status as the UK's most prosperous region and that it should not be milked for its wealth (Assembly's AGM 22 July 1999). SEEDA itself appears to have a more 'prosperity' rather than 'exclusion' driven agenda as implied by its objective of promote business enterprise, competitiveness and innovation. The network of enterprise hubs – linking business to universities and other centres of excellence in research – is a prime example of this imperative (we would need to make a content analysis of RDA websites to substantiate the claim that the South East region is different). The policy positions and statements suggest that regional actors articulate a particular discourse about the regional identity based on the need to ensure economic prosperity and maintain resources 'lost' to other regions. These sorts of argument link to those made in other prosperous regions, such as the north of Italy and Catalonia. Not that such views are particularly developed or highly public in the South East, but they exist in a polite and understated form.

Unsurprisingly, regional actors have discussed and lobbied on transport issues, with the aim of reducing transport congestion. Much of the agenda of the assembly has been dominated by the topic, such as the access to Hastings Multi-Modal, A3 Hindhead, and the M27 South Hampshire. The South East England Regional Assembly, the Government Office for the South East (GOSE) and SEEDA hosted a conference in November 2000, entitled 'Transport: the Ten Year Plan – moving the South East forward', which largely endorsed charging as one of the solutions to traffic problems, perhaps more of a market solution than would be articulated in other regions.

As elsewhere, the region adopted an economic development strategy, *Building a world class region* (SEEDA, 1999a). SEEDA itself has launched a number of activities, such as the Enterprise Hub Network, referred to above, which will contain 30 new hubs, to promote economic growth by providing links between actors, such as universities and entrepreneurs. SEEDA has considered the local draft economic development plans, such as the Draft Chatham Maritime Business Plan. There has also been *Food and drink – A regional and industry review*, based on "harnessing people's cultural attachment to the countryside". Other SEEDA initiatives include a Wired Region Project, being worked up at the time of writing.

The assembly has strayed outside the predictable areas of economic development (planning and transport) and set up a Healthy Region Forum as a partnership between the key agencies in the region. The assembly has also discussed a housing strategy focused on affordable housing. The region has been active in promoting EU matters: SEEDA and the assembly set up an office in Brussels and appointed a European liaison officer in April 2001, having agreed a European strategy in February 2001.

The South East's relationship with London is essential for progress on regional problems, such as planning, housing and transport. London might be seen as an obstacle as its mayor, Ken Livingstone, has immediate priorities in legitimating his role and solving London-wide problems, such as London Transport. In fact, the existence of the mayor's office makes contact between the South East easier because of the single post; and there have already been meetings between the mayor's office and the South East assembly, for instance. Planning issues affecting London and its hinterland are being addressed by a new Advisory Forum for Regional Planning after a pan-regional protocol was signed by the South East England Regional Assembly, the Greater London Authority (GLA) and the East of England. These issues include the first stage of the Spatial Development Strategy, including housing, the mayor's draft Transport Plan for London, and the first findings of the Multi-Modal Study on the M25. Other key issues on the collective agenda for the three new planning bodies include waste disposal across London and its hinterland, and strategies for the future development of airports and ports.

Conclusions

The South East is a regional entity in terms of economic problems and potential. It is not an empty economic and social space created for administrative convenience. The biggest local problems in the region, which are of greatest concern to local authorities and businesses, have a regional dimension. In order to foster local competitiveness, a regional strategy is necessary. In particular, if the South East wants to compete effectively with the rest of Europe and to develop specialised clusters of activity, it needs to start addressing how to use public resources effectively. Although regional identity and mobilisation are weak, the potential benefits are great, an incentive which may create more regional awareness and joint action.

However, it is still too early to tell whether institutional development and interest group mobilisation are going to develop into a stable support and bedrock for regional government. SEEDA and the assembly lobby for South East economic and political interests, yet it is hard to gauge what supports these institutions[1]. In a period when the Treasury is interested in driving the regional government agenda, and with John Prescott in the Cabinet Office, the mobilisation and institutionalisation observed so far could continue to develop.

Note

[1] The survey, conducted while debates about the London Mayor were raging, showed that support was highest in London (60%) and the institutionally strong North East (53%) (cited in Hazell, 2000).

Acknowledgement

The authors are currently engaged in such research, supported by the Economic and Social Research Council (ESRC): 'Building institutions in a vacuum? The devolution of power and the South East', with Adam Tickell (principal applicant), £110,000 January 2001–2004, part of the Devolution and Constitutional Change Initiative. We thank the ESRC for its support.

References

Dowding, K. (1996) *Power*, Buckingham: Open University Press.

Harding, A. (2000) *Is there a missing middle in English governance?*, London: New Local Government Network.

Hazell, R. (2000) *The State and the nations: The first year of devolution*, London: Imprint Academic.

John, P. (1997) 'Sub-national partnerships and European integration: the difficult case of London and the South East', in J. Bradbury and J. Mawson (eds) *Regionalism and European integration*, London: Jessica Kingsley.

John, P. (2001) *Local governance in Western Europe*, London: Sage Publications.

ONS (Office for National Statistics) (1998) *Regional trends*, Newport: ONS.

SEEDA (South East England Development Agency) (1999a) *Building a world class region. An economic strategy for the South East of England*, Guildford: SEEDA.

SEEDA (1999b) *State of the region. An economic profile of South East England*, Guildford: SEEDA.

Tickell, A. and John, P. (2001) 'Building institutions in a vacuum? The devolution of power and the South East', Unpublished paper.

Wokingham District Council (1999) *Economic Development Strategy 1999-2000*, Wokingham: WDC.

TEN

Regionalism in North East England

Paul Benneworth and John Tomaney

Introduction

In many respects, the North East is the key to English regionalism. It has been at the vanguard of demands for new regional institutions, and has the conditions most likely to produce support for elected regional government. The region has been a target for regional policy since the 1930s, as a result of its persistent structural economic problems, and has a tradition of institution building that has focused not only on addressing its economic problems, but has also extended into the cultural and other fields. Measures of opinion suggest that the North East has a stronger sense of regional identity than other parts of England and is more inclined to be supportive of regional government. Whether support is great enough to ensure an affirmative vote in a referendum for a Regional Assembly remains untested.

The main social and economic challenges facing the region

The North East was first awarded its label as a 'problem region' in the period between the two world wars. This period saw the collapse of its traditional industries, coal mining, steel making and shipbuilding. The region's economic history since then has been dominated by a struggle to adapt to structural economic change. A major expansion of regional policy in the 1960s and 1970s modernised its infrastructure, and attracted new mobile investment. An expansion of the service sector also provided jobs, and helped raise levels of female labour market participation. However, the deep recession of 1979-80, followed by low growth throughout the 1980s, saw a further decline in employment in the traditional industries, and the loss of jobs in the newer branches of manufacturing. This decline was only partly offset by service sector growth. These developments left a legacy of high unemployment, low economic participation rates, and associated social and economic problems, resulting in high levels of poverty (Hudson, 1989). In 1999 the North East had the lowest level of income per capita of any region in England. This chapter will examine the set of structural weaknesses that underpin the region's social and economic indicators.

The performance of the North East in attracting new hi-tech companies is especially weak. Successful firms in the region are few and far between. Levels of private sector research and development are the lowest in the country, while general levels of small firm formation are poor. In 2000, the only venture capital company with a presence in the region closed its Newcastle office. The promotion of technology-based industrial clusters is a central theme of government competitiveness policy, but the conditions for achieving this in the North East are especially challenging (Charles and Benneworth, 2001).

Another issue facing the North East is the poor performance of the business service sector, especially financial services. Cities such as Edinburgh, Manchester, Leeds and Birmingham all support significant financial services employment. Although these remain subordinate to the City of London, and occupy different sectoral niches, in each case they support higher value activities and employment, and have substantial spin-off effects in activities such as accountancy, law, consultancy and brokering. The growth of these industries has been a factor in the regeneration of these cities' urban fabric. By contrast, Newcastle, as the main urban centre of the North East region, does not support a significant financial services industry, and faces a major challenge to develop one (Roberts, 2000).

Despite industrial decline, the North East remains relatively dependent on its manufacturing industry. Given the weakness of indigenous industry, inward investment remains an important source of new employment opportunities. High levels of external control, however, and the bias in the region's manufacturing sector toward branch plant activities, means that the region's manufacturing sector is susceptible to closure during periods of rapid economic restructuring. The North East, therefore, faces the constant challenge of finding ways to cope with the threat of plant closure, and consequent major job losses. The future of the sector is likely to require an improvement in the skills and technology components of existing manufacturing activity, in order to survive waves of branch plant rationalisation. However, coping with plant closures is likely to remain a challenge in the future (Charles and Benneworth, 1999; Pike, 1999, 2000; Tomaney, 1999).

The weak state of the North East's private sector means that the public sector plays a relatively important role in the region's economy and society. The North East is likely to remain dependent on this sector, and faces the challenge of turning this dependence to its advantage. The education sector has a major role to play in the emergence of knowledge-based industries. Some of the region's (few) hi-tech firms are the result of university spin-offs and other public sector organisations. The creation of such successful public sector spin-offs in a region such as the North East is far from easy, but is likely to present opportunities for the region (Stone, 2000).

The region's structural economic problems contribute to, and are underpinned by, a set of social factors (Richardson et al, 1999). The lack of job opportunities contributes to low economic participation rates, which means that some communities (notably inner city areas and former mining levels) suffer greater unemployment than the official figures signify. A range of additional social problems – such as high crime levels, physical degradation and isolation, which reinforce problems of social exclusion – typifies such communities. However, these communities are often characterised by high levels of informal and voluntary social and economic action. The contribution of the third sector is likely to be particularly important, although the region lacks a strategy for its development.

A low level of educational attainment is a particular problem in the North East. The region performs poorly in compulsory education, has a weak take-up of post-age 16 education and training, as well as skill shortages, poor graduate retention, and comparatively low skill levels in the labour force. Obviously such factors are interrelated, but the task of separating cause and effect and developing an analysis of the particular nature of the region's problems and a strategy to address them, is a major challenge. Strong voices in the region, however, maintain that nationally determined policies often fail to capture the complexity and particularity of local problems (NEA, 2001).

The North East possesses a large number of communities suffering from multiple deprivation. Although economic problems are at the heart of these difficulties, they are also finding themselves increasingly socially, culturally and politically adrift from the mainstream. (It is notable that the region's record of poor electoral turnouts is a particular problem in disadvantaged communities.) Successive efforts to address the problems of these communities have failed. Tackling the problems of these communities is a massive task. It is likely to demand an intense application of resources, as well as new ways of involving local communities in their own management.

The role of regional strategies

There are at least a dozen regional strategies in operation in the North East, although the force of these varies considerably (see Chapter Twelve of this volume). Four strategies have had the greatest influence in the region. Firstly, the Regional Economic Strategy (RES) – prepared by the Regional Development Agency (RDA), One North East (ONE) – is at the centre of regional regeneration initiatives. As in other regions, the RES provides a framework for the action plans of ONE, and other bodies. As such it depends greatly on the cooperation of a wide range of bodies. The preparation of the strategy was heavily determined by statutory guidance provided by the Secretary of State, and lacks a strong analysis of the specific character of the North East's development problem. Moreover, the strategy labours to define a set of genuine priorities for the region's development, partly reflecting the range of competing interests involved in its preparation, as well as the absence of an overarching political authority. A feature of the RES has been the strong emphasis on Sub-Regional Partnerships (SRPs) for its implementation. For the period 2003/4 some three quarters of total resources are planned to be dispensed in this way, precluding the development of an explicit *regional* strategy.

The Regional Planning Guidance (RPG) has a longer standing strategy, with greater statutory force. The RPG was originally in the hands of local authorities, but since 2000 has been the responsibility of the voluntary North East Assembly (NEA). The RPG is closer to a genuine regional strategy, reflecting the slow pace and iterative nature of its drafting, established policy-making procedures and consolidation of past strategies. The RPG moves towards establishing real development priorities. For instance, it acknowledges the centrality of the Newcastle metropolitan region to the development of the wider North East. A relative weakness of the RPG, however, is that its preparation was largely separated from the preparation of the RES.

Of growing importance is the Regional Sustainable Development Framework (RSDF) developed in the North East by Sustaine, a body which brings together the NEA and the Government Office (GO), among others. In part, the RSDF is intended to bridge the gap between the RES and RPG. It lacks, however, any statutory basis. The RSDF has not gained the influence of its equivalent in the East Midlands (see Chapter Eleven of this volume), and remains a somewhat subsidiary, rather than central, element of policy in the region.

Of particular importance in the North East is the Single Programming Document (SPD), which allocates the £420 million that the region will receive from European Union (EU) structural funds in the period 2001-2005. The SPD is particularly important, because virtually the whole of the North East is eligible for EU structural funding. Much of the funding will be allocated by the SPD to activities specified in the RES. On the face of it, this suggests a high degree of integration between the two documents. In practice, however, this is not the case. The SPD is heavily influenced by the priorities of the European Commission (EC), which are adapted to conditions in the North East. These then need to fit with the priorities of RES, which are heavily determined by statutory guidance.

Despite the existence of several regional strategies, it is doubtful whether they yet add up to a coherent and united vision for the region, reflecting real regional priorities and based on wide debate. The existing strategies, however, do not demonstrate a strong set of priorities for the region's development. This highlights the absence of an overarching body with the authority and capacity to provide the necessary leadership in the developmental process. In the absence of this body, strategies tend to reflect local concerns, with a tendency to stress broad aspirations, rather than clearly defined priorities. The region remains heavily dependent on decisions taken at the national level, with most regional strategies being principally concerned with adapting national priorities to the regional context.

The new institutional arrangements in the North East

The institutional changes which occurred in the North East after 1997 built on a long history of regional institution building. For this reason, the changes after 1997 appeared as less of a revolution in the North East than they did elsewhere. Indeed, continuity was the order of the day. The first chair of the RDA was the former chief executive of the Northern Development Company, which, prior to 1997, existed to promote the region to mobile investors. Many other senior figures in the new organisational set-up were familiar figures from the region's 'economic development industry'. The region's local authorities also had a tradition of voluntary regional working, which meant that the new Regional Chamber arrangements built on existing practices and partnerships.

The existence of strong vested interests around the regional agenda could have generated scope for great dissension in this period of significant change. However, the new institutional arrangements emerged without provoking major conflict. This could be taken as evidence of the evolutionary character of change in the North East. The fact that this did not occur, in part, reflects the desire of the main regional actors to guard their reputation (real or otherwise) for cooperative working. The major stakeholders publicly acknowledge the success of the regional institutions, but privately some voice criticisms. For instance, some business leaders have complained that they are poorly represented in the new bodies, including the RDA, which is designed to be 'business-led'. This issue reached a head in late 2001, when new appointments were made to the board of ONE. A prominent local business figure was replaced, an event which sparked debate in the House of Commons. It is noteworthy, however, that the criticisms levelled at the new bodies concern representation and process, rather than the content of policies. Therefore, although the RES was subject to a wide formal consultation, it is less clear that this involved a wide debate about the region's development priorities. This should hardly be surprising given the absence of significant fora in which such a debate could take place and the central constraints on ONE, which have made the creation of distinctive regional strategy a serious challenge.

The early days of the NEA, established in 1999, were taken up with finding a structure acceptable to local authorities and to social partners in the region. In the period after 1999, however, the NEA undertook a number of distinctive initiatives. It assumed the tasks of a Regional Planning Body (RPB), with responsibility for the preparation of the RPG. It also took the lead in developing the *Case for the North East*, which outlined the region's claim for resources ahead of the Treasury's Comprehensive Spending Review in 2000. This document commanded wide support in the region. Although its direct impact on Treasury thinking was negligible, it contributed to an increase in resources available to RDAs (see Chapter Three of this volume). Its main impact within the region was to further fuel the debate about the alleged inequity of the region's public expenditure settlement (discussed later in this chapter). Another distinctive feature of the NEA has been its willingness to promote the debate about directly elected regional government. In late 2001, the NEA published a discussion paper, *The first English region* (NEA, 2001). In undertaking this initiative, the NEA was drawing on a comparatively long history of regionalist pressure in the North East. In this respect, the trajectory of the new regional bodies can only be properly understood in this context of evolving regionalism in the North East, in which existing arrangements are seen by some regional actors as a staging post to directly elected regional government.

The creation of the new regional institutions prompted a reaction on the part of regional stakeholders. A number of bodies altered their structures in the period after 1997 in order to improve their capacity to act at the regional level. Business organisations became much more engaged with regional policy, and more inclined to debate the prospects for future regionalism. Organisations, such as Northern Business Forum, have taken on a more direct representational role in regional institutions. Other business bodies, such as the Engineering Employers Federation, have devolved financial resources to support more regional working. In the period prior to the publication of the government's White Paper, business organisations such as the regional Confederation of British Industry (CBI), began a more systematic internal debate about regional governance. The voluntary sector, as in other regions, has established a regional structure, and its officers represent the view of the sector in existing bodies, and in debates about elected regional government. The quickening pace of regionalisation has placed new burdens on regional stakeholders, which find themselves called upon to participate in the policy-making process, but often lack the resources to do so. Few organisations currently have the capacity to make significant research-based inputs to regional policy making. (An exception is the regional TUC, which has sponsored a research project designed to improve its understanding of regional policy issues and its capacity to influence them.) It is partly for this reason, perhaps, that stakeholder organisations tend to stress procedural and representational issues, rather then profound disagreements with policy direction.

Although organisations are responding to the process of regionalisation, the enduring influence of local government should not be underestimated. Local authorities dominate the SRPs established by the RDA, to the frustration of other stakeholders, who express exasperation at local authority decision-making procedures. In Durham and Northumberland, the county councils are the dominant players. The use of SRPs reflects in part the limited capacity and resources that ONE has at its disposal, but also the outcome of lobbying by key local authorities eager to find a role for themselves in the new arrangements. In the broader debate about elected regional government, the counties, at times, strike a (muted) note of opposition to any form of change which signals their potential demise.

Until 2002, the North East was largely free of the major public controversies and conflicts that occurred in other regions, such as the East of England and West Midlands (see Chapters Five and Eight of this volume). However, those conflicts that did emerge into the public arena were themselves instructive. A good example is the dispute about the future of the region's two airports that occurred during the preparation of the RES. The dispute focused on whether the role of Teesside Airport was being downgraded in favour of Newcastle International Airport. The Teesside press presented the issue in terms of its airport being relegated to the role of a freight terminal. The draft RES had, in fact, recognised that Newcastle Airport stood a better chance of increasing the number of scheduled flights for the region – in which it is notably deficient – and sought to develop a strategy based on this. In the end, and in face of opposition from the media on Teesside especially, the proposal was dropped. Among other things, this episode demonstrated how the RDA lacked the capacity to overcome local parochialism in order to develop a regional strategy.

To date, no internal regional controversy has appeared more important to the main regional newspapers (notably *The Journal* and the *Northern Echo*) than the question of the regional allocation of public expenditure. Both newspapers regularly support the argument that the North East is disadvantaged by the operation of the Barnett Formula. The argument about the 'unfairness' of the formula lies at the heart of both papers' support for elected regional government, and is a driving force in the debate about regionalisation in the North East (see Chapter Fourteen of this volume). Regular stories appear in both papers' coverage of regional affairs about the North East 'losing out' in the face of central government decisions, or as a result of 'unfair' competition from Scotland and Wales. The basis for these claims is not always clear. For instance, it is axiomatic in this coverage that the North East suffers from the absence of dual carriageway on the A1 between Newcastle and Scotland, although rarely is evidence provided to suggest why this should be a priority for the region. Nevertheless, it appears as such in both the RES and RPG.

Civic regionalism

The North East is characterised by a relatively high level of civic regionalism. The Campaign for a Northern Assembly (CNA) was established in 1992, and played a large part in ensuring that the question of regional government was taken up and debated in the regional media. In 1999, the North East Constitutional Convention (NECC) was established by the Bishop of Durham. Inspired by the Scottish Constitutional Convention, if not exactly modelled on it, the NECC sought to broaden the debate about regionalism, to work toward a more detailed set of proposals on regional government, and to build wide agreement on the way forward (Tomaney, 2000). After 2000, the CNA and NECC formed a joint working party with the NEA to further the case for regional government. These developments, however, drew upon a longer gestation of regionalist sentiment.

Within the North East, the rise of regionalism was a feature of the period following 1979, and accompanied the development of Scottish nationalism (see Tomaney, 1999, for a fuller account). In fact, the origins of North East regionalism lie partly in the conflicts surrounding the Scotland Bill of 1978. Labour MPs in the North East of England had promoted an amendment to the Bill stipulating that a Scottish Assembly had to secure the support of 40% of eligible voters in a referendum. Put simply, key actors in the North East saw Scottish devolution as posing a basic threat to the region, while northern Labour MPs at that time feared a more powerful neighbour would easily win the struggle for investment and resources. Although the threat was seen in explicitly regional terms, the response was organised through parliament.

Thereafter, the North East region played a key role in debates about English regional government. At the end of the 1970s most economic and political interests in the North East regarded the idea of a powerful government in Edinburgh as a threat. This attitude gradually changed for a variety of reasons during the 1980s. The region struggled to cope with its marginal role in the UK political economy, illustrated by rapid deindustrialisation and its social fallout. It found itself politically and culturally at odds with Margaret Thatcher's supporters in 'Middle England'. The region's Labourist voting traditions were reinforced, and Scottish arguments about a democratic deficit began to resonate in the North East. Local authorities, trade unions and business, stimulated partly by European pressures, sought to cooperate and develop distinctive regional institutions (albeit with central government resources) in order to attract new industry to the region. At the same time, the region emphasised its special cultural identity and made claims for regional institutions that reflected such distinctiveness. Together, these conditions planted the seed for the emergence of a new regional politics. In particular, the North East remains the only English region where regionalism has been taken up as a central theme by the media.

Measures of public opinion tend to emphasise that the North East has both the strongest regional identity, and is the most inclined to support regional government. These indicators probably reflect the long-standing nature of the 'regional issue' in the North East. For 50 years the condition of the region has been a central focus of policy and media debate. This concentration on the regional problem has helped to reproduce a sense of regional identity, which draws upon and amalgamates various historical identities. These factors make it most likely that the North East will lead any further development of regionalisation in England.

References

Benneworth, P. and Charles, D.R. (1999) 'Human resources and sustaining competitive advantage in the North East pharmaceutical industry', *Northern Economic Review*, vol 29, pp 63-81.

Charles, D.R. and Benneworth, P. (1999) 'Plant closure and institutional modernisation: Siemens microelectronics in the North East', *Local Economy*, vol 14, no 3, pp 200-13.

Charles, D.R. and Benneworth, P. (2001) 'Situating the North East in the European Space Economy', in J. Tomaney and N. Ward (eds) *A region in transition: North East England at the millennium*, Aldershot: Ashgate, pp 24-60.

Hudson, R. (1989) *Wrecking the region*, London: Pion.

NEA (North East Assembly) (2001) *The First English Region*, Newcastle upon Tyne: NEA.

NEA (2000) *The case for the North East*, Newcastle upon Tyne: NEA.

Pike, A. (1999) 'The politics of factory closures and task forces in the North East of England', *Regional Studies*, vol 33, no 6, pp 567-75.

Pike, A. (2001) 'Corporate retreat and host economy abandonment in the era of the "globalisation" of capital: the case of "ManufacturingCo" in the North East region of England', *Capital and Class*, vol 74, pp 31-59.

Richardson, R., Bradley, D., Jones, I. and Benneworth, P. (1999) 'The North East', in M. Breheny (ed) *The people: Where will they work? Report of TCPA research into the changing geography of employment*, London: Town & Country Planning Association, pp 145-67.

Roberts, J. (2000) 'The knowledge economy in the North East: the role of business services', *Northern Economic Review*, vol 30, pp 17-34.

Stone, I. (2000) 'Universities – at the heart of regional development?', *Northern Economic Review*, vol 30, pp 69-93.

Tomaney, J. (1999) 'In search of English regionalism: the case of the North East', *Scottish Affairs*, vol 28, pp 62-82.

Tomaney, J. (2000) 'Democratically elected regional government in England: the work of the North East Constitutional Convention', *Regional Studies*, vol 34, no 4, pp 383-99.

Tomaney, J., Pike, A. and Cornford, J. (1999) 'Plant closure and the local economy: the case of Swan Hunter on Tyneside', *Regional Studies*, vol 33, no 5, pp 401-11.

ELEVEN

Regional strategy development in the East Midlands

Paul Foley

Introduction

In April 1999 the East Midlands Development Agency (EMDA) commenced operations, and discussions about the establishment of an East Midlands Regional Assembly (EMRA) were in full swing. The establishment of these two organisations has led to a great deal of change in the administrative structure and the nature of liaison between government and non-government organisations in the East Midlands. This chapter reviews some of the background activities that led to the creation of these two organisations. It describes how various organisations in the region were involved in shaping EMRA and EMDA, and how this process of consultation led to the creation of strategies to develop and shape the future of the region.

Unlike many other UK regions, regional thinking, liaison and strategies in the East Midlands were not well established prior to 1999. Many of the processes were therefore working with a blank sheet of paper that has enabled some interesting and significant activities to develop in the East Midlands that have not been observed elsewhere. This chapter examines current strategies and activities to promote regional development, first by examining the characteristics of the region and the resources available to the main strategic organisations. The second part of this chapter investigates the way in which institution building and liaison have taken place within the East Midlands. The third part examines the emergent approach to strategy development adopted by EMDA for regional development in conjunction with regional partners. The final part examines the Integrated Regional Strategy (IRS) approach developed by EMRA and the new forms of subregional partnership (SRP) that are being fostered to advance regional development.

The East Midlands

It is almost tradition that any examination of a region or the activities of regional administrative bodies has to include a review of the key characteristics of the region concerned. Far be it for this chapter to buck this trend. However, these figures can also be used to examine the magnitude of the regional

Table 11.1: East Midlands regional profile

Land area	15,627 sq km. 12% of England's land area. Third largest standard region in England. 80% of the region's land is agricultural.
Population	4.2 million. 7% of UK total.
Employment	2.049 million in 2001. 1.5% in agriculture, 29% in industry, 69.5% in services. 79.5% of people of working age are economically active.
Unemployment	3.3% claimant count rate, 4.9% ILO rate in 2001.
Dwellings	73% owner occupied. UK average 69%.
GDP	£50.9 billion in 1999. Per capita GDP 94% of UK average in 1998.

Sources: ONS (2001); DETR (1997); EMEDF (1997)

development task facing the Government Office for the East Midlands (GOEM), EMRA or EMDA, particularly when considering the limited resources which they have to influence regional development.

The East Midlands consists of the 45 (county, unitary and district) local authorities in the county areas of Derbyshire, Leicestershire, Lincolnshire, Northamptonshire and Nottinghamshire. It is a largely rural region occupying a central position within the country. It is also a very diverse region, stretching from the agricultural fenlands of the east coast, through the densely populated industrial areas in a swathe from Chesterfield to Northampton, and to the Peak District National Park in the West (Cambridge Econometrics, 1996). The region is decidedly average – ranking sixth of 12 regions in the UK, and 43rd of 77 regions in the EU.

The East Midlands is diverse, fairly productive and prosperous. It has significant strengths in textiles (Leicestershire, Nottinghamshire), engineering (Derbyshire, Leicestershire, Nottinghamshire), food and agriculture (Lincolnshire), and leather footwear and the financial services sector (Northamptonshire) (DETR, 1997). Parts of the region, especially in the northern coalfield areas, are affected by restructuring of traditional industries.

The East Midlands has not traditionally had a strong regional identity, a fact that was recognised by many local organisations in the consultation exercise undertaken prior to the establishment of EMDA (DETR, 1997). A Mori/ Economist survey undertaken in 1999 found that only the inhabitants of the East of England region identified less with their region than those in the East Midlands (17% and 31% respectively). Overcoming this problem and attracting inward investment is generally accepted as one of EMDA's core activities.

Resources for regional development are limited and this affects the ability of all agencies to influence development. Regional GDP was £50.9 billion in 1999 (ONS, 2001) and public expenditure in the East Midlands was around £14 billion. GOEM total expenditure in 1999/2000 was £392 million, increasing to £471 million in 2000 (GOEM, 2000, 2001). EMDA grant aid in 1999/2000 was £50 million, rising to £76 million in 2000 (EMDA, 2000a, 2001a).

This level of funding for the two key agencies fostering regional development represented 0.9% of regional GDP in 1999. For EMDA, charged with responsibility for regional economic development, it represented less than 0.1% of regional GDP. For this reason it was recognised at a very early stage in its development that EMDA would have to work closely in partnership with many other groups, such as EMRA, GOEM, local authorities and learning and skills councils to influence economic development and competitiveness (Wallace, 1998). This theme of liaison and partnership has been central in creating regional development policies, and it has received praise from the government (DETR, 2000a) and other observers (Roberts and Benneworth, 2001).

Institution building and liaison

Background to the development of strategies and strategic networks

Even before the publication of the White Paper outlining the development of Regional Development Agencies (DETR, 1997), a great deal of groundwork had been undertaken in the East Midlands to provide preparatory material and networks to assist the development of an RDA and a Regional Assembly.

The East Midlands Economic Development Forum (EMEDF) led much of this development work. It was established towards the end of 1996, stimulated by a Confederation of British Industry (CBI) report published in summer 1996 which called for people in the region to come together and form a multilateral group to look at economic development in the East Midlands (CBI, 1996). Its creation was very opportune and the existence of the EMEDF provided a natural focus for development activities when the RDA was first mooted.

The EMEDF consisted of a wide range of public and private sector organisations, such as CBI East Midlands, East Midlands Chambers of Commerce, East Midlands Training and Enterprise Councils, East Midlands Regional Local Government Association, East Midlands Universities Association and the TUC Midlands Region. They prepared a joint response to the government's proposals to establish RDAs (EMEDF, 1998a, 1998b; East Midlands Local Government Association, 1998). This activity led to the creation of a fairly strong regional partnership (not just local or subregional) prior to development activities (EMEDF, 1998c). Untangling how much of this activity was luck and how much was fuelled by the knowledge of a few key individuals who had access to Labour Party thinking about regional development has been impossible to discern. The Government Office (GOEM) also undertook several extensive reviews of economic and competitiveness issues in the years immediately preceding RDA development activities.

A further impact of the RDA and Regional Chamber development activities was the creation of a Rural Action Group for the region. It included representatives from local government, GOEM, the Countryside Commission, English Nature, the Ministry of Agriculture, Fisheries and Food (MAFF), NFU and many others.

All these activities demonstrate the stimulus to liaison and partnership that preceded the establishment of EMRA and EMDA. In some regions such links had a long history. In the East Midlands, as I have just described, many groups met formally for the first time to discuss key strategic issues (Foley, 1998). They were working with a 'blank sheet of paper' unencumbered by historic roles and animosities that have been evident in some other English regions. This feeling of synergy and democratic consultation was evident throughout the early development activities of both EMRA and EMDA.

In 1998 consultants undertook an independent economic assessment of current and future prospects for the East Midlands. Their report, commissioned in advance of mainstream EMDA activities by the East Midlands TEC/Chamber of Commerce Training and Enterprise Research Group and GOEM, was very advantageous for the newly created EMDA. EMDA commissioned GHK to undertake more analysis of issues facing the region while they were preparing their strategy.

The report, entitled *The East Midlands Regional Economic Assessment* (EMDA, 1999), highlighted future drivers for and barriers to change in the region, including:

• continued competition from globalisation;
• forecast of a short-term downturn in the UK economy;
• uncertain impact of European economic monetary union;
• capitalising on the knowledge economy;
• restructuring European and UK government funding and priorities.

The key implications for the regional agenda (noted in section 6) were:

• maintaining the diversity of the economic base;
• raising GDP and value added across the region;
• promoting, technology, innovation and research and development;
• strengthening clusters and inter-firm linkages;
• raising the skill level of the resident population;
• developing a coherent and integrated approach to physical development;
• developing and promoting a distinctive identity for the region.

These items were all carefully considered by EMDA in their early development activities, and many have become core components of their strategy for the region.

The strategy consultation process undertaken in the summer of 1999, after EMDA was first established on 1 April 1999, has been praised by many local and national observers as being an important element of the overall strategy development process in enhancing ownership and involvement by many partners throughout the region.

The draft strategy and other supporting documents were mailed to 8,000 businesses, agencies and local authorities across the region. It was also published on the EMDA website (www.emda.org.uk). A series of meetings were held with a range of different groups. Open invitation meetings were held in each of the region's five counties, there were meetings with seven established subpartnerships and a series of sector groups were facilitated by EMDA called 'Pathfinders to prosperity' (their views were published as a separate report).

Also of particular note, and another example of good practice, has been the positive partnership that has been established with the East Midlands Regional Assembly. Although the assembly led the preparation of an Integrated Regional Strategy (IRS) it has consulted widely with other organisations, most notably EMDA on issues related to economic regeneration. The IRS provides a broad framework for an extensive range of regional strategic planning, including transport, social and environmental issues. The EMDA strategy, which focuses on economic development issues, produced in tandem with the IRS, provides a key component in the economic input to the IRS.

Strategy and strategic plans in the East Midlands

The first EMDA strategy – *East Midlands prosperity through East Midlands people* – was widely distributed in a pack of materials containing four other documents. The main strategy document – 'Economic Development Strategy for the East Midlands 2000-2010' – provided a profile of the region. It identified key strengths (such as a varied and resilient industrial base, excellent centres of learning, outstanding natural assets, strong locational advantages and good bases for partnerships) and weaknesses (such as poor position in terms of per capita GDP, wide disparity of GDP patterns across the region, below average earnings and skills in manufacturing, overrepresentation in several sectors that are performing badly nationally).

Barriers to economic growth were identified together with key drivers for the regional economy (such as learning and skills, enterprise and innovation, information and communication technologies and promoting a climate for investment).

The initial strategy document was underpinned by a strong central vision that is regarded as "stretching but achievable" (EMDA, 2000c, p 6):

> By 2010, the East Midlands will be one of Europe's top twenty regions. It will be a place where people will want to live, work and invest because of:
>
> - our vibrant economy
> - our healthy, safe, diverse and inclusive communities
> - our quality environment

If nothing else this vision usually elicits a reaction. EMDA regarded it as hugely challenging, with the intention being to raise the sights of people in the East Midlands as much as it was to actually be achieved. Most observers felt it was very ambitious and probably unachievable, since many other areas in Europe would also be trying to advance their position. Nonetheless, it had the impact of broadening the horizons, from the parochial interests, that many people regarded as highly pervasive in the East Midlands.

The first draft of the strategy, circulated in July 1999, was thought by some observers and EMRA to be weak in the areas of sustainability and social inclusion. This was later revised to the satisfaction of most commentators. Most also agreed that the initial analysis was sound, well structured and comprehensive. The audit type approach, which the strategy adopted throughout, was thought to provide a clear framework that was easy to comprehend.

The strategy establishes five key strategic objectives (EMDA, 2000c, section 5.2). These are:

Objective 1 Learning and skills
Objective 2 Enterprise and innovation
Objective 3 ICT revolution
Objective 4 A climate for investment
Objective 5 Develop sustainable communities

Each objective was accompanied by key priorities and actions to enhance and achieve the objectives. Each section was accompanied by a set of commitments (identifying lead partners) and clear performance measures. These were praised by some as an example of good practice in showing progress and achieving 'early success'. The fact that each target had a specific lead partner was also welcomed as good practice. However, it was noted that EMDA was the lead partner for 22 of the 27 targets and the Regional Assembly and Regional Observatory were responsible for four of the remaining five 100 day targets.

Overall most groups felt that in the limited space and time for consultation available the contents of the initial strategy were well presented. Some observers felt that linking actions to objectives was a welcome improvement on previous strategies, but they suggested that little analysis had been undertaken of the actions that will 'make a difference' or those that will be most effective in achieving objectives. Some also pointed out the need to prioritise activities into those that will achieve low level and/or higher level objectives. It was generally acknowledged that there was a careful balance to be struck by EMDA between an emphasis on strategy and operations/action. Most felt that EMDA was just about striking the right balance at present.

Most observers found it difficult to find fault with the initial strategy. The identification of clusters of businesses which in policy terms are, or have the potential to be, of regional economic importance was thought to be sound. Skills issues were thought to have been well handled. The special report on the coalfield area addressed the particular needs of this northern part of the region. Proposals were made for the development of specific strategic sites identified through the planning process that meet business needs. In general the strategy was accepted as well drafted without enough detail to upset anyone unduly. While this may sound slightly critical it was generally regarded as a strength at this early stage of EMDA development.

EMDA have developed an incremental or emergent style of strategy development. Goals, achievements and feedback are carefully analysed on a regular basis (usually annual). This review process enables new opportunities or threats to be considered and action plans to be adjusted to better meet EMDA's strategic objectives. This emergent approach requires coordination

Figure 11.1: Interrelationship between EMDA strategic objectives

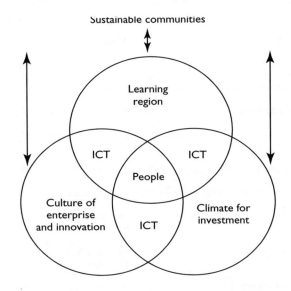

Source: EMDA (2000b, p 4)

and consultation. Meetings and papers are regularly circulated for consultation with all citizens and partners

For instance, the initial strategy (EMDA, 1999) was updated in May 2000 by the *Regional Delivery Plan 2000-2003* (EMDA, 2000b). This update followed a similar approach and structure to the initial strategy document. The interrelationship between the main themes of the strategy are presented in Figure 11.1.

Being the catalyst behind the strategy, EMDA regard a key part of their role as ensuring interconnections are made 'on the ground', through the delivery plan. This same diagram is used throughout the Action Plan with different themes taking the focal point (that is, replacing People at the centre of Figure 11.1), and others rotating around the outside, still showing overlap between all components. The five key priority areas (learning and skills, enterprise and innovation, ICT, climate for investment and sustainable communities) remain the same as those identified by the first EMDA strategy in 1999 (EMDA, 1999).

Each of the five priority areas has an objective encapsulated in a sentence or two, and more details about strategic themes related to the overall objective. For instance the learning and skills objective has three key strategic themes:

- skills;
- learning region;
- attainment in education.

Table 11.2: EMDA baseline data and targets for headline indicators

Headline indicator	Theme	Targets		1997	
		2010	2005	EM	UK
Per capita GDP (cf EU average) (%)	Baseline	111	104	98	102
ILO unemployment rate (cf national average)	Baseline	75	76	77.6	100
Economic activity rate	Investment climate	82	81	80.1	78.8
Foreign direct investment as a proportion of the UK total (%)	Investment climate	10	7.5	4.6	
Workforce qualified to NVQ3 or above (%)	Learning and Skills	50	45	40	43
Workforce qualified to NVQ4 or above (%)	Learning and Skills	27	24	21	24
Business starts per 10,000 residents	Enterprise and Innovation	40	38	36	39
% businesses surviving 3 years	Enterprise and Innovation	65	62	60	61
% businesses exporting	Enterprise and Innovation	4	2	1.5	1.4
% businesses trading electronically	ICT	20	10	4	8
% growth in employment in key targeted sectors **	ICT				
Crime per 100,000 residents (cf UK average)	Sustainable communities	*	8	9187	8841
% Residents in above average living conditions	Sustainable communities	*	*	55	55

* Target to be identified

** Targeted sectors to be identified

Source: EMDA (2000b, annex 4, p 60)

For each theme a list of between two and six commitments (objectives with an endpoint) and proposals (for consideration, no endpoint) are put forward with lead bodies clearly identified.

The May 2000 document also established clear targets and goals. These targets for 2005 and 2010 are presented in Table 11.2. Most have been disaggregated into indicators or variables (such as ILO unemployment rates) that can be clearly measured. These goals (subsequently called headline and pillar indicators by EMDA in their second revision [January 2001] of the initial strategy) also form the basis for the monitoring and evaluation of regional performance.

EMDA take responsibility for the collection of data for monitoring these indicators and therefore regional development progress. This is undertaken during January of each year. The East Midlands Observatory acts as one of the conduits through which the results of this exercise can be channelled, together with the results from the monitoring of other aspects of the IRS. The observatory website (www.eastmidlandsobservatory.org.uk) and newsletter are used for dissemination.

In line with EMDAs emergent strategic planning and review process a second action plan was distributed in January 2001, and during winter 2001 EMDA consulted on the third edition of the plan (Regional Priorities for Action 2002-03), which was published in 2002. As well as these annual revisions progress on the achievement of the regional priorities for action and on their ongoing evaluation is undertaken through a monthly update on the EMDA website (www.emda.org.uk).

Strategy development and liaison with partners

The main economic strategy development documents produced by EMDA have been broadly general in approach. However, they have produced additional documents that focus on specific industrial sectors and others that investigate particular localities or subregional areas. Implementation of this dual approach (thematic and geographical) is difficult to coordinate. In general most of EMDA's partners that have policy making powers or resources (such as local authorities or GOEM) represent specific geographical areas rather than thematic interests. Recent activities have focused more on specific geographical areas, or areas with specific problems (coalfields and textiles), rather than themes or industries.

This emphasis has probably been prompted by two factors, one local and one national. At the local level the positive relationship established between EMDA, the East Midlands Regional Assembly and other partners in developing an IRS has been important in providing a broad framework for an extensive range of regional strategy development activities. It has also been important in offering these groups a regular forum to meet and discuss key strategic issues.

EMRA is leading the preparation of the IRS and the EMDA strategy is a key component in the economic input to the IRS, which is widely drawn and includes social and environmental issues. The IRS is similar in wording to the Regional Planning Guidance (RPG) and takes account of issues raised in the RPG. The IRS takes account of sustainability issues. 'Nesting' the EMDA strategy within the IRS has been seen as a particular strength and a means of ensuring the inclusion of environmental, sustainability, competitiveness and urban issues and also in ensuring consistency between economic development and other strategies produced by EMDA and EMRA.

The second factor has been government's promotion of subregional strategic partnerships, particularly for housing development and economic regeneration (DETR, 2000b). Consequently subregional strategic partnerships (SSPs) have become a key component for economic development in the East Midlands. During 2000 EMDA published with GOEM a discussion paper on SRPs in the East Midlands. In general there was a healthy level of support for strategic partnerships at subregional level. There were some conflicting views about the geographical coverage of such partnerships, but there was support for building on existing partnerships rather than creating new ones.

In spring 2001 a further document was published in close consultation with the East Midlands Regional Assembly that offered guidance and requested proposals for SSPs by the end of June 2001. The document suggested recognition by EMDA and GOEM of the importance of SSPs would be important in "helping to shape the direction of the East Midlands' strategy in the years to come and in prompting partners to bring about change on the ground. This will require investment by many partners to ensure that SSPs are able to fulfil their role effectively" (EMDA, 2001b). The document indicated that this could represent a major change in the delivery of economic development activities in the East Midlands when it stated that

> In the longer term EMDA is committed in principle to giving SSPs greater responsibility, as they prove their added value. EMDA's aim is to make funds available to SSPs from 2002/3 to support the implementation of sub-regional strategies against agreed objectives and outcomes, subject to agreement from Government and to the partnerships proving that they have the capacity to take on the role. (EMDA, 2001b)

The first of the East Midlands' SSPs were approved in November 2001. However, it remains to be seen whether they will represent a major change in the way economic development activity and funding is undertaken in the region.

Conclusions

Despite having been a region with a poorly developed regional identity, perspective and organisations prior to 1999, the East Midlands has developed a relatively sophisticated approach to regional development. Consultation, liaison and partnership have been central in creating regional development strategies and this more democratic approach has received praise from government and other observers (DETR, 2000a; Roberts and Benneworth, 2001).

Central to the development of the region has been the development of an IRS. This has been led by the East Midlands Regional Assembly in partnership with many other organisations, most notably EMDA on issues related to economic regeneration. The IRS provides a broad framework for an extensive range of regional strategic planning, including transport, social and environmental issues. The EMDA strategy, which focuses on economic development issues, has been produced in tandem with the IRS. This strategy, that also acknowledges the requirements of RPG, has been important in providing a framework for EMDA, local authorities and other groups to develop strategies that complement the main IRS. This coordinated approach represents a major advance in regional planning and development in the East Midlands.

EMDA and EMRA regard a key part of their catalytic role as ensuring there is partnership and interconnections at ground level that complement the objectives of the regional development strategy. There has been a good level of support for SSPs, and in the past year several have reached an advanced stage of development. In November 2001 three had their subregional development plans approved by EMDA. It is possible that in the future these SRPs could become a new form of governance, since EMDA has suggested that, subject to approval from government, they will make funds available to these SRPs in 2002/3. This could represent yet another significant change in the structure of governance for regional development in the East Midlands.

References

Cambridge Econometrics (1996) *Regional economic prospects*, Cambridge: Cambridge Econometrics.

CBN (Confederation of British Industry) (1996) *Business Agenda*, London: CBI.

DETR (Department for the Environment, Transport and the Regions) (1997) *Building partnerships for prosperity: Sustainable growth, competitiveness and employment in the English regions*, Cm 3814, London: The Stationery Office.

DETR (2000a) *Regional Development Agency strategies: All systems go*, Press Release, 1 July.

DETR (2000b) *National strategy for neighbourhood renewal: Report of Policy Action Team 7*, London: DETR.

EMDA (East Midlands Development Agency) (1999) *East Midlands regional economic assessment*, Nottingham: EMDA.

EMDA (2000a) *Annual Report 1999/2000*, Nottingham: EMDA.

EMDA (2000b) *Regional Delivery Plan 2000-2003*, Nottingham: EMDA.

EMDA (2000c) *East Midlands prosperity through East Midlands people*, Nottingham: EMDA.

EMDA (2001a) *Annual Report 2000/2001*, Nottingham: EMDA.

EMDA (2001b) *Sub-regional strategic partnerships*, Nottingham: EMDA.

EMEDF (East Midlands Economic Development Forum) (1997) 'Towards a Regional Development Agency for the East Midlands', Nottingham: EMEDF.

EMEDF (1998a) *RDA bulletin*, February, Nottingham: EMEDF.

EMEDF (1998b) *RDA bulletin*, June, Nottingham: EMEDF.

EMEDF (1998c) *Towards a RDA for the East Midlands: Consultation events report*, Nottingham: EMEDF.

EMRLGA (East Midlands Regional Local Government Association) (1998) *Establishing an East Midlands Chamber*, March: Melton Mowbray: EMRLGA.

Foley, P. (1998) 'The impact of the Regional Development Agency and Regional Chamber in the East Midlands', *Regional Studies*, vol 32, no 8, pp 777-82.

GOEM (Government Office for the East Midlands) (2000) *Annual Report 1999/ 2000*, Nottingham: GOEM.

GOEM (2001) *Annual Report 2000/2001*, Nottingham: GOEM.

ONS (Office for National Statistics) (2001) *East Midlands: Region in figures*, Winter, London: ONS.

Roberts, P. and Benneworth, P. (2001) 'Pathways to the future? An initial assessment of RDA strategies and their contribution to integrated regional development', *Local Economy*, vol 16, no 2, pp 142-59.

Wallace, D. (1998) *Towards an RDA for the East Midlands*, Presentation to East Midlands branch of the Regional Studies Association, 27 May, Northampton.

TWELVE

The problem of regional governance

John Tomaney

Introduction

The debate about the reform of the governance of the English regions has tended to hinge on two related assumptions. The first of these is that an extensive tier of government exists within the English regions in the form of a plethora of government departments, quangos and other bodies. To a greater or lesser degree, the policies and actions of these agencies are assumed to provide the framework for regional development. The second assumption is that the fragmented structure of bodies at the regional level contributes to a failure of governance which produces poor public policy outcomes (see NECC, 1999; NEA, 2001). The fragmented character of the policy-making process – together with arguments about the democratic deficit – are the lynchpin of the case for the reform of regional governance in England. Advocates of elected Regional Assemblies, however, have tended to assume rather than demonstrate the existence of governance failure in the English regions. Recently the structure and performance of this existing tier of regional governance has come under more scrutiny in the light of evolving debates about regional governance (for an earlier analysis of regional government, see Hogwood, 1982).

This chapter aims to contribute some empirical detail to the debate about regional governance. It seeks to describe the evolving pattern of governance in the English regions, highlighting emerging and likely future trends. It draws on a detailed study of the patterns and processes of regional governance in North East England[1]. Firstly, however, it begins with an examination of some recent contributions to the debate about regional governance in England.

Joining up: governance failure in the English regions?

> ... initiative de coordination gouvernementale pour simplifier la vie des personnes et des entreprises. (French rendering of 'joined-up' government, cited in *The Guardian*, 13 March 2001)

The alleged deficiencies of governance in the English regions were the subject of research commissioned by the Cabinet Office, which examined the role of central government at the local and regional level. The background to the study carried out by the Performance and Innovation Unit (PIU, 2000) was the government's concern to achieve 'joined-up' government; that is to improve the capacity of government to address strategic, cross-cutting issues and promote innovation in the development of policy and in the delivery of the government's objectives (Cabinet Office, 1999). More specifically, as far as the role of central government in the regions is concerned, a particular issue arises as a result of the proliferation of Area-Based Initiatives (ABIs). These are generally concerned with the renewal of disadvantaged neighbourhoods (or combating 'social exclusion'), but cover a range of interrelated policy areas including employment, health and education[2]. Underlying the PIU (2000) report is the assumption that a greater effort needs to be made to integrate these different policy initiatives in the name of 'joined-up' government.

The PIU report painted a rather damning picture of how the plethora of ABIs were poorly integrated, leading to a waste of local efforts. At the same time ABIs were not coordinated with mainstream government programmes[3]. The planning requirements of mainstream programmes themselves are problematic because they specify detailed action in accordance with the separately conceived interests of central government departments that are tightly specified in Public Service Agreements (PSAs) regulated by the Treasury (PIU, 2000, para 2.21). This problem was described by the PIU's informants, who were responsible for the delivery of policy on the ground. Thus, according to one local authority chief executive, "a lot of the lack of co-ordination is simply reflecting the separate silos at the centre" (PIU, 2000, p 110)[4]. The report argued that these problems were compounded by the fact that the government tends to demand short-term 'outputs' from its initiatives rather than long-term 'outcomes'.

In addition, the PIU report found that a number of officials 'on the ground' doubt how well matched central government initiatives are to local circumstances. For instance:

> Several local authority chief executives argued that education policy-making had become too centralised and insufficiently sensitive to variations in local circumstances. Some took the view that recent increases in funding for schools would, in their locality, have been better spent on dealing with factors outside school which contributed to poor educational attainment. (PIU, 2000, para 2.37; see also NEA, 2001)

Similar observations were made about the role of the Ministry of Agriculture, Fisheries and Food (MAFF). Good links between MAFF and other government activities are deemed to be of greater importance in an age where the emphasis is shifting from agricultural subsidies to sustainable regeneration of rural communities, which requires more integrated local and regional policy strategies (PIU, 1999). Recently similar arguments have been made in relation to health policy, especially public health. Plowden and Greer (2001) have argued that successful public health policies depend heavily on "joining-up" government; that is, using and modifying policies for housing, transport, education, social care or anything else to improve health outcomes, actions best undertaken at the regional level. Among the barriers to such outcomes are performance management, numerical targets, PSAs, privatisation, and other ideas aimed at improving 'delivery', but which further fragment policy, narrowing managerial focus on efficiency rather than effectiveness, and making it harder to create public sector synergies (see also Ross and Tomaney, 2001). These arguments form the case for greater policy integration and more local design of policy. In part, they provide the background to the preparation by the government of a White Paper on regional governance in 2001-02.

The main outcome of the PIU's study of regional governance was a move on the part of central government to strengthen regional Government Offices (GOs). The Conservative government established GOs in 1994, to give a better focus to central government activity in the regions. By 1999, they included the regional activities of the Department of Environment, Transport and the Regions (DETR), Department of Trade and Industry (DTI), and the Department of Education and Employment (DEE). The mission of GOs is "to achieve high and stable levels of growth and employment, and to build an inclusive and prosperous society that can develop in a sustainable way" (RCU, 2001). As a result of the PIU's recommendations, the GOs were expanded to include regional activities of other departments (see Tomaney, 2000, 2001 for an account of this process) which, by December 2001, included the English regional services of the following departments:

- Trade and Industry (DTI);
- Education and Skills (DES);
- Transport, Local Government and the Regions (DTLGR);
- Environment, Food and Rural Affairs (DEFRA);
- The Home Office;
- Culture, Media and Sport (DCMS);
- Health (DoH);
- The newly formed Department for Work and Pensions.

In addition, as a result of planned changes to the NHS, the Health Secretary, Alan Milburn announced in 2001 that public health officers would be based in GOs with, for the first time, a mandate to integrate policy (see Tomaney, 2001).

In order to oversee the GOs, the PIU recommended the establishment of a Regional Coordination Unit (RCU). The RCU was established in 2000 and, following the General Election of 2001, was located in the Office of the Deputy Prime Minister in the Cabinet Office. The main focus of the RCU is to oversee ABIs, to promote closer links between government activity in the regions and the centre, and to manage the GOs.

A further significant step in strengthening the apparatus of regional governance was the creation of Regional Development Agencies (RDAs) in 1999. The significance of RDAs, for the purposes of our analysis, is that they brought together into one organisation a number of hitherto separate bodies, including regional development organisations, regional offices of English Partnerships and parts of the Rural Development Commission. As such the creation of

RDAs represented an effort to 'join-up' previously separate areas of activity. Since their inception in 1999, the resources available to RDAs, and the autonomy to act according to their own priorities, has been increased. However, the boards of RDAs are appointed by the Secretary of State and the activities of RDAs are set in the context of 'outcome targets' agreed with the DTI (see Tomaney, 2000, 2001 for more detailed accounts of the evolving structure of RDAs).

The creation and strengthening of GOs and RDAs are the clearest examples of recent attempts to alter the governance of the English regions in order to improve their social and economic well-being. Certainly they have attracted most attention from academic analysts. However, the findings of the PIU study, although primarily focused on the difficulties of operating area based initiatives, point to a wider problem of governance of the English regions. GOs are but one – albeit important – actor at the regional level. In fact the governance of the English regions is characterised by a plethora of agencies, which together provide the framework for regional development. However, this structure of regional governance reproduces on a larger scale the fragmentation identified by the PIU as a characteristic of the departments of central government. The following section looks into this wider structure of governance, attempting to chart its evolution and performance.

The pattern of regional governance

This section reports the results of an audit of regional institutions in North East England, based on interviews with directors of regional bodies and surveys of official literature[5]. The pattern of regional government in the North East, and the connections between departments and agencies, are illustrated in Figure 12.1. The figure shows the complex wiring of regional government that already exists. Focusing only on the main bodies with an explicit regional remit, it shows that there are at least 21 agencies of one type or another operating at the regional level. These bodies are sponsored, (sometimes via national quangos) by a variety of central government departments. Figure 12.1 demonstrates the multiplicity of lines of accountability connecting central government policy with regional 'outcomes', giving an insight into the problem of policy 'silos' described earlier.

Figure 12.1 also draws attention to the contribution of central government departments, via agencies at the regional level, to a variety of regional strategies, indicating the large number or organisations contributing to regional strategies, and suggesting further the complexity of regional governance. Recent years have seen a proliferation of regional strategies, of which only the main ones are visible in the illustration. A fuller list of regional strategies is reported in Table 12.1. There are currently some 12 regional strategies in the North East, which are largely replicated in other regions. These strategies vary significantly in terms of their legal status. Regional Planning Guidance (RPG), for instance, has a statutory authority, whereas the Regional Cultural Strategy currently represents little more than an agreed set of aspirations. Most of the regional

Figure 12.1: Governance of North East England

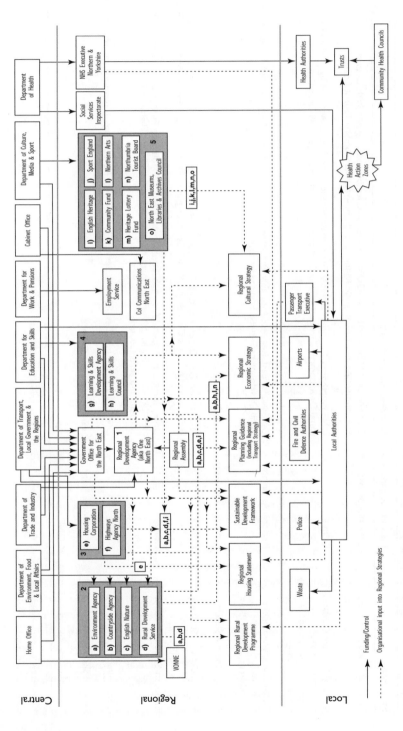

© Centre for Urban and Regional Development Studies, University of Newcastle upon Tyne, 2001 (version 4)

Table 12.1: Regional strategies

Strategy	Leading organisation	Key regional partners*
Regional Economic Strategy	ONE North East	Government Office North East (GONE), Regional Assembly, Learning and Skills Council, Environment Agency, Countryside Agency, Northern Arts, Northumbria Tourist Board.
Regional Planning Guidance • Transport Strategy • Spatial Development Strategy • Waste Strategy	GONE	ONE North East, Regional Assembly, Environment Agency, Countryside Agency, English Nature, Rural Development Service, Housing Corporation, English Heritage, NHS Executive.
Sustainable Development Framework • Biodiversity Action Plans	Regional Assembly	ONE North East, Regional Assembly, Environment Agency, Countryside Agency, English Nature, Rural Development Service, English Heritage.
Regional Housing Statement	Housing Corporation	GONE.
Regional Cultural Strategy	GONE	ONE North East, English Heritage, Community Fund, Heritage Lottery Fund, North East Museums, Libraries and Archives Council (NEMLAC), Sport England, Northern Arts, Northumbria Tourist Board.
European Structural Funds	GONE	ONE North East, Regional Assembly, Environment Agency, Community Fund, Heritage Lottery Fund, NEMLAC, Sport England, Northern Arts, Northumbria Tourist Board, Highways Agency, Learning and Skills Council.
Rural Development Programme	GONE	ONE NorthEast, Rural Development Service, Environment Agency, English Nature, Countryside Agency.
Regional Skills Strategy	ONE North East	Learning and Skills Council.
Regional Crime Reduction Strategy	GONE	

NB: Indicative list of main regional partners. Other partners, such as local government, are not listed.

Source: Tomaney and Humphrey (2000 I a)

strategies listed in Table 12.1 were introduced in the period after 1997. They represent an explicit effort on the part of central government to impose greater coordination of the design and execution of public policy at the regional level. Table 12.1 indicates the main organisations, which make inputs to the regional strategies. In addition to those listed, there exists the possibility of additional strategies being formulated, such as Regional Public Health and Social Care Strategies (as a result of announcements by the Secretary of State for Health), and River Management Strategies (developed by the Environment Agency and partners in some regions), all of which draw on the activities of a range of regional actors.

Regionalisation in practice: the case of cultural policy[6]

Figure 12.1 attempts to group some agencies, in part according to the degree to which they have regular contact in the preparation of regional strategies. For instance, one group (5) includes the main bodies (for example, English Heritage, Northern Arts, Northumbria Tourist Board, among others), who, in addition to the GO and RDA, make a significant contribution to the Regional Cultural Strategy. The regional significance of cultural activities is manifold. Cultural activities are central to the quality of life in all regions, but reflect diverse heritages and identities. At the same time, cultural, tourism and sporting businesses and creative industries make a very significant contribution to the economic and social regeneration of regions, and different natural and cultural assets present regionally varied economic opportunities. Tourism's potential contribution to income generation and employment is particularly important. For the government, cultural activities can also play a part in tackling social exclusion.

The preparation and development of the Regional Cultural Strategy is the responsibility of Culture North East (the North East Regional Cultural Consortium), which was established by the DCMS to coordinate cultural and creative interests in the North East. Regional Cultural Consortiums were established in each of the English regions in 1999. The Board of Culture North East is made up of representatives from archives, arts, heritage, libraries, museums, sport, tourism, local authorities, the creative industries, the RDA and higher education. The Regional Cultural Strategy seeks to provide a framework for the actions of a range of other bodies, while at the same time seeking to complement the range of other strategies that are concerned with regional development (see Figure 12.2).

The organisations contributing to the production of the Regional Cultural Strategy are varied in character but in some notable cases altered their structures in the period after 1997 in order to better engage with the process of regionalisation. A good example of this process is English Heritage, which, after 1997, made its boundaries coterminous with those of the GO region and also devolved some budgets and decision making to the regional level. It remains, however, the regional office of a national non-departmental public body, sponsored by the DCMS, whose national governing board is appointed

Figure 12.2: Regional Cultural Strategy and its linkages with other regional activities in the North East

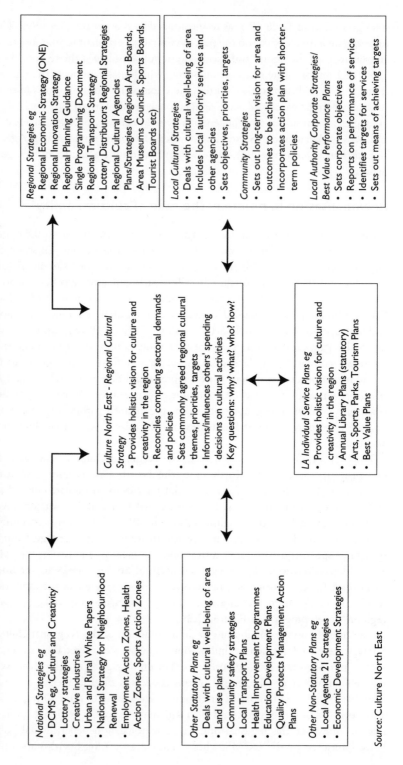

Regional Strategies eg
- Regional Economic Strategy (ONE)
- Regional Innovation Strategy
- Regional Planning Guidance
- Single Programming Document
- Regional Transport Strategy
- Lottery Distributors Regional Strategies
- Regional Cultural Agencies Plans/Strategies (Regional Arts Boards, Area Museums Councils, Sports Boards, Tourist Boards etc)

Local Cultural Strategies
- Deals with cultural well-being of area
- Includes local authority services and other agencies
- Sets objectives, priorities, targets

Community Strategies
- Sets out long-term vision for area and outcomes to be achieved
- Incorporates action plan with shorter-term policies

Local Authority Corporate Strategies/ Best Value Performance Plans
- Sets corporate objectives
- Reports on performance of service
- Identifies targets for services
- Sets out means of achieving targets

Culture North East - Regional Cultural Strategy
- Provides holistic vision for culture and creativity in the region
- Reconciles competing sectoral demands and policies
- Sets commonly agreed regional cultural themes, priorities, targets
- Informs/influences others' spending decisions on cultural activities
- Key questions: why? what? who? how?

LA Individual Service Plans eg
- Provides holistic vision for culture and creativity in the region
- Annual Library Plans (statutory)
- Arts, Sports, Parks, Tourism Plans
- Best Value Plans

National Strategies eg
- DCMS eg, 'Culture and Creativity'
- Lottery strategies
- Creative industries
- Urban and Rural White Papers
- National Strategy for Neighbourhood Renewal
- Employment Action Zones, Health Action Zones, Sports Action Zones

Other Statutory Plans eg
- Deals with cultural well-being of area
- Land use plans
- Community safety strategies
- Local Transport Plans
- Health Improvement Programmes
- Education Development Plans
- Quality Protects Management Action Plans

Other Non-Statutory Plans eg
- Local Agenda 21 Strategies
- Economic Development Strategies

Source: Culture North East

by the Secretary of State. Another example is the North East Museums, Libraries and Archives Council (NEMLAC), the result of a merger in 2000 of the regional museums service and the regional library service. NEMLAC was created to better integrate activities at the regional level. The bulk of its funding, however, comes from Resource, the national council for museums, libraries and archives, a body sponsored by the DCMS. These examples are part of a broad trend toward regionalisation that can be identified across the range of organisations represented in Figure 12.1, albeit one in which ultimate decision making remains with national organisations.

However, the regionalisation trend is by no means a universal one. A counter example from the cultural field was the decision of the Arts Council of England (ACE) to abolish local authority dominated Regional Arts Boards (RABs). In an announcement in mid-March 2001, ACE announced plans to abolish the ten RABs in England, by merging them with ACE. RABs currently make regional arts policy, and dispense arts funding. (The RAB in the North East [and Cumbria] is Northern Arts, which has its origins in the North East Arts Association, founded by the poet Basil Bunting in the 1960s. It has a board dominated by local authority representatives, but 80% of its income comes from ACE.) The proposal was to create a single, new arts development organisation for the arts in all of England, by uniting the 11 organisations and constituting the 'arts funding system' into a single, new Arts Council of England[7].

In general though, since 1997, organisational change in the field of cultural policy has been in the direction of greater regionalisation, a process that was largely welcomed by actors in the region. However, the outcomes of recent changes fall far short of 'joined-up' regional governance. As noted previously, the Regional Cultural Strategy does not carry statutory force. Its effectiveness is entirely dependent on the actions of a number of organisations with separate budgets and lines of accountability, which are determined by national bodies.

The DCMS identified the scale of the problem in a paper it published in 1998. The paper reviewed regional cultural provision in the light of the government's then Comprehensive Spending Review. It concluded that:

> [T]he importance of the regions under the Government's new constitutional agenda, and recognition of the economic importance of DCMS sectors, highlight the fragmented nature of the administration of DCMS sectors in the regions, and the fact that many relatively minor decisions, affecting both Lottery and grant-in-aid, are still taken at the national level. The work of the cultural agencies in the regional context is both overlapping and complementary. They already share the cultural objectives of promoting access, pursuing excellence and innovation, nurturing educational opportunity and fostering creative industries.... Yet as small fragmented bodies they are often constrained from turning these shared objectives into joint practical action. (DCMS, 1998)

Many senior figures involved in the cultural sector in the North East would agree with this analysis. Regional Cultural Strategies represent only a small step toward addressing this situation. In the same 1998 discussion paper, DCMS proposed the creation of new cultural bodies that could exercise executive functions for grant-in-aid and lottery money, involving "the distribution of a considerable proportion of grant-in-aid to regional bodies". These bodies could "act as a strategic planning body for the interests it represented and maintain relationships with regional funding partners". Such an agency was envisaged as having at its core the RABs, area museums councils and regional library functions, funded by DCMS. It also suggested the regional activities of English Heritage and Sport England as possible candidates for inclusion. Although these proposals were not acted upon, they point to outstanding issues and would gain some support from actors in the cultural arena in the North East.

Broader regionalisation

The issues that I have described as affecting the cultural sector can be identified in the other policy subsectors highlighted in Figure 12.1. In each case, the processes of regionalisation are underway, albeit with enduring central control. In the environment sector a number of organisations are addressing the implications of regionalisation for their structures and practices. For instance, English Nature increased its regional research and policy capacity in 2001. The Highways Agency made its 'Network Strategy Division' coterminous with GO boundaries in order to facilitate their involvement in regional transport planning in 2001. As part of its five yearly financial, management and policy review the Environment Agency announced it would review its regional operations in light of the government's evolving regional policy. Most organisations, in order to make their boundaries coterminous with those of GOs (and RDAs), are increasing their capacity to engage in regional policy making. The stimulus for this is the growth of regional strategy making. This is not a universal or uncontested process, but it did appear to be the dominant one in the period 1997-2001[8]. In most cases those involved in regional agencies – including those heavily dependent on national decision making and budget procedures – accept the merits of more integrated regional structures. Indeed, there was great enthusiasm for improved regional working and expectation that the process was likely to go further. However, most believed that there is some way to go before genuine integration is achieved at the regional level and expressed scepticism about the real commitment of actors in central government to follow the process of regionalisation to its logical conclusion.

The problem of regional governance

A lack of joined-up government has been assumed to be an important aspect of the problem of governance in the English regions. Our survey of regional agencies reveals that there is an empirical basis for this assumption. The research reported here has demonstrated a slow regionalisation of governance in England since 1997, but one which falls short of genuine integration. One danger of the situation that had developed by the end of 2001 was that a high level of enthusiasm for regional working could be dissipated because of growing frustration with the limited forms of regionalisation that had been established.

The fractured character of regional structures was only one factor at play in frustrating efforts to create 'joined-up' regional policy. However, it interacts with, and contributes to, other problems in the system of regional governance. One factor raised repeatedly in interviews with regional directors was the lack of an authoritative and overarching policy framework at the regional level, which could guide the activities of agencies. In this context, each agency tends to approach regional strategy making in terms of the opportunities that they present for their own organisation. Regional directors themselves regarded this as a reversal of the ideal situation, where generally agreed regional priorities should guide the activities of regional agencies. Among regional directors in the North East, there was a working assumption that such leadership would be given by an elected Regional Assembly. For instance, one regional director of a traditionally centralised non-departmental public body said:

> "From my perspective we need to grasp the nettle and develop some innovative ideas about the way forward. The only way that will come is if the Regional Assembly actually tasks certain groups and certain people with pieces of work. If I were tasked by a Regional Assembly to do something I could say 'we've been asked to do something', I could go back to my organisation and say: 'we've been asked to take a lead on this, is this something we can do?' I'm quite sure they'd be supportive." (quoted in Tomaney and Humphrey, 2001a, p 25)

The need for an overarching regional vision that can unite diverse – and at times disparate – planning efforts has also been stressed by the Local Government Association, Town and Country Planning Association, the Royal Town Planning Institute, the Council for the Protection of Rural England, as well as the Sustainable Development Commission. It was also a theme of Peter Mandelson's pronouncements on regional government in 2001. Mandelson has argued, for instance:

> By introducing a level of political accountability and democratic scrutiny, a new regional authority would provide a stronger sense of vision and leadership for the North East. They would provide a focus for disparate departmental initiatives and resources. And the authority could win consent for public investment in infrastructure, generating the human and social capital that is necessary to sustain a high enterprise regional economy. In short, a regional authority would deliver better government by providing a strong, clear, authentic voice of the people, and of the interests it is representing. A regional authority, as I envisage such a body is a strategist, galvaniser, advocate and manager rolled into one. (Mandelson, 2001)

This connects the issue of the structures of improved governance with the issues of *democratic government* (see Marquand and Tomaney, 2001). A regional body capable of undertaking the role ascribed by Mandelson is likely to require the legitimacy that can only be derived from being democratically elected. It is for this reason that debate about Regional Assemblies increasingly is central to the debate about how to improve subnational public policy outcomes.

Notes

[1] This chapter is based on research, conducted with Lynne Humphrey, and commissioned by the NEA as part of its contribution to the government's deliberations on regional government in England (see Tomaney and Humphrey, 2001a, 2001b). We are grateful to Stephen Barber of the NEA for assistance, and to John Adams of the Institute of Public Policy Research and Mark Sandford of the Constitution Unit for comments on the research findings.

[2] Examples of ABIs include: Health Action Zones, Employment Action Zones, Education Action Zones, Sure Start, Single Regeneration Budget and New Deal for Communities.

[3] One effect of the proliferation of ABIs and lack of oversight in relation to them was revealed in a study conducted in Sheffield in 1997, which demonstrated, among other things, that projects could be funded several times through different ABIs in support of the same outputs (PIU, 2000).

[4] The general thrust of the PIU's analysis of the fractured nature of regional governance and the inefficiencies it generates, is endorsed by a number of other sources. For instance, the Local Government Association (LGA) conducted its own inquiry into regional government. The witnesses to LGA's 'hearing' emphasised the problems arising from the absence of key departments from GOs, and the uneven capacity of GOs to engage as a genuine partner with local and regional organisations (LGA, 2000, para 45).

[5] These interviews have focused on bodies with an explicit regional focus. There are many other 'quangos' in the region, which we have not looked at in this study. For a review of the broader picture of the 'quango state' in the region see Robinson et al (2000), who raise important questions about the democratic accountability of these bodies.

[6] For more detailed analysis of the cultural sector (and other sectors) see Tomaney and Humphrey (2001a, 2001b)

[7] It is worth noting that in its initial announcement the ACE suggested that its proposal commanded wide support in the regions. It rapidly emerged that this was far from the case. Among the first to condemn the proposal were the London Mayor, Ken Livingstone and the chair of the London Assembly, Trevor Phillips. Members of Parliament, the RABs themselves, and other actors in the regions (notably Regional Assemblies) also

opposed the changes. In the face of this opposition, the ACE moderated its proposals, but ultimately ensured the abolition of the RABs.

[8] Previous studies of regional government in England (for example, Hogwood, 1982) have emphasised the lack of coterminosity between the boundaries of government departments and agencies in England. As part of the *Modernising government* agenda, the Labour government made the achievement of coterminosity a policy target. To wit:

> [W]orking to align the boundaries of public bodies. More than 100 different sets of regional boundaries are used in England alone. This complicates administration, reduces efficiency and frustrates joined up government. It also confuses the public. Wherever possible, boundaries should coincide with local authority boundaries at local level, and with Government Office regions' boundaries at regional level. The Government will work from a presumption that geographical boundaries should be aligned in this way whenever public bodies next review their administrative, managerial or delivery arrangements and structures. We will only make exceptions when there are strong over-riding considerations, for example where we have already committed ourselves as a result of recent reviews. We expect all newly created bodies to aim to meet these requirements from the outset and will review progress in 2002 (Cabinet Office, 1999, para 23).

References

Cabinet Office (1999) *Modernising Government*, Cm 4310, London: Stationery Office.

DCMS (Department for Culture, Media and Sport) (1998) *The Comprehensive Spending Review: A new approach to investment in culture* (now available at www.culture.gov.uk/role/).

Harding, A. (2000) *Is there a 'missing middle' in English governance?*, London: New Local Government Network.

Hogwood, B. (1982) *Regional Government in England*, London: Unwin.

LGA (Local Government Association) (2000) *Regional variation: Report of the LGA's learning on the regions*, London: LGA.

Marquand, D. and Tomaney, J. (2001) 'Regional government and sustainability: taking devolution in England forward', *New Economy*, vol 8, no 1, pp 36-41.

Mandelson, P. (2001) 'The state of the English regions', Keynote address to the State of the English Regions Seminar, Centre for Urban and Regional Development Studies, University of Newcastle upon Tyne, 21 June (available from Rt Hon Peter Mandelson MP, House of Commons, London, SW1A OAA).

McQuail, P. and Sandford, M. (2001) *Unexplored territory: Elected Regional Assemblies in England*, London: University College London, Constitution Unit.

NEA (North East Assembly) (2001) *The first English Region. A discussion paper on Regional Government* (www.northeastassembly.org.uk/publications/ publications.html), Newcastle upon Tyne: NECC.

NECC (North East Constitutional Convention) (1999) *Time for change: Proposals for Elected Regional Government*, Newcastle upon Tyne: NECC.

PIU (Performance and Innovation Unit) (1999) *Rural economics*, London: Cabinet Office.

PIU (2000) *Reaching out: The role of central government at the regional and local level*, London: Cabinet Office.

Plowden, W. and Greer, S. (2001) *Regional government and public health*, London: University College London, Constitution Unit.

RCU (Regional Coordination Unit) (2001) *Introducing the Government Offices*, London: Office of the Deputy Prime Minister.

Robinson, F., Shaw, K., Williams, S. and Hopwood, B. (2000) *Who runs the North East now?*, Newcastle upon Tyne: University of Northumbria.

Ross, W. and Tomaney, J. (2001) 'Devolution and health in England', *Regional Studies*, vol 35, no 3, pp 265-70.

Tomaney, J. (2000) 'Regional governance in England', in R. Hazell (ed) *States and nations review: The first year of devolution in the United Kingdom*, Exeter: Imprint Academic.

Tomaney, J. (2001) 'Reshaping the English regions', in A. Trench (ed) *The States and nations review 2001*, Exeter: Imprint Academic.

Tomaney, J. and Humphrey, L. (2001a) *Powers and functions of a Regional Assembly*, vol 1: main report, Newcastle upon Tyne: NEA, (www.northeastassembly.org.uk/ publications/publications.html).

Tomaney, J and Humphrey, L. (2001b) *Powers and functions of a Regional Assembly*, vol 2: main report, Newcastle upon Tyne: NEA, (curdsweb1.ncl.ac.uk/files/ 4708rgnee2.pdf).

THIRTEEN

Elected regional government: the issues

Paul McQuail and Mark Sandford

So, then, let's strike a northern light
To blind those armies of the night
Who always place a southern spin
Around the state we're living in.

(*A Northern Assembly*, Sean O'Brien, 2001)

This book has so far outlined the present state of play on the governance of the English regions. This chapter examines the processes required – and decisions to be made – in order to establish directly elected assemblies in any or all of the regions[1].

During the 2001 General Election campaign, the Deputy Prime Minister announced a commitment to publish a White Paper on the subject, holding out the prospect of a timetable similar to that for devolution in Scotland and Wales. This complemented the statement in the Labour Party Manifesto, repeating that of 1997, which constituted a clear commitment:

> In 1997 we said that provision should be made for directly elected regional government to go ahead in regions where people decided in a referendum to support it and where predominantly unitary local government is established. This remains our commitment. (Labour Party, 2001, p 35)

In the months prior to publication, the government has remained very tight-lipped about the contents of the Regional Government White Paper. The minister responsible, Nick Raynsford, won praise for his extensive efforts of consultation over the paper, but very little public support was forthcoming from colleagues. The issue was relegated well behind the totem of second-term service delivery and finally appeared in May 2002.

The more complex departmental responsibilities for regional government put in place after the 2001 General Election may not in themselves advance the cause. The public commitment to a White Paper and (implicitly) to early legislation, with the continuing lead responsibility of the Deputy Prime Minister (the only senior member of the government with a known personal commitment to elected regional government) mark a long step forward from the ambiguous record of the 1997 government.

Even so, giving effect to the Manifesto Commitment was not going to be plain sailing. Some of the reasons for this are noted as reservations in the statement on the subject approved at the 2000 Party Conference:

> [C]areful consideration will need to be given to ensuring that elected assemblies do not create additional tiers of bureaucracy; to the responsibilities, powers, type and size of assembly; to the appropriate test of public consent; to the types of voting system; and to the relationship between assemblies and other democratic institutions, including local government and Westminster.

These reservations reflect awkward facts. One is that there have been, over the years, competing and not fully reconciled strands in Labour Party thinking – broadly speaking, economic and democratic – about the purpose of regional government. The actions of the 1997 government made clear that priorities for the English regions were heavily on the economic side. The lack of a clear lead from government on the democratic front has handed the agenda for public debate to advocates of directly elected government in the regions (though some Regional Chambers/Assemblies are making a late dash for the line.

The second awkward fact is that there is still little reliable evidence of strong public demand in most of England for regional government. A BBC poll of March 2002 registered healthy majorities in favour in all regions, in particular the three northern regions. Just as striking, however, was the level of scepticism revealed by the poll. Almost 50% of those questioned, for instance, expected any Regional Assemblies created to add to bureaucracy and/or to be 'talking shops'. Meanwhile, the Campaign for the English Regions (CfER) produced its own White Paper in January, but to little public interest. Certainly there has been nothing like the pressure for devolution in Scotland, and to a lesser extent in Wales, before 1997. Consequently, there has been a lack of serious public engagement, beyond the political classes, with the issues that must be settled before a seaworthy project can be launched.

Beyond these tactical points, there is the general position of the government as a whole. The Labour government has overwhelmingly stressed service delivery as the priority for its second term. This was already a preoccupation in the 1997–2001 government, and a steady flow of targets for, and intervention in, local government services led to descriptions – often accurate – of a centralising tendency. The essence of devolution is to remove choice about policy priority from the centre. Devolving the high-profile services on which the government has staked its reputation would be a bold and risky step.

The most outstanding and important issues about regional government are:

- What is regional government for?
- What would it do if established?

Establishing the rationale for regional government is not, as it might seem, a theoretical or academic question. For on it turns a number of intensely practical questions, notably:

- What form should regional government take?
- What powers should it have?
- How to bring it about?

Furthermore, the basic political question remains:

- What good would it do to the lives of the people of England?

The first task for the promised White Paper is to set out the government's thinking on the purpose of having elected regional government. Without explicit and persuasive rationale, the instruments chosen will be defective, expectations will be unrealistic, and the project will falter.

The argument for directly elected regional government has three separate but overlapping and mutually reinforcing strands:

- it would correct the significantly different life opportunities between the regions of England;
- decentralisation of power is a democratic necessity which would produce solutions better suited to individual regional needs;
- it is anomalous, even perverse, that England has been left out of the devolution settlement for Scotland, Wales, Northern Ireland – and London.

The *economic* case rests on the twin propositions that people living in the regions furthest from London are materially worse off; and that giving them control would reduce the disparities. Even the first of these strands has been challenged by those who argue that differences within even prosperous regions are greater than those between regions. Certainly there is much poverty and deprivation in London and other cities outside the northern regions. They have a lower per capita GDP than any other region. They have a higher standardised mortality rate; and educational attainment is lower. The structure of employment, based on declining industries, is unfavourable. Beyond the facts, there is resentment, particularly in the North, about London-based decision making which is difficult to overestimate.

The *democratic* case is that decisions affecting people in the regions are taken remotely and without proper regard to the diversity of conditions, needs and wishes between different parts of the country. Naturally, this is seen as wrong in itself, and also likely to produce worse decisions not just in the individual regions, but in the interest of England as a whole. One especially resented aspect of this situation has been the powers exercised on the government's behalf by quangos and other agencies, working in the regions but with accountability only through Westminster.

Elected assemblies are proposed as a means of overcoming remoteness in decision making and making policy delivery responsive and effective. Attempts by central government to be directly concerned with delivery on the ground through Area Based Initiatives (ABIs), national inspectorates, policy 'guidance' and the Best Value project have heightened the sense of local authorities and others in the regions that central intervention is perverse. Hopes are also expressed that regional government, with wide functions, would attract fresh blood into the political process, a new group of people rising to new challenges and opportunities.

The democratic group of arguments does not in itself settle which functions ought to be carried out over which areas, for reasons of efficiency or of common interest or identity; or the relationship between new regional bodies and the existing democratically elected local authorities. Nor are these questions settled conclusively by the other leading arguments advanced for elected regional government. These include:

- the example and influence of Europe;
- popular demand and regional identity;
- the existence of an unelected – though incoherent – level of administration at regional level by central government and its organs;
- the anomaly (as some see it) of England's regions being left out of the devolution settlement for the other nations of the UK.

A European example is instructive without being particularly helpful. Some European nations have elected regional governments with a uniform set of powers (Germany and France), while others have very different levels (Spain and Italy). German Länder and the three historic Spanish regions have very extensive powers; French regions by comparison are very limited in their functions. As in England, many regions in each of these countries have no clear identity. This does not in itself reduce the effectiveness of their functioning. Furthermore, the European comparison underlines the fact that England is by far the largest unit of government in the EU without an elected regional tier.

The advocates' case for regional government is well summed up by Marquand and Tomaney (2000) in four related propositions:

1. A tier of regional government exists (Government Offices and a range of quangos and agencies), but is fragmented and poorly coordinated.
2. Too much public policy is designed centrally in ways that do not match local conditions.
3. There is insufficient democratic scrutiny of the hidden regional state.
4. English politics needs to accommodate greater diversity and pluralism if it is to survive and generate wide interest.

The implicit claim is that devolution to elected regional bodies would improve performance and satisfaction. It must also be accepted, however, that priorities will not necessarily be those of the UK government, as the performance of the Scottish Parliament has begun to demonstrate.

Before going on to consider the key question of the functions of regional government, realism requires a look at the obstacles and objections to be removed or overcome. The reservations noted in the Labour Party resolution reflect genuine concerns, based on political assessment, that regional government should not become an additional layer of bureaucracy or an extra cost, drawing resources from the provision of services. It is reasonable also to expect evidence of public support for as radical a change as regional government.

The chief objection in principle to powerful regional government is based on equity: the unfairness of different opportunities and outcomes as a consequence of being on either side of a boundary that is arbitrary from the point of view of the individual (the 'postcode lottery') resonates deeply. The strongly centralising actions of the present government, further emphasised in the April 2002 Budget announcement of an expanded health service under close central supervision, owe much to this impetus. There are also practical objections: change on this scale could not be undertaken without turbulence, and without risk. There are also vested interests to be overcome, from Whitehall departments (and their ministers), and from inertia, a form of vested interest in the way in which England's administration, famously centralised, hangs together; and the weakness of regional identity that is another aspect of inertia. The other side of the coin is wide dissatisfaction with the delivery provided by the existing machine and its arrangements and interventions.

What would regional government do?

It would be regrettable if the White Paper did not deal adequately with the rationale for regional government, though it would not be the first time a government had fudged difficult steps in an argument. What cannot be avoided is clarity about the functions of proposed Regional Assemblies. No precise criteria for the choice of functions for regional government are appropriate, but questions need to be asked:

- For which function is the region the most appropriate unit?
- Do the proposed functions make a coherent and intelligible whole?
- What will be the effect on quality of decision making and service delivery?
- What will be the effect on overall governance, including revival of democratic effectiveness?
- If there is a specific economic goal, such as increased prosperity for the most disadvantaged regions, how is that reflected in the functions?

The fundamental issue is whether the functions would permit the assembly to make choices that would make a real difference, for better or worse, to the region. Just as important is the question of whether they are enough to encourage people to vote in a referendum or in subsequent elections.

Advocates of regional government have naturally used as points of reference the examples of Scotland, Wales and London. The proposals of the North East Constitutional Convention (NECC) are representative in proposing that an assembly would set "a strategic policy framework for the development of the region", with responsibility for planning, economic development, transport and infrastructure, training and arts and culture. It would also "exert influence over" health and education. It would be funded by a single block grant from central government, and perhaps also independent financial resources though initially no taxation powers (NECC, 2000, pp 5-6). Later in this chapter we refer to proposals made by Marquand and Tomaney (2000), and it is right here to acknowledge the most substantial contribution to the debate so far by a senior political figure: Peter Mandelson's speech at a seminar at the University of Newcastle upon Tyne in June 2001 (Mandelson, 2001).

In order to take the decisions forward, as the White Paper must, we have set out three conceptually distinct models with progressively greater levels of devolution. We stress that these, and particularly the second, are illustrative cases. However, we have tried to give enough detail about functions and resources to expose the choices to be made, and their consequences:

1. *Strategic/coordination:* with a range of strategy-setting functions;
2. *Strategic/executive:* adding executive functions taken from unelected bodies;
3. *Wales:* as for the National Assembly.

Strategic/coordination

This model, with one possible exception, would have purely strategic functions. The assembly would act primarily through influence, coordination and cooperation with a range of partners including the voluntary and business sectors, Government Offices and agencies in the regions, and local government. Its strategies would have statutory force or would require overt backing from central government in influencing or directing the actions of quangos and other agencies still in government control. The exception mentioned could give it executive control over the Regional Development Agency.

Funding, as for the Greater London Authority (GLA), could be by precept on local authorities. The costs of running a full-time, elected assembly would need to be substantially more than those of the existing Regional Chambers. Some indication of scale is suggested by the GLA's running cost budget of £36 million, which suggests that the functions proposed could, for a typical region, be of the order of £20 million to cover the cost of research and strategy preparation, member support, communication and administration.

Strategic/executive

This model draws on the proposition in Marquand and Tomaney (2000). It adds executive responsibility for regional agencies, including the regional arm of a number of national quangos with their accompanying budgets. Most functions of Government Offices, and those of the Regional Development Agencies (RDAs), would pass to the assembly, as would those of the learning and skills councils and Small Business Service. The agencies from which the assembly could take over defined functions include the Environment Agency, Highways Agency, Housing Corporation, Countryside Agency, English Nature, English Heritage, Forestry Commission, English Tourist Board, Resource, Sport England and the Regional Arts Boards (in their future form). Considerable structural change would be required: some do not have regional structures or budgets, while others have different boundaries from those of the standard regions.

Such a model is admittedly schematic, and the precise functions set out are illustrative: the principle underlying it is that of a body with sufficient clout to attract support in a referendum and afterwards. It illustrates a step change in influence and resource from the earlier model. Assumptions about the allocation of resources to regions are required in several cases, but the assembly could expect to command a budget of £1.1-2.5 billion according to size of region. This could provide the basis for a formula for a block grant for each region to cover running as well as programme costs.

Wales

An assembly on this model would mirror the functions of the National Assembly for Wales. It would control the entire domestic policy agenda and would, in the full model, have powers of secondary legislation. Since the functions include health, education and local government including social services, there would be a large increase in the resources compared with the previous model, ranging from £6-14 billion according to the size of region.

The process of establishment for an English region would be more complex than in Wales itself where there existed a complete and for many purposes self-contained set of functions and an administrative machine to match. Complexity apart, such a major change even for one region would require a radical reappraisal of resource allocation within England.

Functions

Table 13.1 summarises the three illustrative models of assembly. It includes figures for the size of assembly and executive implied (using the East Midlands as an example); these are assumed to increase with the size and scope of the task.

Of the three, election makes even the first a marked advance in legitimacy on existing Regional Chambers. There is a prospect that its members would act from a regional, not a local authority delegate, standpoint. However, without executive powers (even with the RDA) it runs the danger of being seen as a talking shop. In the vital test, it is doubtful whether it would attract enough support from the electors in a referendum or an election.

The Welsh model goes far beyond any hint given in ministerial or Labour Party statements. As suggested above, it would go strongly against the grain of important strands in government thinking as demonstrated in Labour's first term, notably:

Table 13.1: Summary of key features of the three models

Essential features	Model 1	Model 2	Model 3
	Strategic/ coordination	Strategic/executive	Wales
Type of functions	Strategic	Strategic and executive	Mainly executive
Functions additional to Model 1 and Model 2		*Executive responsibility for:* Single Regeneration Budget Regional Selective Assistance Environment Housing investment Highways Agency Culture, Sport, Tourism	Health Education (including higher and further education) Local government Police Fire and emergency Agriculture
Size of assembly	27	37	79
Size of executive	6	8	10
Annual budget for East Midlands	£20 million	£1.1 billion	£7.5 billion

- distrust of local government's capacity to deliver services to the required standard without inspection, reporting and central intervention;
- in particular, concern to provide an NHS and an education system with consistent and improved standards. Handing either of these to new bodies consisting of either a new political class or members of the old one would be an astonishing reversal of position.

It is hard to imagine the government going as far as the Welsh model; and the Strategic/Coordination model in its pure form is so far short of the aspirations of advocates of regional government that that also seems unlikely to be the central proposition for the White Paper. The functions of the latter, however, seem bound to be at the centre of the proposals. The question then is how far down the executive road, represented here as Model 2, the White Paper proposals go: there have been few clear clues about that. Control of the RDA is obviously a front runner; the planning Green Paper of December 2001 proposes statutory planning powers for elected assemblies.

Beyond these the test will be how radical an attempt is made to devolve functions, primarily from Government Offices, and the range of centrally-owned agencies listed above. A crude measure of the scale of devolution to assemblies, and therefore of their potential for effecting change, will be the size of each budget. However, clarity and coherence of the package as a whole will be important also, as will the degree of freedom from central control and inspection that is proposed.

Other issues

Apart from the rationale and the powers of regional government, other important issues need to be faced:

- *Constitutional questions of size, electoral system, and internal governance.* Recent precedents suggest that the assemblies should be as small as the competing claims of representation and efficiency permit. It is thought that the government considers that assemblies of around 30 members, elected by the Additional Member system used in Scotland, Wales and London, are preferable. There is room for doubt as to whether 30 members, in any of the English regions, could adequately represent the diversity of their region – particularly as the Additional Member system implies some 10 of those members being elected via top-up lists.
- *Boundaries.* There is a strong practical case for adopting the existing boundaries of the Government Offices as those of regional assemblies. A more wide-ranging review from first principles would certainly be time-consuming and so contentious as to lead to no better result. Some parts of the country, however, notably the wider South East and South West, for different reasons, require more detailed review. For important economic and geographical reasons, the South East including London is a single entity, but an entity with a population of about a third of England. It would likely be unworkable as a single region, but special provision for coordination might be required. In the South West, Cornwall has an active campaign aiming to resist incorporation into the standard region. Provision for boundary changes at the margins between regions should also be made.
- *Financing the assemblies.* Methods of financing the assemblies would depend on the proposed functions. Of the models described earlier, the Strategic/ Coordination model could be financed either by block grant or by precept on the local authorities in the region. There are arguments for preferring the latter. The two models with substantial programme expenditure would need to be financed mainly by block grant.

There is no necessary connection between financing Regional Assemblies and the issue of resource distribution between the nations of the UK or the regions of England. However, establishing regional government with devolved budgets would heighten already existing demand for a new needs assessment and redistribution of resources within the UK and between the English regions:

- *The effect on local government.* It is understandable that local authorities are nervous about regional government, particularly in the light of the Manifesto proposition that elected regional government requires a predominantly unitary pattern of local government. This condition might be interpreted as already being met in the three northern regions: in the North East and North West some two-thirds of the population live under unitary authorities, rising to nearly 90% in Yorkshire and the Humber. Contrary to indications in early

2001, the government's concern to avoid 'too many tiers' appears to have risen up the list of issues around Regional Assemblies.

- *Clear proposals for the status and further development of regional governance in those regions with little prospect of a successful referendum.* The Regional Chambers (now Assemblies) would expect to play a central part in these. The proposals in the 2001 Planning Green Paper may be an example. Even the Strategic/ Coordination model would have some impact on local government functions in the fields of strategic planning and economic development. The relationship between regional and local government would need continuing negotiation.
- *'Asymmetrical devolution'.* This implies permitting assemblies to be established in one or more regions but not in all, as the referendum route implies. This is likely to be the most difficult of the issues, apart from the functions themselves. Even with modest functions, an elected assembly will give the region a greater and more legitimate political voice than regions without one. The Greater London Assembly and its mayor demonstrate this even with their modest and constrained executive role. However, it seems the government are untroubled by the prospect. Ministers have indicated that they would like to see at least one assembly up and running before the next General Election, indicating that a staggered approach is the preferred one.

In practical terms, the establishment of even one directly elected assembly would require the construction of a framework for the devolution of resources for the whole of England. Even a mild form of devolution to a single region would create demand elsewhere. Devolution envy is already potent under the label of the 'Berwick effect' in the north. One or two devolved regions might be readily enough manageable. But at a certain point, variety of practice between devolved regions would point to universal devolution. In Spain, the 'rump' territories were obliged to take on devolved powers after the leading regions had set the pace.

Under an advanced model, as in Wales, full freedom of virement (the ability to move resources between budget heads) between programmes would also inhibit the construction of central policy initiatives in devolved areas of competence. In Spain and Italy this is addressed by tying substantial tranches of grant to specific broad programme areas, such as health.

Getting from here to there

The White Paper will need to make decisions concerning such issues as:

- whether there are referendums in each region at once, or (more probably) where demand has been established;
- if on demand, by what criterion. For example, initiation by the Regional Chamber, or petition by a specified number of voters, as with the 2000 Local Government's provision for elected mayors;
- assembly functions in outline at least – with enough detail to make the proposition clear to voters;

- method of financing assemblies, audit, inspection, reserve powers of intervention by the UK government;
- constitution of assemblies, electoral system and cycle, size of assembly and its executive;
- procedure following a 'Yes' vote.

There are two possible legislative routes. Were the London precedent to be followed, there would, after consultation, first be a referendum bill which would deal with the procedure for a number of potential referendums, including criteria and timetable as for the White Paper. The referendum itself would require a public statement of key features proposed for assemblies, probably in more detail than in the White Paper. The scope of such a statement might be set out in the referendum bill. The conditions for having a referendum would presumably be open-ended so that one might be held at an indefinite time in the future provided the criteria were met. After the first referendum resulting in a 'Yes' vote, there would be a second bill, different from London, in that it would need to provide for the staged introduction of assemblies across the regions. The second bill would provide for:

- an assembly to be set up in any region where there had been a 'Yes' vote;
- functions and powers; these could be in defined tranches set out in the bill; with provision for each assembly to be established by order with one or more tranches of functions;
- financial and constitutional arrangements;
- consequent arrangements for regions without assemblies. If the functions of the assemblies were on the lines of the Strategic/Coordination model, consequences would be modest. Were they on a larger scale, with resources to match, they could be considerable, requiring a framework for progressive transfer of functions and resources from central government to the regions.

The two stages for London have necessarily become three: two bills and an order to establish each assembly, adding to the time required. By this route, from legislation in 2002, the earliest date for establishing an assembly would be July 2005 (as demonstrated in Table 13.2).

The alternative legislative route would be to compress the whole process, including authorising the referendums, into a single bill. Although technically feasible, it would mean that popular demand is not tested in any region until after the full (and elaborate) legislation is passed. That was one reason why the 1997 government chose to test the level of demand first.

Political pitfalls

A bill confined to setting up referendums could be narrow and precise, though requiring prior decisions on key matters of substance. However, the main legislation, by either route, would be complex and controversial. There would be debate on powers and functions: pressure from regions wanting more than

Table 13.2: Possible timings for the establishment of Regional Assemblies in England

	London pattern	Single-stage legislation
May 2002	White Paper	White Paper
August 2002	End of consultation	End of consultation
November 2002	Bill for referendums	
February 2003	Royal assent	Bill for referendums and substantive issues
May 2003	Referendum in any region where demand established	
October 2003	Substantive and procedural bill introduced	Royal assent
December 2003		Referendum
January 2004		Order to establish assembly(ies) where 'Yes' vote obtained
May 2004		Elections for assemblies
July 2004	Royal assent	Assemblies take up powers
October 2004	Order to establish assembly where 'Yes' vote obtained	
May 2005 (first date for General Election)	Elections for assemblies	
July 2005	Assemblies take up powers	

was on offer, and pressure from regions, mainly in the south, who saw little prospect of a 'Yes' vote, or were opposed in principle and feared competition from the north. There would be acute political pressure on matters not strictly related to the setting up of assemblies – most notably the distribution systems for central government resources through the Barnett Formula[2] and Standard Spending Assessments. Not all of the pressure would come from England: Scottish and Welsh MPs would have their say on things that affected their interests – however remote the prospect of clawing back resources from their nations.

Whichever route were followed, there must be at least a chance that, even in the North East, the package on offer is not attractive enough to secure a 'yes' vote in a referendum; or a high enough vote to carry conviction. To have gone through the whole process of legislation and referendum with that result would be a severe embarrassment at best. That was the path followed by the Callaghan government in the 1970s, when huge quantities of political capital and parliamentary time were spent in pushing through devolution legislation, only to have it rejected at the referendum. This is a powerful reason for preferring the London route of two stages of legislation. However, even the two-stage model has the implication that a tide of regional government is set in train by a referendum in a single region without other regions (some of which may be strongly opposed to the project) having a say except in parliament. On balance, the advantage lies with two stages.

The risk points to at least considering an alternative approach. It would of course be difficult (perhaps impossible) to depart from the commitment to referendums as tests of public opinion. However, if the government were willing to concede no more than purely strategic functions to the assemblies, and further soundings of opinion at the White Paper stage revealed that support or likely turnout was low, it would be worth considering doing without referendums. Either a different (and less demanding) test of public support could be devised; or provision could be made for elected Regional Assemblies in all regions with a standard set of strategic powers. This was the route followed in France: although the regions there have taken time to establish themselves, they are now doing so. The action would be clear-cut and decisive. It could be presented as the first stage of a process to be developed organically, depending on demand.

Conclusion

Within the framework of the government's fundamental commitment to service delivery, the challenge for the White Paper is twofold:

- to make proposals for elected assemblies in regions where there is demand that will potentially make a real difference to people's lives;
- to provide convincing alternatives for development of governance at regional level for those regions where the prospect of elected regional government is remote.

The choice before the government is not altogether comfortable. It rests between proposing devolution to elected regional government of much more than there has so far been any sign of their contemplating; and proposing a 'strategic' set of functions that will please nobody. The first of these choices may seem to them to put at risk the emphasis on delivery, which is the watchword of their second term. The second raises the prospect that, after a bruising legislative passage, the voters in the regions will turn their backs.

Notes

[1] The argument of this chapter is explored in greater detail in our volume *Unexplored territory: Elected regional assemblies in England* (McQuail and Sandford, 2001).

[2] The Barnett Formula, contrary to popular (and press) opinion, is not the source of higher public spending in Scotland, Wales and Northern Ireland. Rather, this derives from historical spending patterns. The Barnett Formula is purely used to allocate *new* government spending, under any budget head, between the four nations (although the

devolved assemblies can vire those funds). It is not used to allocate expenditure between the regions of England. The original hope that incremental change at the margin would bring about convergence of levels of spending between the nations has not been realised.

References

Labour Party (2001) *New ambitions for our country*, Election Manifesto, London: Labour Party.

McQuail, P. and Sandford, M. (2001) *Unexplored territory: Elected regional assemblies in England*, London: Constitution Unit, University College London.

Mandelson, P. (2001) 'The state of the English regions', Keynote address to the State of the English Regions Seminar, Centre for Urban and Regional Development Studies, University of Newcastle upon Tyne, 21 June (available from Rt Hon Peter Mandleson MP, House of Commons, London, SW1A OAA).

Marquand, D. and Tomaney, J. (2000) 'Democratising England', Regional Policy Forum, London, October.

NECC (North East Constitutional Convention) (2000) *A time for change: Proposals for a directly elected North East Assembly*, Newcastle upon Tyne: NECC.

FOURTEEN

Barnett plus needs: the regional spending challenge in Britain

Peter Jones

Introduction

British political debate about public spending has concentrated on two main issues: whether there is too much – or too little – public spending; and the distribution of spending between functions, such as defence, education, and health. Questions concerning the efficiency or the effectiveness of public spending have tended to be variations on these issues. Now a third and rather different issue is looming large: the geographical distribution of spending between the regions and the nations of Britain.

Devolution has pushed this issue up the political agenda. The creation of the Scottish Parliament, the Welsh Assembly, and, to a lesser extent, the Northern Ireland Assembly, plus the pressure for regional government in England, has exposed three facts that pre-devolution British constitutional arrangements had brushed under the carpet:

1. There is a fiscal mechanism for distributing public spending to the nations of Scotland, Wales and Northern Ireland;
2. There is no equivalent mechanism for distributing spending to the regions of England;
3. When existing spending levels in the three devolved nations are compared to existing spending in the English regions, it appears that some regions get a raw deal, and that the devolved nations get a good deal.

Increasing awareness of these facts has provoked considerable debate. Mainly, this has focussed on the national fiscal distribution mechanism, known as the Barnett Formula. In North East England, a vocal lobby led by *The Journal*, Newcastle upon Tyne's daily newspaper, wants spending in the region raised to Scottish levels (see Chapter Ten of this volume). This has a varying amount of support from all political parties and other groups, such as trade unions. Business organisations are increasingly aware of the issue. West Midlands First, an umbrella group of business organisations representing the region, has told ministers that they "believe it is unfair that Scotland Wales and Northern Ireland receive a higher per capita spend" and that "English regions are disadvantaged by the

Barnett spending formula" (Guthrie, 2000). Even in Wales, which, from an English viewpoint, is thought to get a relatively good deal, there is a demand for a review of the Barnett Formula. In a report on social exclusion, the Commons' Select Committee on Welsh Affairs said: "The Barnett Formula should be replaced with a formula for public funding which accurately reflects the levels of need in the various parts of the UK" (House of Commons, 2000, para 118). These pressures have been recognised by some in government. John Prescott, the Deputy Prime Minister, has said that the Barnett Formula is not "written in stone" and should be reviewed, perhaps alongside a review of local government finance in 2001. His comments also implied that the review would cover disparities in English regional spending, and that there would be "blood on the carpet", as there would be losers as well as winners (Prescott quoted in Hetherington, 2001). Against that, the Prime Minister, Tony Blair, and the Chancellor, Gordon Brown, said during the 2001 General Election campaign that there would be no change to the Barnett Formula.

Thus, it appears that a genie is struggling to get out of the bottle. It is equally clear that moves to English regional government, due to be given momentum by a White Paper expected in 2002, will uncork the bottle. Questions about what regional government will do will be rapidly followed by questions about what it will spend and how it will get that money. Questions about whether the money likely to be available to any one region represents a fair allocation will inevitably invoke comparisons with Wales and Scotland, especially since Scotland is the most generously funded part of mainland Britain. This White Paper will therefore look at two principal questions:

1. Can the Barnett Formula survive in its present form?
2. Is there a need for an English regional version of the Barnett formula?

Pre-Barnett spending distribution

The use of an arithmetic formula for distributing public spending in Britain on a territorial basis has a long history. It first appeared in 1888, when Sir George Goschen, as Chancellor of the Exchequer, introduced a formula which became immediately known as the Goschen Formula. It was required because Scotland had in 1885 acquired a territorial administration, the Scottish Office, which took charge of the distribution of central government grant-aid to local authorities. Although Ireland had managed to survive without such a formula until then, Goschen extended it to Ireland in 1888. Wales, at this time, was considered to be part of England.

The Goschen Formula decreed that the proceeds of the wheel tax, the horse tax, and half the revenue from probate duty should be allocated to England, Scotland and Ireland in the ratio 80:11:9 respectively. This formula was based neither on population, nor on needs, but on the contribution each country made to probate duty revenues (McCrone, 1999). Although slight allowance was made for the relative poverty of Ireland, it was not a redistributive formula, but simply a means of recycling some taxes back to the territory where they

Figure 14.1: Indices of Scottish versus English public spending 1889-1977 (England = 100)

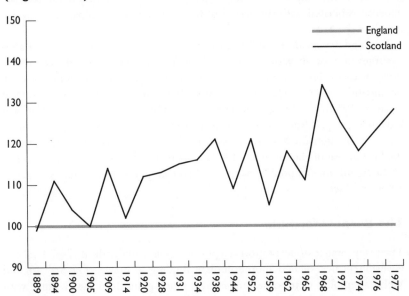

were collected. With changing forms and patterns of taxation, and changing patterns of population, the formula became out of date in the 20th century. But in amended form, it still managed to survive Irish secession in 1922, and endured as a Scottish and Northern Irish formula until 1958, by which time it was wildly out of date and was abandoned. Thereafter, funding for the Scottish, Northern Ireland and Welsh Offices (the Welsh Office was established in 1964) became the subject of annual negotiation between the three territorial Secretaries of State and the Treasury, as was the norm with all Whitehall ministries.

Chancellor Goschen also introduced public accounts which enable local expenditure by central government to be geographically identified. Figure 14.1 shows how identifiable spending by central government in Scotland compares with the same spending in England since the Goschen Formula was introduced (McCrone, 1999). It should be noted that, prior to the introduction of the welfare state and the National Health Service in the late 1940s, public spending was only about 10-15% of GDP – compared to around 40% at present – and that geographically identifiable spending was at most 40% of total central government spending. Two points emerge:

1. Public spending per capita in Scotland has risen in comparison to England;
2. The increase is not steady, but shows peaks and troughs.

There are two possible explanations for the peaks. One is that they are the result of specific government programmes. For example, the peak in 1968 may result from the introduction of an economic development programme following a 1963 White Paper. (A similar programme for North East England was introduced following a 1965 White Paper.) The 1953 peak may result from the expense associated with the arrival of the NHS and the comparatively worse health of the Scots.

A second explanation could be that the peaks represent political responses to upsurges in Scottish nationalism. The 1953 peak comes immediately after a wave of nationalist sentiment expressed in pro-home rule meetings of civic organisations (1947, 1948), the theft from Westminster Abbey of the Stone of Destiny (1950), and the gathering of 2.5 million signatures for the National Covenant, a pro-home rule petition (1949-50). The 1968 peak comes immediately after the Scottish Nationalist Party (SNP) sensationally captured the Labour seat of Hamilton in a 1967 parliamentary by-election. (For accounts of the significance of political factors in Scottish spending decisions, see Levitt, 1999, and McLean, 2000, pp 76-80.)

The Barnett formula

The reappearance of devolution as a political policy under the 1974-79 Labour government necessitated another look at funding formulae. The Scottish and Welsh assemblies were to be funded by a block grant from the Treasury with no taxation powers of their own. Evidently, if there were annual negotiations between the assemblies and the Treasury, these would become highly charged politically. Even with assembly administrations of the same political complexion as the central government, opposition demands in those assemblies for more money would have rapidly increased political friction between Scotland, Wales and England. This would have defeated the central policy objective of devolution, which was to reduce political friction caused by the surge in support for the Scottish and Welsh nationalist parties in the 1970s.

A solution was produced by Joel Barnett, then chief secretary to the Treasury: the Barnett Formula. Although it was introduced in 1978, its use was kept secret until the Scottish Secretary, George Younger, disclosed it to the Scottish Affairs Select Committee in 1980 (Wigger, 1998). Essentially, for any spending programme where there is a territorial division of responsibility (such as education), any increase to the English budget results in an automatic increase to the Scottish, Welsh and Northern Irish budget. The Barnett Formula's purpose is simple: that for every £1 per capita extra spent in England, £1 per capita extra should also go to each of the devolved territories. England's population is the base unit for this calculation. In principle, the population of each territory is expressed as a fraction of England's population (not as a fraction of the total UK population), and the territory receives a sum of money equivalent to that fraction of the English budget increase.

Despite this simplicity, the Barnett Formula is widely misunderstood. It does not define all public spending in the devolved territories. For example, in 1998-99, £25.7 billion was identified by the Treasury as having been spent in Scotland. But only £15.6 billion of this was in the block of spending controlled by the devolved Scottish Executive, and is affected by the Barnett Formula.

Most of the remaining £10.1 billion is social security spending, which comes from central government (Scottish Executive, 2000). Even within the Scottish Executive's budget, about 14% of spending is not covered by the Barnett Formula. This is mainly spending on agriculture, which is determined by EU decisions and geographical factors rather than by domestic political decisions (Midwinter, 2000). In Treasury terminology, Barnett-covered spending is Departmental Expenditure Limit (DEL) and the rest is Annually Managed Expenditure (AME).

Neither does the Barnett Formula determine overall levels of spending in Scotland, Wales and Northern Ireland. It only determines the changes made to the overall spending totals. The spending that each nation receives each year is determined in two ways:

1. In any year, the previous year's total spending is taken as the inherited baseline total expenditure;
2. For spending programmes which are divided territorially (such as health), the Barnett Formula is applied to any change in the English spending element so that the populations of Scotland, Wales and Northern Ireland receive, on a per capita basis, the same change in spending. This is added to the inherited baseline total.

Thus, if there is no increase in English spending programmes, the three devolved territories receive no increase. If there is a reduction, the three nations also have their spending reduced.

The Barnett Formula is not based on any assessment of needs for public spending, but on population. It is intended to ensure that the three territories get, according to their share of the UK population, a fair share of any marginal change in public spending. It is also intended to gradually reduce the differential in per capita public spending between Scotland and England, which, by 1978 had grown to 22%.

This is a simple function of arithmetic. For example, say that Scotland's population is the equivalent of 10% of England's population. Say also, that it has been decided to add £50 million to an English domestic programme for which the existing budget is £1000 million, a rise of 5%. Scotland should therefore get 10% of the £50 million, or £5 million extra. If existing per capita spending on the equivalent Scottish programme matched English per capita spending, the existing Scottish budget would be £100 million. So a £5 million increase would also be a 5% rise. But if existing Scottish per capita spending is 20% higher than in England, that is, £120 million rather than £100 million, then the £5 million increase becomes a rise of just over 4%. Over time therefore, the advantageous Scottish differential ought to have been eroded. However, as Figure 14.2 shows, this has not happened. In fact, per capita Scottish spending was slightly higher in 1998 than equivalent English spending (23% higher), than in 1978 (McCrone, 1999; Scottish Executive, 2000).

Figure 14.2: Index of Scottish public spending relative to English public spending 1978-1998 (England = 100)

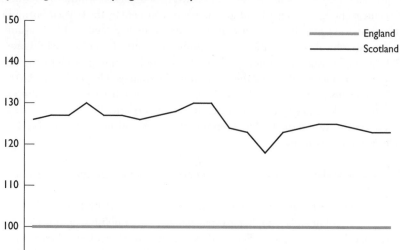

The failure to apply Barnett

In fact, in the form in which the formula was intended to be used, it has only applied in 1992 and the years since 1997. A number of reasons why the Barnett Formula did not work as its creator envisaged can be identified (McCrone, 1999):

1. *The original fractions were greater than warranted by Scotland's population.* Barnett decided that Scotland should get 10/85 (11.79%), and Wales 5/85 (5.88%) of comparable English programmes. Where a programme covered England and Wales, such as law and order, the Scottish increment was 10/90 (11.11%). In fact, Scotland's population in 1979 was 11.1% of England's population, and it continued to decline relative to England's population so that in 1992, Michael Portillo, then chief secretary to the Treasury, reduced the figure from 11.79% to 10.66%. In 1997, the New Labour government's chief secretary, Alistair Darling, reduced it further – to 10.45% – and decided that it would thereafter be reviewed annually. But between 1979-97, Scotland was getting higher spending increases than its population entitled it to.

2. *Few spending increases.* The last 20 years have generally been years of small spending increases, so the formula has had little to bite on, and cause convergence.

3. *Real increases.* From 1978-85, the formula applied to real increases only. The Treasury rolled the inherited baseline figure forward from year to year with

an in-built allowance for inflation. Since 1985, the formula has applied to cash increases.

4. *The formula has occasionally been bypassed.* This has occurred either because the Treasury has been persuaded to fund pay awards to public sector workers in full, or because it has been persuaded that a lump of money is needed for some specific problem.

5. *Some Welsh and Scottish spending may have no English counterparts.* This necessitated some other basis for determining spending increases. For example, water and sewerage services in England were privatised in 1989 but have remained in the public sector in Scotland. Without some special means of allocating money to Scotland for water and sewerage, spending on this service in Scotland would have to be allocated at the expense of some other service (Heald, 1994, pp 168-9).

The lessons are fairly obvious. First, if a population-based formula for distributing public spending is to work, it has to be based on real population figures, not approximations. Second, even in such a case, the formula can be subverted by politicians.

The Barnett Formula's future

The tendency, noted earlier in this chapter, of the Barnett Formula to produce convergence in spending levels between Scotland and England should have started to come into effect in 1997 with the introduction of an annual review and adjustment of population figures. In Scotland, this tendency has been dubbed the 'Barnett squeeze' (Cuthbert, 1998; Kay, 1998, p 42). The phrase carries the implication that the government in London is being mean-minded and is squeezing Scottish public spending. From an English perspective however, England is getting a 'Barnett boost' and will catch up with Scottish spending. In rough terms, a 4% increase in England translates into a 3% increase in Scotland.

This might seem perfectly acceptable – but there are two problems. The first is inflation: if inflation was running at a 4% annual rate, then a 4% cash increase to an English programme results in a 1% cash cut in Scotland in real terms. The second is that in the long term, Scottish public spending levels will come to match those in England and any differential implied by needs will disappear.

In the period covered by the present Comprehensive Spending Review until 2003-04, the first matter is not a problem. Spending increases for both England and Scotland are above inflation levels and should remain so if inflation remains at its target rate of 2.5%. There is debate, however, about whether or not the second problem will occur. One argument contends that there are enough factors, such as central government spending on programmes which are not covered by Barnett, which will offset a 'Barnett squeeze' so that it becomes negligible (Midwinter, 2000, p 46). Only 86% of the budget controlled by the Scottish Executive is affected by Barnett; the remainder is largely agriculture spending which is determined by EU decisions.

This argument does not seem terribly convincing. It relies on chance by-products of government and EU decisions counteracting a relentless arithmetic progression. There is ample evidence that disparities in the Barnett-controlled spending programmes are gradually being reduced. Scottish health spending, while it will continue to increase in real terms, will reduce as a proportion of UK health spending, from 10.5% in 1994-95 to 9.7% in 2003-04 (Scottish Parliament, 2001). In another way of looking at it, the Scottish Executive's DEL spending in 2003-04 will be £920 million less than it would have been if the rate of growth in Scottish spending since 1999-2000 had been the same as the rate of growth in spending in the UK as a whole (Bell, 2001, p 6).

Devolution of central government powers also appears to have produced a division of government interests. The Treasury no longer has the same interest in funding expensive decisions by the Scottish Executive which it had when these decisions were taken by ministerial colleagues in the pre-devolution Scottish Office. An expensive pay package for teachers agreed in 2001, which previously might have been wholly funded by the Treasury, now has to be funded out of the existing devolved financial settlement.

Generally, devolution has introduced transparency into the geographical distribution of public spending, which makes the kind of previous political bypassing of the formula much more obvious and therefore politically more difficult. Since the 1997 changes to the Barnett Formula, there has only been one such political bypass. In July 2000, the Treasury announced that an additional £272 million was being allocated to the Welsh Assembly over the three years until 2003-04 to permit the assembly to meet its spending obligations under the EU Objective 1 regional aid programme for west and south Wales. However, this occurred under unusual political pressure caused by the resignation of the Welsh Executive's First Minister, Alun Michael.

Such exceptions apart, convergence of spending levels might well happen quite rapidly. According to one simulation (Bell, 2001, p 9) if public spending in England continues to rise at a nominal annual rate of 5.25%, then, assuming a 3% inflation rate, a 25% Scottish spending advantage would reduce to 13% after 12 years. Similarly, a Welsh spending advantage of 18% reduces to 10% after 12 years. The rate of convergence on this model is fast in the initial years and slow in later years.

If this does turn out to be the pattern, pressure for reform of Barnett will grow. The logic of Barnett is to "set in motion a long-term tendency towards convergence of expenditure relative to the UK average, provided that there was growth in the expenditure aggregates to which the formulae were applied" (Heald, 1994, p 164). The Scots and the Welsh will become increasingly restive as their present comparative advantage over England erodes. It is clear that a situation in which all parts of Britain received the same average spending would be politically unacceptable as any notion that different parts had different needs and therefore different spending requirements would have disappeared. Before that point is reached, however, pressure for reform of Barnett will have become irresistible because the rough justice implied in the present system will be severely eroded. However, there is no means of judging when the greater spending needs of Scotland and Wales are no longer being met by additional spending.

The English regions

There is little history of central government distributing public spending to the regions of England according to defined criteria or by formulae. Distributive mechanisms do operate in the NHS and in local government finance. The operation of the local government Standard Spending Assessment mechanism is a constant subject of debate, sometimes quite heated, between local and central government. It is also extremely complex and beyond the scope of this chapter to analyse, although it may have some lessons to offer when considering regional spending.

This aside, there is little guidance available about how the government distributes public spending in the regions, beyond the following statement:

> It is a long-established principle that all areas of the United Kingdom are entitled to the same level of public services and that the expenditure on them should be allocated according to their relative needs. (HM Treasury, 1979, p 4)

But needs do not figure in how Scotland, Wales and Northern Ireland get their share of spending. It is also difficult to see how they feature in the share of England's regions. If needs were the main criterion, we would expect that the poorest regions and nations of the UK would get the most public spending.

Figure 14.3 plots relative prosperity among the regions and nations (measured by per capita GDP), against per capita public spending on what can be broadly defined as domestic services (such as education, health, and so on) (HM Treasury, 2000; ONS, 2001). Social security and agriculture payments are excluded. Both data series are indexed to a UK average of 100 to allow for comparisons.

The poorest regions are at the top. You would expect therefore that, going down the figure, public spending totals would fall as prosperity rises. Generally speaking, that does happen. But there are obvious anomalies. One is that Wales and Scotland, despite being richer than North East England, receive substantially more public spending. Scotland's position looks particularly anomalous in light of the fact that Scotland has become more prosperous since Barnett came into operation. Scottish per capita GDP has risen from 85% of the average UK per capita GDP in 1979 to about 96% of the UK average at present (ONS, 2001). Much of this growth in wealth is attributable however, to the growth in offshore oil-related activity in the Aberdeen area and the growth in financial services around Edinburgh. The spending level is defensible when factors such as the relative sparsity of population, the poor levels of health, and the high levels of public sector housing are taken into account. London, despite being the richest region, also receives a high level of public spending. That can be explained by the high level of congestion costs in the capital which make the provision of services more expensive. Nevertheless, the

Figure 14.3: Nations and regions – prosperity and public spending 1998 (UK average = 100)

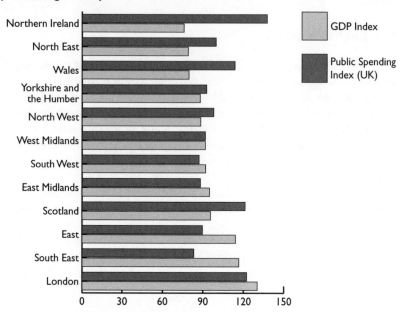

pressure in the North East for regional public spending to be increased is understandable when seen in this context.

The need for a needs assessment

The discussion so far points inexorably towards the conclusion that an assessment of the spending needs of each of the regions and nations of the UK is required. Devolution has already introduced much greater transparency into the operation of Barnett which, pre-1999, was an internal UK government mechanism. Commentators who have examined this subject have agreed that yet more transparency is needed. The model which is generally advocated has a simple structure and operating principles (Heald and Geaughan, 1996; McLean, 2000):

1. A Territorial Exchequer Board should be set up. It should operate independently of the government. It should report to a governing council or commission comprising representatives of the UK government and the devolved governments of Scotland, Wales and Northern Ireland. Representatives of devolved English regional governments, should they be set up, would also join. Independent members with particular expertise could also be appointed.
2. Its statutory job should be to conduct a periodic assessment (say, every five or ten years) of spending needs in each of the devolved territories and, as English regional government evolves, in the English regions.

3. Annual changes to spending programmes could be governed by population-based fomulae, similar to Barnett, which the board would set.

Something of this proposal has already found its way into the political arena. The Liberal Democrats advocate a Finance Commission for the Nations and Regions: "Its Revenue Distribution Formula will allocate funds from central government to the nations and regions on the basis of need" (Liberal Democrats, 2001). A working example of this type of system is the Australian Commonwealth Grants Commission. Its task is to see that "state governments should receive funding from the Commonwealth such that, if each made the same effort to raise revenue from its own sources and operated at the same level of efficiency, each would have the capacity to provide services at that same standard" (quoted in McLean, 2000, p 77).

Assessing needs is by no means easy. The difficulties are amply illustrated by a Treasury study conducted between 1976 and 1978. It was driven by the government's intention to introduce devolved assemblies in Scotland and Wales. It also encompassed Northern Ireland as the reintroduction of devolved government remained a long-term goal after the suspension of Stormont in 1972. The government explained the study's aim as being to collect "objective information on needs and standards of public services in all four countries of the United Kingdom. The Government hopes this information will help them and the devolved administrations to make informed judgements on levels of expenditure and to explain them publicly" (HM Government, 1977, para 71).

In the event, the study was never implemented. A look at the broad conclusion explains why. Table 14.1 presents two sets of figures. The first row shows comparative levels of actual public spending at the time in the four nations of Britain, indexed to English spending set at 100. The second row shows what the Treasury estimated to be the need for spending in the four nations, again indexed to English spending set at 100.

Scotland and Northern Ireland turned out to have actual spending which was higher than their assessed need; and Wales to have spending lower than its assessed need. Although the Conservative government elected in 1979 was committed to reducing public spending, implementing this study would have given it serious political problems. Reducing Scottish spending faster than it was being reduced elsewhere would have risked re-igniting Scottish nationalism, which appeared to have been extinguished as a serious political threat in 1979.

Table 14.1: Actual and needs assessed levels of public spending

	England	Scotland	Wales	Northern Ireland
Index of actual public spending, 1977-78	100	128	100	141
Index of Assessed Need for public spending	100	116	109	131

Source: HM Treasury (1979, pp 5, 28)

Conservative seats, which had been won from the SNP, would have been threatened. A similar reduction in Northern Ireland would have given the Republican cause considerable grist to its mill. So the study was shelved and Barnett continued to operate unmodified by needs and with the flaws already noted.

Nevertheless, the study is well worth reading now. It was confined to the "technical question of the implications for relative expenditure requirements of following the same policies and standards in Scotland, Wales, and Northern Ireland as are followed in England" (HM Treasury, 1977, p 1). The introduction hints at the difficulties encountered by those who drew it up (parallel teams of officials from the Treasury and the Welsh, Scottish and Northern Ireland Offices):

> The departments who have carried out the study agree that the methods of assessment are a long way from providing a wholly definitive means of expressing the relative expenditure needs of the four countries. There is no 'right' answer either overall or *a fortiori* for the individual programmes from which the assessment is built up. (HM Treasury, 1977, p 1)

The problems of needs

The Treasury study aimed to provide spending assessments for six main programmes which were proposed to be devolved in the 1978 Scotland and Wales Acts. These were health and personal social services, education (excluding universities), housing, other environmental services, roads and transport (excluding railways), and law order and protective services (excluding the police). There are methodological problems:

1. *The notion that objectivity can underpin a needs assessment is fanciful.* Subjective judgements have to be made. The Treasury study distinguished between objective factors (those outside the control of a public authority) and subjective factors (those which can be affected by a policy decision). Thus in education, objective factors included pupil numbers, their age distribution, geographical location, and so on. Subjective factors included such things as pupil-teacher ratios, and bilingual schooling in Wales. These were ignored by the study, as were factors that were not obviously subjective or objective, such as denominational education in Northern Ireland (HM Treasury, 1977, p 7). But subjective judgements are bound to intrude: are low pupil-teacher ratios good educational practice or an inefficient use of teachers?
2. *Some factors are difficult to quantify.* The example cited by the study is that of towns suffering from environmental stress because of through traffic. Such towns might be described as having an objective need for a bypass. But can such a need be quantified (HM Treasury, 1977, p 7)?

There are also more fundamental political problems:

1. Some policies and traditions in the devolved nations have no counterpart in England. An example at the time was compulsory English/Welsh bilingualism in Welsh public bodies. The Treasury study simply ignored such differences. But since then, both the range of policy devolved, and the divergence of policy has increased. Such divergences can have major spending implications. Responsibility for the universities has been devolved. In England, Wales, and Northern Ireland a three-year undergraduate degree is normal, but in Scotland a four-year degree is traditional. The Scottish Parliament has decided to abolish up-front student tuition fees payable everywhere else and substitute a form of graduate tax. Water and sewerage services have been privatised in England and Wales, but not in Scotland and Northern Ireland. The number of people eligible for free eye tests in Wales has been greatly increased by the Welsh Assembly. The questions raised by these examples are of fundamental importance. How should a spending 'need' be assessed in one part of the UK which has no counterpart in the other parts? To what extent should all UK taxpayers be expected to fund a public service which is only available in one part of the UK?

2. The underlying principle behind the Treasury study was to assess the level of spending required to enable the same policies to be pursued in each part of the country. Therefore, for example, it looked at the effect that sparsity of population had on increasing the spending needed to ensure the same level of health service provision (access to hospitals, GPs, and so on) in all parts of Scotland and Wales. The unspoken assumption behind this was that service provision in England was the yardstick for service provision elsewhere. But this was at a time when there was a strong political consensus about public services: a universal and publicly-funded free NHS, comprehensive education, and so on. This consensus is now much weaker, if not completely fragmented. Again, this raises a fundamental question: to what extent should service provision in England be the standard for service provision elsewhere? If, for example, the Westminster government decides that private health firms should play a much bigger role in the health service in England, to what extent should that policy drive spending allocations to Scotland, Wales and Northern Ireland, whose governments may reject that policy? And if regional government arrives in England and produces policy divergence, how can any standard for service provision be set?

Although the Treasury study has assumed a highly authoritative status in recent years, its text is littered with qualifications. It is quite clear that the authors regarded it only as a first stab at an answer which required a lot more work. Discussions with two of the civil servants who worked on it reveal that many of its quantitative outcomes were arrived at not so much through statistical rigour, as by negotiations between the departments. A memory was evoked of a Secretary of State for Scotland who, in another context, used to bring discussions about numbers to an end by invoking the "Athine Formula": "Ach, to hell, it's near enough" (personal communication).

Nevertheless, the Australian example already cited shows that it can be achieved. Assuming the methodological problems can be resolved, the political problems can also be addressed. Solutions to them invariably involve questions of devolved taxation. But before looking at that, the variable pattern of English regional spending needs to be brought into the equation.

The needs of the regions

Without a proper needs assessment it is impossible to know whether existing patterns of spending in the regions are a good or a bad match with regional needs. However, a rough idea can be gleaned by using figures for per capita social security spending in the regions. These offer a rough guide to how poverty varies from region to region. Since poverty is associated with poor health, bad housing, and low educational attainment, social security figures are a reasonable proxy for regional needs. How needs, on this proxy measure, match with existing per capita regional spending (excluding social security and agricultural spending), is shown in Figure 14.4. Both sets of figures are indexed to a UK average of 100 for comparison.

The same pattern as in Figure 14.3 is evident here. The poorest regions are at the bottom and therefore you would expect levels of spending to increase

Figure 14.4: Nations and regions – deprivation and public spending 1998 (UK = 100)

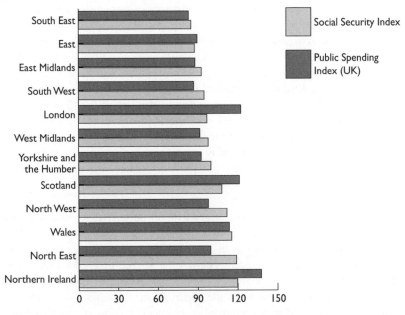

Source: HM Treasury (2000)

with levels of poverty. London, Scotland, and Northern Ireland stick out as having levels of spending which are well above the social security spending indicator of need. London's spending level is attributable to congestion costs, Scotland's to inherited historically high levels of spending, and Northern Ireland's to security costs. The North East and North West regions stick out as having spending levels which are well below the level required on this indicator of need.

The scale of the problem

If these disparities are to be regarded as a problem which needs solving, we need to know something of the scale of the problem. Then an assessment can be made about the practicality of any proposed solution. The available data on identifiable public spending in the regions and nations can be used to calculate scale. This section uses 1998-99 Treasury data on identifiable regional public spending, excluding spending on social security and agriculture.

One implication of the debate on the geographical distribution of public spending is that some regions are over-funded and some are under-funded. Table 14.2 shows the winners and losers if spending throughout the UK was at the UK average.

Redistributing public spending according to a UK average turns out to involve re-allocating some £9 billion. Despite the focus on Scotland and Wales in the debate about Barnett, the biggest loser would actually be London. And despite the loudest complaints about Barnett being heard in the North of England, the North East and North West would gain comparatively little, the biggest gainer being the South East. This may be why John Prescott said there would be "blood on the carpet" in any review of Barnett. Quite apart from

Table 14.2: UK winners and losers with UK average public spending

	Per capita spending (£)	Gain (£m)	Loss (£m)
North East	2,466	31	
North West	2,425	365	
Yorkshire and the Humber	2,295	923	
East Midlands	2,182	1,234	
West Midlands	2,272	1,098	
East of England	2,222	1,377	
London	3,035		4,003
South East	2,061	3,338	
South West	2,157	1,573	
Wales	2,814		986
Scotland	3,005		2,698
Northern Ireland	3,408		1,570
UK average	**2,478**		

Source: HM Treasury (2000) and author's calculations

Table 14.3: English winners and losers on English average spending

	Gain (£m)	Loss (£m)
North East		282
North West		468
Yorkshire and the Humber	312	
East Midlands	729	
West Midlands	453	
East of England	725	
London		4,872
South East	2,369	
South West	980	

Source: Author's calculations

this not being the result desired by those calling for reform of Barnett, it is clearly politically impractical. The political cost to any government would be far greater than the political gain. The current New Labour government would face the loss of the Scottish Parliament and the Welsh Assembly to nationalist parties, and an unwanted spanner would be thrown into the Northern Ireland peace process.

What would be the effect of confining the averaging experiment to England? Table 14.3 shows the winners and losers, were spending in England redistributed according to English average spending.

London is again an enormous loser, but so too, somewhat surprisingly, are the North West and North East regions. The London figures, incidentally, showing that, on per capita figures, London receives about £4.9 billion more than English average spending, and about £4 billion more than UK average spending, providing something of a counter to the claim, raised in the first London mayoral election campaign, that London needs to receive still more public spending. Again, obviously, redistributing spending within England according to an English average is impractical.

Looking at it another way, could average English regional spending be raised to the Scottish average? Table 14.4 shows the cost of doing so.

The total cost of doing this turns out to be £32.5 billion. Since this represents about 10% of total government spending, it is impractical to expect any government to indulge in an increase of this scale. Even if a government was so minded, such a distribution does not take into account varying patterns of need.

Possible solutions

It is clear that any solution to the problem of English regional spending disparities has to take into account the question of needs. It is equally clear that a comprehensive solution which does so will take years to formulate and implement. Is there a quicker and more practical way to deal with the most

Table 14.4: The cost of "going Scottish"

	Gain (£m)	Loss (£m)
North East	1,396	
North West	3,997	
Yorkshire and the Humber	3,580	
East Midlands	3,431	
West Midlands	3,909	
East of England	4,210	
London		216
South East	7,556	
South West	4,516	
Wales	560	

Source: Author's calculations

obvious problems? It has been shown that politicians have stopped Barnett from causing convergence between English and Scottish spending by political decisions to direct extra cash north of the border. The same method could be used to deal with the worst disparities. A comparison between the index used as a measure of deprivation and the index for per capita public spending is shown in Table 14.5.

If Scotland is taken as the benchmark, there are only four parts of the UK where the deprivation index shows that needs are greater: Northern Ireland, Wales, the North East and the North West. However, Northern Ireland can be discounted, since public spending is higher there than in Scotland. That leaves Wales, the North East, and the North West where needs look to be greater than in Scotland, but where public spending is lower. Using the figures in

Table 14.5: Indices of deprivation and spending (UK = 100)

	Index of deprivation	Index of public spending
Northern Ireland	120	138
North East	119	100
Wales	115	114
North West	112	98
Scotland	108	121
Yorkshire and the Humber	100	93
West Midlands	98	92
London	97	122
South West	95	87
East Midlands	93	88
East of England	88	90
South East	85	83

Source: HM Treasury (2000) and author's calculations

Table 14.5, the cost of raising spending in these three regions to Scottish levels would total £5.9 billion – £1,396 million for the North East, £3,997 million for the North West and £560 million for Wales. Arguably the required level of spending ought to be greater, since needs in these three regions are greater than in Scotland. However, £5.9 billion is a reasonably manageable figure (about 2% of total public spending).

The present government has shown that it is prepared to indulge in this kind of politics. In 2000, political outrage was caused in the North West by a government decision to locate a new research facility – a synchotron – in Oxfordshire rather than in Daresbury, Cheshire, where there was an existing synchotron. In response to that, the government announced a year later that it was prepared to allocate £150 million for scientific research in the North West, including money for projects to keep the Daresbury synchotron gainfully employed (Carter and Meek, 2001). The North West is the only English region to have this fund. Similar devices could be used to direct other spending; for example, to dual the undualled sections of the A1 in the North East, extend the metro network in Newcastle, extend the tram system in Manchester, and so on. Additional resources might also be directed to education and health services in the two regions.

Such measures would be, however, a temporary political fix. There is no means of knowing, if they were adopted, whether they would meet regional needs. That brings the argument back to the necessity for a needs assessment. It has been shown that a Barnett-style formula, if it were adopted to distribute spending to the English regions, would result in eventual convergence towards an average. But a population-based formula could be used to distribute spending if it is modified to take needs into account. Such a formula would take the population of each region and nation of the UK as a base figure. Each regional population figure would then be weighted by a figure derived from the needs assessment. So, for example, if a needs assessment found that the North East of England required spending which was 19% above UK average spending, the weighting factor would be designed to ensure that a 19% spending advantage in the North East was preserved. The needs assessment would be periodically reviewed to determine whether needs have changed and whether the weighting factor needs to be changed.

Conclusion

A system which combined population figures with needs weightings might be presented as Barnett Plus. It would be difficult to move towards it because, as has been shown, there are major difficulties in defining needs. Moreover, any needs assessment is bound to show differentials between what is actually spent in each region, and what ought to be spent. Adjusting spending so that needs and spending coincide would be painful, as there would be losers as well as winners. Administrative reorganisation would be required within England, as the boundaries of the English regions used by the regional Government Offices (also by the Treasury for regional spending statistics) do not coincide with the regional boundaries used, for example, by the health department (Hogwood, 1996). The time required to introduce such a system could be used, however, to meet existing regional spending grievances by political decisions to increase spending in the most obviously deprived regions.

However, a Barnett Plus system would have many advantages. It would introduce fairness and transparency into the system for distributing spending geographically. The kind of grievance politics used by nationalist parties in Scotland and Wales and increasingly by regional politicians in England would become more difficult to sustain. Barnett Plus would also deal with the Barnett squeeze effect in Scotland and Wales. That such systems are used in countries such as Australia shows it can work. Sooner or later, and preferably sooner, the government will have to move towards such a system.

References

Bell, D. (2001) 'The Barnett Formula', Mimeo, University of Stirling.

Carter, H. and Meek, J. (2001) '£150m boost for science in the north', *The Guardian*, 3 March.

Cuthbert, J. (1998) 'The implications of the Barnett Formula', *Saltire Paper no 1*, Edinburgh: SNP.

Guthrie, J. 'Byers urged to review regional funding formula', *Financial Times*, 25 May.

Heald, D.A. (1994) 'Territorial public expenditure in the United Kingdom', *Public Administration*, vol 72, pp 168-9.

Heald, D.A. and Geaughan, N. (1996) 'Financing a Scottish Parliament', in S. Tindale (ed) *The State and the nations: Politics of devolution*, London: Institute for Public Policy Research.

Hetherington, P. (2001) 'Scots and Welsh face subsidy axe', *The Guardian*, 24 April.

Hogwood, B.W. (1996) *Mapping the regions*, Bristol: The Policy Press.

House of Commons (2000) *Third report: Social exclusion in Wales*, House of Commons Select Committee on Welsh Affairs, London: The Stationery Office.

HM Government (1977) *Devolution: Financing the devolved services* (Cmnd 6890), London: HMSO.

HM Treasury (1979) *Needs Assessment Study – Report*, London: HMSO.

HM Treasury (2000) *Public expenditure statistical analyses 2000-01* (Cm 4601), London: The Stationery Office.

Kay, N. (1998) 'The Scottish Parliament and the Barnett Formula', *Fraser of Allander Quarterly Economic Review*, vol 24, no 1, pp 32-48.

Levitt, I. (1999) 'The Scottish Secretary, the Treasury and the Scottish Grant Equivalent 1888-1970', *Scottish Affairs*, vol 28, pp 93-116.

Liberal Democrats (2001) *General Election 2001 Manifesto*, London: Liberal Democrats.

McCrone, G. (1999) 'Scotland's public finances from Goschen to Barnett', *Fraser of Allander Quarterly Economic Review*, vol 24, no 2, pp 30-46.

McLean, I. 'Getting and spending: can (or should) the Barnett Formula survive?', *New Economy*, vol 7, pp 76-80.

Midwinter, A. (2000) 'Devolution and public spending: arguments and evidence', *Fraser of Allander Quarterly Economic Review*, vol 25, no 4, pp 38-48.

ONS (Office for National Statistics) (2001) *Regional Trends No 36*, London: The Stationery Office.

Scottish Executive (2000) *Government expenditure and revenue in Scotland, 1998-99*, Edinburgh: Scottish Executive.

Scottish Parliament (2001) *Scottish Parliament Official Record: Written answers report*, vol 11, no 5, March 29.

Twigger, R. (1998) 'The Barnett Formula', *Research Paper 98/8*, House of Commons Library.

FIFTEEN

Conclusion: prospects for regionalism

John Adams, Simon Lee and John Tomaney

The rise of regionalism?

The aim of this book has been to cast a spotlight over the current state of regionalism in England. This inevitably presents only a snapshot of an evolving situation. The varied contributions in the book, however, make clear that the pattern of regionalism is highly uneven. At the same time, there are forces at play that are likely to ensure that regionalism remains a part of the political scene in England. In fact, by mid-2002, there was evidence that the interest of the English in regionalism was starting to grow. Indeed, a poll commissioned by the BBC in March 2002 showed growing support for regional government across England. Nearly two thirds of the population (63%) were in favour of elected regional assemblies, with support even higher in the four regions of the West Midlands (73%), the North East (72%), North West (72%) and Yorkshire and the Humber (72%). Least support was found in the South East (49%) and the Eastern region (55%). Support for devolved government comes from the belief that it will provide regions with a stronger voice in Westminster and Brussels (72%), help economic development in the regions (64%), bring government closer to the people (60%) and increase pride in people's areas (58%).

The debate about English regionalism, awareness of regional diversity and understanding of the government's proposals for strengthened regional governance were only just emerging as the 2002 White Paper was published. This book is a contribution to this important ensuing debate.

Towards regional assemblies?

By far the most important source of future dynamism in the politics of regionalism is likely to be the attitude of central government to devolution within England. In this respect the publication of the White Paper in May 2002 was of special consequence (Cabinet Office/DTLR, 2002). Its publication was significant if only because it demonstrated that previous reports of the death of the devolution project had been greatly exaggerated. And it has been significant in other ways. Notably, in the face of some Whitehall scepticism, the Deputy Prime Minister, John Prescott and his allies appeared to have fought a subtle and patient campaign, not least in the Cabinet's Committee of Nations and Regions, to extract a package of powers for regional assemblies from a reluctant Whitehall machine. At the same time, the nature of this struggle means that the White Paper presented a mixed bag of powers and responsibilities, reflecting the uneven gains which the Cabinet Office and the Department for Transport, Local Government and the Regions (DTLR) were able to make.

The White Paper raised the prospect of at least some regions obtaining elected regional assemblies during the lifetime of Labour's second term. In his speech to the House of Commons, announcing the publication of the White Paper, John Prescott for the first time set out a timetable for achieving an elected assembly in at least one English region. He stated:

> We intend ·to introduce legislation to provide for referendums and local government reviews as soon as parliamentary time allows. We intend to allow a referendum to be held before the end of this Parliament. After a region has voted for an elected assembly, we intend to introduce further legislation enabling assemblies to be established. That would make it possible for the first regional assembly to be up and running early in the next Parliament – under a Labour Government, of course. (House of Commons Debates, 9 May 2002, col 278)

North East England was the region that the government had in mind. In fact, the White Paper was replete with references to the North East. Furthermore, it is noteworthy that while launch events were held in all regions of England, the Deputy Prime Minister and the Secretary of State for the DTLR, Stephen Byers, chose to attend a launch in Newcastle upon Tyne. It was there that both ministers made it explicit that the North East was the only region which would be expected to achieve an elected assembly in the medium run. The Deputy Prime Minister stated:

> I would hope that the North East will want to carry the torch, although we will be consulting all the regions over the coming months to gauge what the level of demand is elsewhere. To be first in line – to be in the vanguard – is an opportunity that happens very rarely. From the mood here tonight I think it's a challenge you want to take, and one which – for all the right reasons – will put you in the spotlight. (Prescott, 2002)

The government's proposals in the White Paper, if enacted, would change the landscape of the British constitution and the terrain of English politics. In one sense they are potentially more radical than the proposals for Scottish and Welsh devolution, insofar as they represent a more fundamental challenge, albeit initially modest, to the dominance of Whitehall over all aspects of English life. Scottish and Welsh devolution involved making separate departments accountable to elected assemblies. In the longer run, English regional government would suggest a dismemberment of Whitehall, and departments have struggled hard to resist the allocation of their functions to regional assemblies. The range of powers proposed for assemblies reflects, then, the outcome of these Whitehall turf wars, with few Whitehall departments willingly entertaining the prospect of handing over powers to elected assemblies (see Chapter Thirteen in this volume).

The shape of things to come?

John Prescott fought a war of attrition in order to extract the maximum range of possible powers that he could for regional assemblies. Full control over the budgets and activities of Regional Development Agencies (RDAs) was a minimum requirement for a credible model of regional government (see Chapter Thirteen). Therefore the main proposals of the White Paper could be widely predicted. RDAs have seen their budgets steadily increased since they were established and their financial flexibility extended. RDA finances were envisaged initially as providing the core budgets of RDAs. In the northern regions, where support for regional government is strongest, these economic development powers are likely to receive significant support.

The planning powers proposed for regional assemblies contained few surprises. The government had already signalled its intention to create new regional planning structures in its Green Paper on Planning, published in early 2002 (Cabinet Office/DTLR, 2002). The government proposed that mandatory Regional Spatial Strategies should be produced in all regions and that assemblies would have responsibility for these where they existed. Previous arrangements were criticised for the lack of coordination between the strategies of RDAs and land-use planning. An elected regional assembly, along the lines of the government's proposals, could potentially address this weakness of the existing arrangements.

A further significant power proposed for regional assemblies is control over European Structural Fund expenditure. Structural Fund expenditure, although likely to diminish in scale over time, remains an important element of regeneration funding, especially in the 'poorer' regions such as Scotland, Wales and the northern regions of England. An assembly would take these powers from Government Offices for the Regions, where they currently reside.

In some areas the proposed powers go beyond what was expected. For instance, the proposed housing powers have exceeded most predictions, with assemblies to take a central role in the allocation of housing investment. These were powers that the Mayor of London, coveted but was denied by the 2000 Greater London Authority Act. The Mayor and his advisers had argued that successful regeneration policy requires the integration of economic development and housing policies with the planning system, and the government's new package now holds out that possibility in the English regions. Consequently, the creation of elected regional assemblies is likely, therefore, to add a further dynamic to the pressure for greater devolution in London.

In a conscious acknowledgement that devolution is a process and not an event, the government made it clear, however, that the range of powers outlined in the White Paper was likely to evolve over time.

The package of assembly functions reflects the way in which these functions are currently organised. However, the Government is keen to further decentralise responsibility for policy and delivery where this will improve regional outcomes. As a consequence, it is likely that there will be ongoing developments in regional governance and organisational changes in the way functions are delivered. The government will therefore build into policy development the new opportunities offered by the creation of elected assemblies. (Cabinet Office/DTLR, 2002, para 4.5)

The package outlined in the White Paper provided a starting point on which some in the regions would hope, over time, to build. There were a number of areas where early pressure to strengthen the powers of assemblies was expressed. For example, transport and skills were areas where, in the regions, there was a widely held feeling that, to quote John Prescott and Stephen Byers: "Whitehall does not always know best" (Cabinet Office/DTLR, 2002, Foreword). Indeed, the White Paper made a strong case for these activities to be exercised at the regional level.

In the case of training and skills, the White Paper noted that:

Developing the skills of the workforce plays a vital role in economic development. So improving the skills base and equipping people to take up opportunities being created in a region will be an important component of delivering an elected assembly's objectives. (Cabinet Office/DTLR, 2002, para 4.28)

According to the White Paper, assemblies are to be given responsibility for the production of Frameworks for Regional Employment and Skills Action, but the assembly's relationship with the main delivery arms for training policy, notably local Learning and Skills Councils, will be only a consultative one.

Similarly, the White Paper notes:

Good transport is essential for sustainable economic success, a better environment, and an enhanced quality of life.... To achieve this, transport needs to be integrated with policy economic development, planning, and housing. (Cabinet Office/DTLR, 2002, para 4.37)

Yet the potential powers outlined in the White Paper would restrict assemblies to a mainly consultative role in relation to the activities of central government and its agencies. The past 20 years or so have seen an increasing recognition of the significance of transport beyond the field of transport itself: for the environment, economic development, regeneration, urban renewal, social inclusion, and even housing. Furthermore, the RDAs have emphasised the importance of transport in their Regional Economic Strategies (RES) – both in the congested South and the deprived North. The regional transport agenda – of linking the economic, social and environmental agendas, of returning UK-wide policy to the different circumstances of individual regions, of brokering deals between subregional interests – is impossibly complex and too voluminous to handle at the national level, whether that be the UK or England (Wenham Smith, 2002). It is noteworthy that at a meeting between DTLR ministers and RDA chairs shortly after the publication of the White Paper, the chairs called for a strengthening of training and transport powers (Tomaney et al, 2002).

The government's proposals for regional assemblies to be accompanied by a move to a single tier of local government were well trailed prior to publication of the White Paper. However, the notion that this signalled "the end of county councils", as prior press speculation suggested, was not been entirely borne out in the White Paper. Under the terms of the proposals it is possible that counties could survive in some places while districts disappear. This issue is likely to prove more of a stumbling block in some regions than others. In the North East only the rump of Durham and Northumberland counties remained by 2002, while 70% of the population already lived in single tier local authority areas. The government's proposals in the White Paper were designed to neutralise the charge that regional government would mean an extra tier of bureaucracy. It would actually be up to voters in the regions to decide whether the prize of regional government made reform of local government worthwhile. The early signals from local government leaders in the North East, the only apparent candidate for an early referendum, indicated that they would not oppose the provisions of the White Paper in order to defend existing local government arrangements (see *The Journal* [Newcastle upon Tyne], 10 May 2002).

The White Paper made clear that assemblies would be elected by proportional representation. The government proposed to use the same electoral system as used in Scotland and Wales. Even John Prescott, a noted supporter of first past the post, bowed to arguments for proportional representation. Such a proposal would have far-reaching consequences in Labour heartland regions. Labour does well under the first past the post in regions such as the North East, but the mayoral elections there in 2002 revealed that when new voting systems were introduced Labour came in for a shock, losing all three.

The level of support for regional assemblies remains uneven at best. Even under the most positive prognosis, some regions are likely to remain unconvinced of the charms of devolution. The government's approach has raised the likelihood that some regions will not proceed towards elected regional assemblies in the foreseeable future, and those regions which do would not see actual assembly elections for some years. The White Paper therefore contained proposals to strengthen regional structures, even in regions where there is currently no appetite for elected assemblies.

However, the government's strategy for regional governance short of elected assemblies appears solely to build up the role of the Government Offices in each region. It seems that no added responsibilities will be allocated to, for example, the regional chambers (see Chapter Three). Many of the proposed extra responsibilities identified in the White Paper will be assigned to the Government Offices: working with the Home Office on crime reduction and drugs; a new role in the 'community cohesion' fund; and the enhanced role in emergency planning (Cabinet Office/DTLR, 2002, paras 2.31, 2.33). The

Government Offices, however, are to be given "extra responsibilities in working with and monitoring the performance of" the RDAs' planning (Cabinet Office/ DTLR, 2002, para 2.31), and a responsibility to "provide a forum for other public sector bodies in a region to review their high-level strategies and improve read-across by identifying mutual aims and removing any inconsistencies or duplication between them" (Cabinet Office/DTLR, 2002, para 2.27). Each of these functions would seem to fit better with the regional chambers, bodies which, despite their drawbacks, are more representative of the regions than the Government Offices, which inevitably look to Whitehall for political direction.

Limits to regionalism?

The UK, it is traditionally claimed, is one of the most centralised of developed nations – and the control of HM Treasury over public expenditure and taxation is high even by the standards of other unitary nations. Very little fiscal activity eludes the Treasury's control. The publication of *Your region, your choice* is an important statement of the Blair government's commitment to devolution for the English regions. However, one should not lose sight of the fact that the White Paper has done little to alleviate central control over policy and resources institutionalised during New Labour's first term by the Treasury's Comprehensive Spending Reviews, the accompanying tide of Public Service Agreements (PSAs), and the government's modernisation of government agenda. This should come as no surprise to the English regions given that one of the most important attempts by New Labour in opposition to define how they could deliver its vision identified three 'engines at the heart of government' which would be capable of driving policy implementation. These were "No 10, the Cabinet Office and the Treasury" (Mandelson and Liddle, 1996, p 240). Mandelson and Liddle argued that these institutions need to be used together by a Blair-led government in a coordinated, even 'Napoleonic', manner. Devolved institutions were conspicuous by their absence in this vision of how a future Labour government's policies might be formulated. In practice, the Blair government's ambivalence towards English devolution has reflected this analysis.

Since the 2001 General Election, the trend towards centralisation in the government of England has been further deepened. To some extent this was driven by a Prime Ministerial desire to recapture some sovereignty over policy making from the Treasury, especially over reform of the public services – New Labour's key priority for its second term of office. The 'new centre' was strengthened immediately after the 2001 General Election, possibly as a bulwark against the Treasury's influence. To units such as the Performance and Innovation Unit and the Social Exclusion Unit were added the Office of Public Services Reform, the Forward Strategy Unit and the Prime Minister's Delivery Unit (based in Number 10). Moving the Deputy Prime Minister to his own office in the Cabinet Office, along with the Regional Coordination Unit and the responsibility for the Government Office for the Regions, might also be seen as a strengthening of the 'new centre'.

Following the resignation of Stephen Byers in May 2002, this centralisation has been taken a step further with separation from the Cabinet Office of the Office of the Deputy Prime Minister. The former may become a Prime Minister's Department in all but name, while the latter has now been expanded to include responsibility for English regional policy, local government and its finance, planning, housing, urban policy, the Neighbourhood Renewal Unit and the Fire Service. Yet again, at a stroke the central architecture in Whitehall for managing the government of England has been fundamentally restructured.

In parallel with this organisational centralisation within Whitehall, the government has resisted anything other than administrative devolution for the English regions in relation to the key public services and policies which can influence the pattern and alleviation of regional inequalities – health, education, employment, crime and transport. Thus, Blair has defined his agenda for public services' reform in terms of central governmental provision of an 'overall vision', that is, policy design and specification of 'national standards' (for England), and local delivery of that vision, that is, policy implementation "by devolution and delegation to the front line" (Prime Minister's OPSR, 2002, pp 2-3). The principle underpinning this notion of devolution for England has been "earned autonomy for schools, hospitals, local government and other public services" (Prime Minister's OPSR, 2002, p 17). While devolved governments in other parts of the UK "are able to take their own approaches to public service reform", in England, "Devolved delivery can only operate with national standards and accountability" (Prime Minister's OPSR, 2002, p 28). Furthermore, while the government has readily acknowledged that devolved power in Scotland, Wales and Northern Ireland has enabled "locally-elected representatives to adopt approaches to public services reflecting their own national priorities and concerns" (Prime Minister's OPSR, 2002, p 6), such national priorities in England are assumed to be the sole province of Whitehall, dominated by 10 Downing Street, the Cabinet Office and the Treasury. The possibility that there might exist pluralistic and diverse English subnational priorities and concerns has not been entertained. The Blair government seems hesitant to take a risk with the crucial marginal constituencies of 'Middle England' where the 1997 and 2001 General Election landslides were secure and where the prospects for a third or fourth term are deemed to reside.

Financing regionalism

Faced with the forces of centralisation which have dominated England, the degree of fiscal flexibility contained within the White Paper was a surprise. In some ways the financial powers of the proposed regional assemblies are stronger than those available to the other devolved institutions in the UK. For example, the fact that funds will be granted to assemblies via a 'block grant' provides for substantially more fiscal flexibility than that available to the Greater London Authority, as, under the terms of the Greater London Authority Act, the Mayor is unable to switch funds between different budget heads. This provision severely limits the opportunity for divergent and innovative policies and is undermining the Mayor's ability to achieve 'joined-up' government.

The proposal for block grant was influenced by the example of the 'single pot' made available to RDAs in March 2001. During the initial period of their existence, RDAs were constrained by Whitehall's accountability mechanisms. Monies spent had to remain within the programmes for which they were assigned by the relevant Whitehall departments, and there was little room to switch money between different activities. RDA leaders felt that this was a significant restriction on their ability to 'do their job' and made the single pot one of their top priorities. Following a successful lobbying campaign the decision to grant the RDAs their single pot was announced by both the Deputy Prime Minister (when he was responsible for RDAs in the DETR) and the Chancellor of the Exchequer in 2001 (see Chapter Three).

The White Paper also proposes significant borrowing powers for regional assemblies, another example of significant financial flexibility. Such powers have not been made available to the Scottish Parliament or the National Assembly for Wales in their respective legislation. In one of the most significant changes to the UK devolution settlements, the Chancellor of the Exchequer and the Prime Minister visited Belfast in May 2002 to announce that a 'prudential' system for capital spending will allow the Northern Ireland Executive to undertake borrowing to help remedy its deficiencies in infrastructure investment, so long as it can service that borrowing from its revenue base. The fact that Northern Ireland does not have the same system of local government as the rest of the UK would undoubtedly have influenced this decision. Similar powers were also signalled for regional assemblies, although a 'prudential' borrowing regime for the regional assemblies may well have tighter limits than those available to local authorities. Nevertheless, this would give the administrations of regional assemblies options to invest in their region's infrastructure.

The White Paper also proposed to grant revenue raising powers to regional assemblies, via a precept on the council tax, although it is unclear how much the proposed assemblies would be able to raise through this method. The council tax precept is the means by which the Greater London Authority raises additional funds, although as constituted it is not the most progressive of taxes. Neither the Northern Ireland Assembly nor the Welsh Assembly were granted revenue raising powers when established, and powers of the Scottish Parliament to raise revenue remained unused in its first term.

It is only then the Greater London Authority, which has both revenue raising powers and has taken the opportunity to use them. Mayor Livingstone has increased both the police precept and the transport precept, using the money to fund increased numbers of police officers and to freeze London underground fares respectively. From 2003 the Mayor is also proposing to introduce a congestion charge in central London, and will use the £150 million per annum proceeds for public transport. Clearly the proposed revenue raising powers of the proposed assemblies would be limited, but would also be subject to a 'capping regime' (Cabinet Office/DTLR, 2002, para 5.9).

The degree of fiscal flexibility proposed for regional assemblies surprised most commentators and has potentially radical implications. Having room at the margins to enable assemblies to decide their priorities enhances fiscal responsibility and concentrates the minds of elected politicians about just how important particular expenditure really is. It also increases the potential for greater divergence in public policy (Heald and Geaughan, 1996).

A space to be different?

Despite the historic centralised nature of taxation and public expenditure within the UK, the centralising instinct of Whitehall manifests itself in different forms. Perhaps the most surprising proposal contained in the White Paper was that:

> We will expect each assembly to help achieve in their region a small number – perhaps six to ten – of targets agreed with the Government. These targets will be relevant to an assembly's responsibilities and will leave it open to the assembly to establish how to achieve them. Some additional money will be available to reward elected assemblies which achieve or exceed the targets. Targets and rewards will be agreed between central government and each assembly, along the lines of existing local public service agreements. (Cabinet Office/DTLR, 2002, para 5.3)

Neither the Scottish Parliament, Welsh Assembly nor the Northern Ireland Legislative Assembly have to negotiate their priorities for public policy with the centre and the proposal in the White Paper appears to undermine the autonomy of priority setting in the devolved territories. The government also proposed that assemblies should produce an annual report for the regional electorate on their progress in meeting these objectives, a stipulation that does not apply in Scotland, Wales and Northern Ireland (Cabinet Office/DTLR, 2002, para 4.7).

The government's initiative in target setting within Whitehall, via the PSAs, has had many critics. A summary of these might be (see Robinson, 2002):

- that the government are apparently unable to set out a clear and consistent set of priorities, especially when different targets potentially conflict;
- that there is a government tendency to commit itself to policies with significant implications for public spending without thoroughly thinking through those implications;
- that the targets can create perverse incentives which distort priorities;
- that they can generate unrealistic public expectations;
- that the government would have difficulties in avoiding the temptation to match top-down target setting with the micro-management of public services from Whitehall;
- that it was a lost opportunity to use the process to open up decision making in Whitehall to a wider range of influences.

These are all valid comments and may well apply to regional governments, but while there is a contrary argument that PSAs concentrate minds in Whitehall and in the front-line public services, there is also a principled argument against government targets being set for directly elected assemblies. As Taylor and Wheeler (2002) argue in relation to the local level, the pluralist argument for directly elected regional assemblies is underpinned by the ideal of a creative tension between the democratic authority of the centre and the democratic authority of regional government, and the need for a diffusion of power within the national polity.

The pluralist case for regional government would seem to be undermined by the necessity of a democratically elected regional body being obliged to enter into negotiation with the centre. The simple fact that Whitehall has an institutional locus via which it can influence the political priorities of a devolved administration would seem to be contrary to the general spirit of devolution. In particular the use of financial incentives, which can be used to bargain with the devolved administrations, would give Whitehall 'the upper hand' in negotiations.

Best value

The PSA target is not the only means by which the centre could restrict the autonomy of the regional assemblies. The government proposed that it:

> ... will apply the principles of 'best value' to assemblies, building on the lessons learned from local government and tailoring requirements to the particular circumstances of assemblies. (Cabinet Office/DTLR, 2002, para 5.12)

Best value required local authorities to seek continuous improvements in economy, efficiency and effectiveness, and to do this by reviewing services periodically in order to gauge whether they were still necessary, and whether current approaches to service delivery were the most appropriate. While these may be objectives, which many would support, the best value regime is a significantly centralising force, which has restricted the freedom available to local authorities. The government would doubtless 'tailor' the best value regime for regional assemblies in its own way, and the potential would remain for this to be a centralising provision.

The proposals of fiscal flexibility in the White Paper could be undermined by the fact that assemblies will be subjected to PSA and best value requirements. The government may not strictly deserve its reputation for centralism, especially as it devolved power to Scotland, Wales, Northern Ireland and London. Nevertheless, the two provisions contained in the White Paper could tempt it to intervene in regional politics and policy making. Successor governments could use these provisions with enthusiasm.

The White Paper did not discuss the vexed issue of the Barnett Formula, although, as noted by Peter Jones, it is likely that moves toward elected assemblies would be accompanied by increased interest in the issue (see Chapter Fourteen in this volume). Significantly, though, the government commissioned a major study of the territorial flow of public expenditure in the UK in early 2002, linking it explicitly to the prospect of regional assemblies.

The political challenge

As a government document the White Paper could not enter the debate about how political parties respond to regional devolution. They are, however, an important part of the devolution process and two areas are noteworthy: the referendum campaign and the selection of candidates.

In publishing the White Paper the government signalled its intention to hold its referendum in one region at some stage prior to July 2006, with the North East the favoured candidate. The North East was characterised by the existence of a number of organisations campaigning and pressing for regional devolution – most notably the Campaign for a North East Assembly and the North East Constitutional Convention (see Chapter Ten). Despite the recent polling evidence, described above, showing 72% support for regional devolution in the North East, a "Yes" was by no means assured and therefore the political parties will have a crucial role to play. The referendum will be held on the Labour government's proposals and it is a policy that has been supported by the Liberal Democrats (and their precursors) since the days of Gladstone. However, there was little evidence that preparations had been initiated for a referendum 'yes' vote that could draw on all the resources of the main actors in the region, despite the fact that the North East is home to the Deputy Leader of the Liberal Democrats and the Deputy General Secretary of the Labour Party.

Membership of an elected assembly will be an important job, requiring high-calibre people. The government's proposals were for backbench members of the assembly to be part-time only. Whether this is enough to attract the necessary calibre of member remained to be seem. But the possible advent of elected assemblies provides new challenges for the political parties in the regions to ensure that their selection processes are devised in such a way that people of the requisite ability are chosen to stand in the election. A particular challenge lies in the need to ensure greater participation by women, members of ethnic minorities and disabled people than is currently achieved by local authorities, especially in the northern regions. At the time of the publication of the White Paper there was scant evidence that the main parties have even begun to think through these issues.

References

Cabinet Office/Department for Transport, Local Government and the Regions (DTLR) (2002) *Your region, your choice: Revitalising the English regions*, Cm 5511, Norwich: The Stationery Office.

Heald, D. and Geaughan, N. (1996) 'Financing a Scottish parliament', in S. Tindale (ed) *The state and the nations – The politics of devolution*, London: Institute of Public Policy Research, pp 167-83.

Mandelson, P. and Liddle, R. (1996) *The Blair revolution: Can new labour deliver?*, London: Faber & Faber.

Prescott, J. (2002) 'Your region, your choice', Speech at the launch of the White Paper in the North East, International Centre for Life, Newcastle upon Tyne, 9 May.

Prime Minister's OPSR (Office of Public Services Reform) (2002) *Reforming our public services: Principles into practice*, London: OPSR.

Robinson, P. (2002) 'Comment', *New Economy*, vol 9, no 1.

Taylor, M. with Wheeler, P. (2002) *In defence of councillors*, London: IdeA.

Tomaney, J., Hetherington, P. and Humphrey, L. (2002) *Monitoring the English Regions*, Report No 7 (May), London: Constitution Unit, University College London.

Wenham-Smith, A. (2002) 'Building regional institutional capacity for integrated transport planning', Paper presented to Transport 2000 Seminar, 21 March, London: Institute of Public Policy Research.

Index

Also available from The Policy Press

Rural homelessness
Issues, experiences and policy responses

Paul Cloke, School of Geographical Sciences, University of Bristol, and **Paul Milbourne** and **Rebekah Widdowfield**, Department of City and Regional Planning, Cardiff University

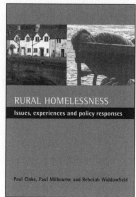

"This book makes an extremely valuable contribution to our existing knowledge in this area. It will become a key reference point for material on rural homelessness for some years to come." Mark Goodwin, Institute of Geography and Earth Sciences, University of Wales

Rural homelessness explores the shifting policy context of homelessness and social exclusion in relation to rural areas. Drawing on the first comprehensive survey of rural homelessness in the UK, the book positions these findings within a wider international context.

Paperback £17.99 • ISBN 1 86134 284 5
Hardback £45.00 • ISBN 1 86134 346 9
216 x 148mm • 256 pages • March 2002

Urban competitiveness
Policies for dynamic cities

Edited by **Iain Begg**, Business School,
South Bank University
Foreword by **Lord Falconer**

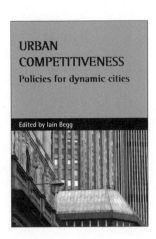

*"... deserves a wide readership among policy
makers as well as students."*
Ian Gordon, London School of Economics and
Political Science

Bringing together leading experts on urban
economic performance, *Urban competitiveness*
provides a new look at the issue of urban competitiveness and offers invaluable
insights into the factors that shape competitiveness.

Although previous work has explored particular facets of competitiveness, this
volume is the first to do so in a systematic way that combines theory, evidence
and policy implications.

Paperback £17.99 • ISBN 1 86134 357 4
Hardback £45.00 • ISBN 1 86134 358 2
216 x 148mm • 352 pages • February 2002

For further information about these and other titles published by The Policy Press,
please visit our website at: www.policypress.org.uk or telephone +44 (0)117 954 6800

To order, please contact:
Marston Book Services
PO Box 269
Abingdon
Oxon OX14 4YN
UK
Tel: +44 (0)1235 465500
Fax: +44 (0)1235 465556
E-mail: direct.orders@marston.co.uk